WRITING *the* LOST GENERATION

WRITING
the
LOST GENERATION

EXPATRIATE
AUTOBIOGRAPHY AND
AMERICAN MODERNISM

by CRAIG MONK

UNIVERSITY OF IOWA PRESS

Iowa City

for BRENDA

CONTENTS

ACKNOWLEDGMENTS

As a boy in Newfoundland, attending university was a vast ambition for me, and the thought that I might work at one and assist in its running was more than I dared imagine. Had Gordon and Violet Monk, my parents, not supported me without question, I could not have found my way. I have, at the University of Lethbridge, a home and an ideal scholarly environment. Bill Cade, Seamus O'Shea, and Andrew Hakin have fostered a community of scholars to compete with any comprehensive university in North America while staying true to the values of liberal education that defined our first years. Because of Christopher Nicol, I can teach things about which I know, research the topics that interest me, and continue to influence our faculty through my administrative work. It is a privilege to work for someone whom I so admire. I appreciate his generous and tireless support of this project.

I have had five excellent mentors over the past twenty years: Shane O'Dea, Bill Barker, Stephen Adams, Mike Weaver, and John Woods. I am grateful for the faith they have placed in me and the patience they have always shown me, and I trust that this book will justify their support.

This book has benefited immeasurably from the generosity of friendship provided by Malcolm and Bonny Greenshields. There is evidence of Malcolm's gentle criticism on every page, and my life is richer for knowing the Greenshields. Many other friends and colleagues have helped me along the way, including William Andrews, Rene Barendregt, Edward Bishop, Adam Carter, Martha Campbell, Agnieszka Graff, Heather Gunn, Christoper Hosgood, Raymond Huel, Cathy Kanashiro, Cliff Lobe, Mary McGillivray, Maria Ng, Barbara Pell, Clare Pettitt, Christian Riegel, Ches Skinner, Demetres Tryphonopoulos, and Catherine Turner. Lynn Ambedian, Jeanie Baczuk, Cheryl Calver, Chi Chi Cameron, Linda Gilbert, Beah Ramtej, Kim Skura, and Corinne Steele have endured my divided attention at work. I developed many of the ideas here in seminar classes I taught in 2000, 2002, and 2005. The fifty-one students in these classes deserve credit, but I wish to offer special thanks here to Nicole Baxter, Jason Bennett, Shannon D'Agnone, Shannon Dube, Dalziel Frisky-Whipple, Shane Larratt, Tanya McRae, Brett Parker, Jeremy Robinson, and Melissa Sexsmith. I am grateful to Stacey Gaudette-Sharpe and Trista Green for assistance with the manuscript; Joshua Dedora, Mary Greenshields, and Kali McKay provided additional insight.

Much of the initial work on this project was undertaken in Halifax, Nova Scotia, a wonderful place to live and work. I would like to thank the residents of Bishop's Row who tolerated a grown man living like a graduate student for eighteen months. The Nova Scotia College of Art and Design University granted me an Honorary Research Fellowship during my time in Halifax, and the librarians at Dalhousie University, Mount Saint Vincent University, and St. Mary's University helped me take full advantage of the resulting access to their facilities. The members of the English Department at MSVU were notably welcoming. I am, of course, indebted to the Social Sciences and Humanities Research Council of Canada for its generous support of my research. In addition, I also held a Mellon Fellowship at the Harry Ransom Center, University of Texas at Austin, and a Helm Fellowship at the Lilly Library, Indiana University, in support of this project.

Over the past five years, I have come to the slow realization that I am a tremendously deliberate writer. I have tried to make every sentence of this book sing, though it remains to be seen whether its song is in tune, of course. Unfortunately, the writing is only half the battle, and I have accumulated many debts of gratitude in the publishing world. Holly Carver, Joseph Parsons, Allison Thomas, Charlotte Wright, and the rest of the staff at the University of Iowa Press took in my "little yellow dog," as I came to call my developing manuscript, and gave it a happy home. I am also most grateful to Sue Breckenridge for carefully untangling my affected prose and patiently correcting those errors I failed, time and again, to catch myself. Parts of chapter 6 appeared as "Textual Authority and Modern American Autobiography: Robert McAlmon, Kay Boyle, and the Writing of a Lost Generation," *Journal of American Studies* 35, no. 3 (December 2001), and are reprinted here with the permission of the University of Cambridge Press.

Finally, I would like to thank Brenda Hubley. Virtually every word of this book was written, rewritten, and rewritten again within her earshot. Many of these words were coaxed out at her dining room table in Halifax. She has not yet known me to be preoccupied by a scholarly subject other than American autobiography, and I hope she will not now be put off by my return to the world of little magazines. Our future will surely be cluttered with microfilm. Only love could take two people from the Atlantic coast to the windy prairies, and I thank Brenton and Hazel Hubley, her parents, for understanding why we had to steal away. A man must have ambition, and I resolve to live by the ocean once again, someday.

PREFACE

This project began almost a decade ago at the book fair of the Congress of the Humanities and Social Sciences. The "Learneds," as many of us still call it, is the Canadian equivalent of the annual meeting of the Modern Language Association in the United States. I purchased there a copy of the new printing of Robert McAlmon and Kay Boyle's *Being Geniuses Together*, a text I first read as a graduate student at Oxford University. My doctoral research dealt with the expatriate American magazine *transition*, and I read for context countless autobiographies written by its contributors. While I flatter myself that I handled the material then with the savvy and skepticism necessary for reading life narrative, it struck me as I reread McAlmon and Boyle that critics had never really interrogated this influential text as autobiography. Short of an excellent article by Christine Hait on the topic, no one had examined what it meant to modernist life narrative for Boyle to incorporate her own story with McAlmon's original tale.

There has been, over the past thirty years, remarkable work done on autobiography. Generally speaking, critical texts have constructed theories of life narrative by illustrating their ideas with examples from primary texts. What I have attempted to do here, however, is use a number of these theories to unlock books I believe to be important to the development of twentieth-century American literature. My basic argument is that from the appearance of Alfred

Kreymborg's *Troubadour* (1925) to the publication of Maria Jolas's *Woman of Action* (2004), readers have been heavily influenced by Lost Generation autobiography as they developed ideas about life in Paris between the World Wars.

Obviously it was sometimes difficult to choose the appropriate tools to use in the discussion of each text. Gertrude Stein achieved remarkable success in the 1920s and 1930s with texts that are read today as an important early contribution to feminist studies. Yet, Stein's autobiographical writings suggest to me, first and foremost, modernism's equivocal relationship with commercial success, and so I have deferred a more comprehensive reading of women's autobiography to a subsequent discussion of Sylvia Beach and Janet Flanner. My approach privileges a chronological narrative throughout. This, in itself, may appear ironic, in light of modernism's preference for nonlinear stories. However, the unfolding of the movement, and the public's changing perception of it, makes a compelling historical narrative, and it was important for me to organize my analysis as one would a story. I beg the indulgence of readers with a detailed knowledge of the Lost Generation who might have preferred a study organized around those various theories of life narrative, a study that brings in examples from different autobiographies throughout. This approach, in my judgment, could never do justice to the depth and richness of my primary material.

My chosen strategy obdurately refuses to privilege one critical approach, and this reflects the way I treated all source material. I read as many autobiographies written by Americans abroad as was reasonably possible—from that of Ernest Hemingway, perhaps the greatest modern novelist from the United States, to that of Bill Rogers, a doughboy who met Gertrude Stein and Alice Toklas after the First World War—and still failed to use them all in a meaningful way. But I also read extensively in the theories of autobiographical writing. Thus, I have attempted here to write something that reflects an inquisitive scholar using theoretical insights to explore and connect a long series of related texts. To the extent that I have succeeded in my task, *Writing the Lost Generation* is a detailed look at eighty years of American autobiography intended to appeal both to readers of life narrative as a subject of critical inquiry and readers of literary history fascinated with the 1920s in Paris, a distant time in a distant place that truly reshaped art, and the way in which art is regarded, in the United States.

WRITING *the* LOST GENERATION

INTRODUCTION

The Lost Generation and
the Critical Function of Autobiography

"All of you young people who served in the war. You are a lost generation," Gertrude Stein proclaimed.[1] That, at least, was how Ernest Hemingway remembered her words more than thirty years later. Students of twentieth-century literature will attest, however, that the Lost Generation refers today, albeit loosely, to American writers who spent some time in Europe between the World Wars. As eminent a scholar as Noël Riley Fitch takes up the phrase with little question in her literary biography *Sylvia Beach and the Lost Generation* (1983), where an index entry for those words guides readers to "*see* Expatriates, American."[2] Responding to concerns about such apparent critical inexactness, Philip Young provides an insightful, if cranky, reevaluation of the phrase, noting that if one defines its implicated members narrowly as having "had experience of World War I" followed by "some bohemian period in Paris," the generation would consist only of e. e. cummings, John Dos Passos, and Hemingway, himself.[3] In reality, as Lawrence Broer and John Walther observe, because the Lost Generation remains one of the "convenient labels" utilized in discussions of the 1920s,[4] broad understandings of what the designation might signify continue to persist. Indeed, Marc Dolan points out that the influence of the Lost Generation has resonated "far beyond academic and literary circles in popular films, television series, used-clothing shops, and even theme bars."[5]

Careful discussions of the phrase in recent years, like Dolan's own *Modern Lives: A Cultural Re-Reading of "The Lost Generation"* (1996), also underline the manner in which these words have consistently "illuminated too limited a grouping to explain the full sweep of the American 1920s."[6] The journey by which postwar disillusion in the United States was but temporarily assuaged by the dizzying temptation of excess could never be described simply as loss; however, the ambivalence with which that prosperity was embraced, even in its greatest moments of overindulgence, was evident in the fiction of F. Scott Fitzgerald long before it was proven illusory on the floor of the New York Stock Exchange. This may have been the reason Fitzgerald himself preferred the label "Jazz Age" for the years that "bore him up, flattered him and gave him more money than he had dreamed of, simply for telling people that he felt as they did, that something had been done with all the nervous energy stored up and unexpended in the War."[7]

Because the meaning of the Lost Generation shifted very quickly from "youth culture," broadly conceived as "the younger generation," to allude to expatriate Americans with "literary or aesthetic aspirations,"[8] Dolan is justified in doubting the usefulness of the phrase for understanding any representative component of American society in the first half of the twentieth century. While emphasizing only the skepticism with which expatriate writers themselves viewed these words, he concludes that the phrase "may have already outlived whatever discursive utility it had ever possessed,"[9] even while so-called Lost Generation authors remained prolific. By concentrating solely on the ambiguity inherent to the words themselves, Dolan overstates significantly this important conclusion. For while he believes that "few Lost Generation authors" consciously set out to "engage the concept," he acknowledges that they may have inadvertently addressed these words by "writing books that sought to elucidate the historical significance of their own lives."[10] It is difficult, in fact, not to understand this frequent and sustained interest in writing and rewriting the history of modern American expatriation as a clear indication, instead, of the extent to which these writers were actually engaged in shaping the perception of their place in literary history. One can argue that beyond the admittedly useful discussion of how the concept of the Lost Generation fails to provide a definitive understanding of social conditions in the United States and Europe after the First World War, a connection between the role of its alleged participants in framing their own cultural achievement and the manner in which the term proliferated still has not been investigated thoroughly. The persistent desire of expatriate Americans to chronicle their experiences abroad, the emergence of the Lost Generation as a phrase with undeniable currency, and the determined efforts of implicated writers to control those very words—and thereby shape any wider sense of community surrounding it—testified to the critical impulse that gave rise to the self-conscious writing that established modernism as the dominant cultural enterprise of the first half of the twentieth century.

American modernism, of which the contribution of expatriate writers is best understood as an essential element, must not be read as synonymous with modernism as an international movement in the arts, now acknowledged as the institutionally sanctioned cultural response to the industrialized world. It is, instead, an important component of that wider movement. Bruce Robbins points out that some readers view such attempts to situate writers from the United States in this cultural context as a critical Trojan horse of sorts, an "Americanism in sheep's clothing" that promises the opportunity to assert covertly the primacy of American artists among those foreign writers who might best be understood as having influenced them.[11] The efforts during the first decades of the twentieth century of Americans like Ezra Pound to promote in Europe writers from the United States must not overshadow the fact that expatriates like Pound, T. S. Eliot, and Gertrude Stein left their country in the early years of the last century precisely because of a paucity of indigenous creative activity, as they judged it. American writers who went abroad in subsequent waves of expatriation shared a similar sense of disillusionment, clearly, but they also sought more optimistically to experience firsthand the conditions that gave rise to the creative upheaval represented by the European artists whose works were displayed at the Armory Show in 1913. Many audience members in New York and, later, in Chicago and Boston saw there for the first time the paintings of Paul Cézanne, Marcel Duchamp, Henri Matisse, and Pablo Picasso. Emerging from the widespread bewilderment with which the general public had received these works, American writers confirmed for them a suspicion that the twentieth century warranted new approaches to their disciplines as well. And once the tumult of those years in Europe gave rise to the Great War, a cataclysm that seemed to threaten all Western culture, American artists sought to preserve fragments of a shared cultural heritage and find a path forward in what Malcolm Bradbury, echoing Hugh Kenner, describes as "a homemade way."[12] By doing so, American artists forged a modern art that both extended their own national tradition and participated in a wider, international enterprise. The coming of age of American writers between the World Wars, then, coincided with the experience of the Lost Generation, but if Dolan's observations prove anything, it is that American modernism must not simply be equated with the Lost Generation, either.

All these threads of cultural currency do come together, however, with the sense in which both "modern" and "Lost Generation" emerged as pejoratives in the interwar period. The adjective "modern" has a long pedigree to refer to what is contemporaneous, of course. Malcolm Bradbury and James McFarlane lament famously "the inappropriateness of applying so semantically mobile and indeed febrile a term to a historical phenomenon we now wish to root in time."[13] If we accept "modern" today as simply an adjective to refer to all cultural production that engaged the world that gave rise to it, there can still be no doubt that in the first decades of the twentieth century, the term was often used as a reproach in reference to contemporary art whose difficulty was understood, at best, as signifying its willful estrangement from tradition. Similarly, by growing consensus, the lost quality of the Lost Generation referred to its morality; American writers abroad between the World Wars had supposedly abandoned their "moral bearings" once in Europe and estranged themselves from traditional principles.[14] But if, as Tom Wood argues, virtually all expatriates saw the Lost Generation idea "as a happenstance of chronology" and consistently denied "being lost" in any sense,[15] is it any wonder that expatriate writers showed an interest in addressing the opinions created and propagated by this persistent label? The change from modern as a negative judgment to connote, instead, challenging or even representative was an important step in establishing modernism as a movement, as its participants sought to define and position themselves by shifting from a point of resistance to eventual complicity with the evolving dominant culture. Similarly, the attempt to give shape and direction to stories of expatriation reflected a desire to frame the achievement of Americans abroad within a developing understanding of modernism.

Modernism, in fact, appears in most accounts now as a tremendously self-conscious undertaking. Hugh Kenner proclaims clearly that the movement was written "by the canonized themselves, who were apt to be aware of a collective enterprise, and repeatedly acknowledged one another."[16] More recently, Lawrence Rainey marvels at how "literary modernism was unusual in the degree to which its principal protagonists interacted with one another through shared institutional structures."[17] The critical gestures necessary for the definition and redefinition of the movement were evident, in fact, across a range of public and private discourses flourishing throughout the first half of the last century, including editorials, letters, manifestos, translations, and, most notably, erudite essays. Edmund Wilson is widely acknowledged to have done a great deal to frame the early reception of modern literature in *Axel's Castle* (1931), but conscious certainly of the problems with which the word "modern" was fraught even then, he chose to extend the term "symbolist" to examine "the origins of certain tendencies" in literature that were to him "contemporary."[18] Laura Riding and Robert Graves actually anticipated this effort some years before with *A Survey of Modernist Poetry* (1927). A comprehensive and systematic apology for the works of its time, that study challenged the perception that the difficulty of modern art, the seeming "differences from traditional" works that define modern texts, presented no justifiable reason in and of itself to resist their resounding innovations.[19] Because their criticism sought in its own way to normalize modern art on its own terms, Riding and Graves took particular issue with the position of Louis Untermeyer who, they charged, placed too much emphasis on "simplicity" where he found it and treasured a "modernism no longer modern."[20] It is remarkable to read here of a movement already shabby and tired before it was properly named; Riding and Graves used "modern" and "modernist" almost interchangeably, and Peter Childs argues that their attempt to define modernism fell victim to a looseness of terminology and thus "failed to gain currency."[21] But in that their work singled out explicitly a number of their contemporaries for individual praise, an international catalogue of archetypes including Hart Crane, James Joyce, Marianne Moore, and Paul Valéry, *A Survey of Modernist Poetry* went well beyond simple appreciation, as too would Wilson's text four years later. The identification of a smaller, exceptional set of modernist writers represents a potent example of the gestures that continued to contribute to establishing modernism in subsequent decades.

Similarly, as the idea of the Lost Generation emerged and persisted in the popular imagination, self-conscious critical responses from expatriates were inevitable, especially as fictional portraits placed Americans abroad in an unflattering light. While *Dry Martini: A Gentleman Turns to Love* (1926), John Thomas's humorous, "Edwardian" portrait of expatriate life written from a safe distance on the well-heeled Right Bank, caused hardly a ripple, its author was regarded clearly as an outsider among those who lived, wrote, and socialized across the Seine.[22] It was Hemingway's *The Sun Also Rises* (1926) that introduced the "Lost Generation" phrase into general currency and provided from within the Left Bank enclave itself a damning portrait of recklessness and waste. In the first of the novel's three segments, American narrator Jake Barnes leads us on a tour along the Boulevard du Montparnasse, where there are altogether "too many . . . writers and artists,"[23] as far as his apartment on the Boulevard St. Michel. This short walk takes readers through scenes of excess, past La Rotonde, Le Sélect, the Café du Dôme, and the Dingo, located nearby on the rue Delambre. But it is on a tranquil fishing trip near Burguete in the Spanish countryside, far from the Parisian nightlife, that the normally lighthearted Bill Gorton upbraids his friend Jake and provides what would prove a representative condemnation of the expatriate lifestyle:

> You know what's the trouble with you? You're an expatriate. One of the worst type. Haven't you heard that? Nobody that ever left their own country ever wrote anything worth printing. Not even in the newspapers. . . . You're an expatriate. You've lost touch with the soil. You get precious. Fake European standards have ruined you. You drink yourself to death. You become obsessed by sex. You spend all your time talking, not working. You are an expatriate, see? You hang around cafés.[24]

Writing as Genêt in the *New Yorker*, Janet Flanner reported without exaggeration that the book "stirred Montparnasse, where, it is asserted, all four of the leading characters are local and easily identifiable."[25] The mainstream media in the United States worried that the book would become a "Bible" for disaffected youth, "callow cynics who were old enough to shave the down off their chins but not old enough to vote."[26] Richmond Barrett thus wrote of visiting the Left Bank, intent on observing expatriates hoping to "do magnificent work wherewith to startle the whole civilized world and make the United States put on mourning for having sent its rarest spirits into exile." He reported, not surprisingly, of dissipation and wasted potential. "They traipse lackadaisically from one café in the Montparnasse district to the next," he wrote of expatriates. "They go the rounds every day as patiently as a policeman on his beat." What was intended as freedom from American subjugation led instead to new limitations, shaped in an environment of largesse.

"Into this atmosphere, the neophyte from New York or San Francisco comes to breathe the ozone of fresh ideas," he continued. "It soon proves to be the stalest sort of carbon monoxide, that ozone; it makes him sleepy, dead-and-alive, languid."[27] Louis Bromfield defended against these charges "young writers" who went abroad to "find a way to live" by taking advantage of favorable exchange rates, surrounded as they found themselves "by people, by music, by good plays, by good pictures and the stimulation of intellectual companionship, in comfort and in certain quarters in luxury for less than it costs him to live in poverty in America."[28] Still, Barrett's observations were sufficiently notable that Frederick Lewis Allen cited his article in *Only Yesterday* (1931), his influential history of the American 1920s, in which Allen too lamented "a lost generation" who through "revolt against stupidity and mediocrity" still "could not find peace."[29]

In fact, through the end of the 1920s, a surfeit of American novels appeared—like Nathan Asch's *Love in Chartres* (1927), Harold Loeb's *The Professors Like Vodka* (1927), and Solita Solano's *This Way Up* (1927)—that drew extensively on experiences gleaned abroad. Asch's novel, in particular, invoked a number of motifs that became commonplace in discussions of expatriation, effectively contradicting Bromfield's optimism. A young American blueblood, bored with Paris, ventures southwest to Chartres, where she falls in love with a writer from the United States who finds inspiration from the Gothic cathedral's stained glass. While "he drank too much, and smoked all the time, and he looked as if he did not have enough to eat," she is enamored of him precisely "because he was so mysterious, so different" from the society boys back home.[30] The two become lovers as he nurses her through an illness, and the girl is both fascinated and horrified at the thought of how she thus estranges herself from the world her parents know, even as her mother tries to coax her home. "I know it costs father a good deal to keep you there, and you might at least get the most you can out of this trip, since you may never get another opportunity," she writes. "Business isn't too good, he says wages are going up, and people don't seem to buy as they used to. Anyway he isn't going to build the annex till next year. And he says he's going to get tired of this nonsense pretty soon, and *send for you*" (*LC*133).

Meanwhile, the young man's self-doubt prevents him from writing. "Can I do it? Can I? Am I capable of it?" he frets to himself. "Thrown up home, thrown up friends, thrown up what I used to do. Couldn't go back if I tried to" (*LC*59). He eventually blames his indolence on his relationship, observing that artists "are not fit for human intercourse, human companionship" (LC160). His resentment of the girl estranges them further, and he teeters near total collapse. "He was terribly drunk, could hardly sit straight in his chair, could hardly recognize the people around him," as he is described in the midst of one notable binge. "When he picked up another glass of brandy he spilled part of it and with his sleeve wiped the moist spot on his coat. Just terribly drunk" (LC136). Eventually, the young man abandons love to return to Paris, where life seems more tired than inspiring:

> . . . slowly the café had filled with people returning from the restaurants for their coffee. Their faces had been for the most part unfamiliar to him. In that café people came and went. One could never be sure how long anyone would stay, nor whom one could meet on any particular day. The people who had come in now, had seemed to him younger than himself. They seemed just to have come from America, the home dust not yet blown off them. Some had seemed just as assertive in embryo as the older, more experienced ones he was waiting for. And others had had unsure looks. Perhaps they also did not know what to do, how to go about accomplishing the things they were dreaming of. Looking at these people from home, who were very much like he himself had been when he had first come to Paris, had made him still more depressed, had made things still more helpless. (LC211)

By the time Kay Boyle's My Next Bride (1934) and F. Scott Fitzgerald's Tender Is the Night (1934) were published, many of the expatriates on whose experience such stories were modeled had returned to the United States, but any further unflattering portraits of life abroad only confirmed views prevalent in the American media, especially those printed following the suicide death of Harry Crosby in 1929. While the press had long held skeptical views of expatriates, as we have seen, an unprecedented scandal erupted in the wake of the notorious poet and publisher taking his own life and that of his socialite lover during a visit to New York. "Couple Shot Dead in Artist's Hotel," the New York Times declared on the morning of Wednesday, December 11. "Suicide Compact Is Indicated between Henry Drew Crosby and Harvard Man's Wife." But city tabloids like the Daily Mirror blamed the tragedy on the "sometimes half-mad thoughts on love and life" espoused by "the band of exiles" in Paris.[31] Immediately, a series of related articles popped up in Hearst papers throughout the country. Within the next decade, the idea of the Lost Generation began to emerge more systematically in academic circles as well. In Philip Horton's *The Life of an American Poet* (1938), his biography of Hart Crane, the author defined expatriate Americans, for example, as "fumbling for convictions and values among the spiritual ruins of post-war Europe."[32]

Louis Bromfield had predicted that, as young American writers grew more worldly, "the expatriate will be as extinct as a Dodo." Visitors from the United States would recognize each other and be accepted as global citizens in an Americanized world.[33] In fact, while Americans abroad between the World Wars continued to foster a particular identity, the growing perception that they might represent a cohort of note, and expatriates' own ambivalent musings about this possibility, coincided with what John Downton Hazlett understands as an unprecedented sense of "generational self-consciousness" among American writers. And, as he further acknowledges, "numerous memoirs and reminiscences" helped in "the construction of that generation's now legendary identity."[34] Sidonie Smith and Julia Watson recognize that life narratives compose a sort of "history" in that, among other things, authors may seek "to explore a certain time period, or to enshrine a community." Presumably, autobiography can thus create communities in their narratives that never actually existed, at least not by any formal endorsement. In this way, they can be seen to realize subjective "truth" rather than achieve historical "fact."[35]

To best understand autobiography as a framing discourse, the proliferation of texts that address life abroad in the 1920s might be read more broadly as critical acts. Indeed, autobiography as critical gesture has been pondered by readers like Anita Grossman, for one, who sees its defining characteristics in the "selection, interpretation, and imaginative re-creation" of its subject matter.[36] "The critical act and the autobiographical act share the same structure," Candace Lang argues further, "for both criticism and autobiography are discourses of language on—'about'—language." But Lang also acknowledges that the most persuasive and persistent objection to such a reading might be that while the critic always deals "with the language of another," the autobiographer "turns back upon his own discourse."[37] The implicit belief here, that the autobiographical subject enjoys some privileged ontological position, is one at the basis of earliest scholarly readings of life narratives. It is for this reason, for example, that Roy Pascal in *Design and Truth in Autobiography* (1960) believes that "critics are in no great difficulty to define their subject-matter when they write about autobiographies," narratives that seek "the reconstruction of the movement of a life, or part of a life, in the actual circumstances in which it was lived."[38] The subsequent implications for scholars as eminent as Philippe Lejeune is that "the *author*, the *narrator*, and the *protagonist* must be identical" in autobiography, and so the critical issue remains the responsibility assumed by autobiographers to faithfully render their stories for their readers.[39] Were this really the case, a perfect correlation between author and subject would differentiate autobiography from other forms of discourse, including criticism.

More recent readings of autobiography have forever changed the way we view this issue, of course. For Smith and Watson, "the emphasis of reading" life narratives has moved "from assessing and verifying knowledge to observing processes of communicative exchange and understanding."[40] The self as subject no longer enjoys the privileged position it had heretofore been granted. This dramatic shift is in no small part a result of Paul de Man, who argues convincingly that the self in autobiography on whom the reader has depended is nothing more than a "linguistic structure" created once an "author declares himself the subject of his own understanding." The "self-knowledge" seemingly reflected in autobiography is simply a "tropological structure" like any other thought, and so the defining feature for all autobiographical texts in de Man's view is their frequently frantic attempt to assert an elusive authority.[41] Whereas earlier enquiries, safe in their faith in a self in the text, concerned themselves with whether the words themselves represented an adequate medium for the expression of that self, one is justified today in considering further the status of the self created by that medium, a self that emerges as a critical construction in a web of social and linguistic connections. When Donna Perreault talks now of autobiography's "self-consciousness in language," she is acknowledging how the narrative represents a "turning back of the self upon itself" to realize provisional identities with no greater standing than the subjects of all other discursive constructions.[42] For expatriate Americans writing autobiography, not only are the selves they fashion submitted always to further revision within their narratives, but because they emerge in the context of a discussion of a cultural enterprise in whose creation they believed themselves to be participating by the writing of autobiography, these selves become forever connected to tendentious definitions of the Lost Generation—and, in fact, the modernism with which it is so inexorably implicated. It is not surprising that de Man despairs of the attention afforded autobiography as a literary genre, claiming that it "always looks slightly disreputable and self-indulgent" when "compared to tragedy, or epic, or lyric poetry."[43] Indeed, with perhaps a couple of notable exceptions, as we shall see, the autobiographical works of expatriate Americans pale in comparison with the great works of modern American fiction. But it is the accumulated impression of that time created by these autobiographies—impressions of the time that gave rise to its fiction and that shape our responses to it—that remains today most formidable.

To read modern American autobiography as criticism, one must also acknowledge how modern writers themselves worked hard to extend conceptions of critical discourse. Pound, for example, viewed "criticism by translation" as one of five viable "categories" that also include "discussion," "exercise in the style of a given period," "via music," and "in new composition."[44] T. S. Eliot looked for "criticism in the work of creation itself." In fact, he maintained that "the labour of sifting, combining, constructing, expunging, correcting, testing" one's own work represents "the highest kind of criticism."[45] But this is not to suggest that autobiography enjoyed universal acceptance, even among Americans abroad. John Pilling observes that "the most canvassed twentieth-century writers" neglected autobiography, in fact, contributing to a developing canon of texts "indirectly" through more marginal works.[46] "It [would] not interest me in the least to write my literary autobiography," Pound asserted in a letter in 1927, for example. "I don't see how that form of introspection [could] be expected to count as part of my own mental life, and I have no inclination to start dying before it is necessary."[47] However, as a relatively underutilized form, it soon proved itself receptive to the kind of aesthetic innovation that came to define modern literature. Olav Severijnen believes, for example, that works undertaken by writers in the first decades of the twentieth century "show the first essential renewal" of autobiography since its roots in antiquity.[48] By remaining receptive to modern artistic unrest, the works of expatriate Americans contributed to the distinctive techniques of modern narrative; on the other hand, Albert Stone finds in autobiographies that are less aesthetically challenging "a trend away from the modernist experiments" proliferating at this time,[49] revealing something of the ambivalent radicalism in some quarters by which the movement would be known. In an age whose literature was concerned with identity, autobiography was nothing if not a versatile form.

If one accepts that autobiography came to represent for modern writers a formidable framing gesture, a critical act heretofore underutilized and subsequently overlooked, there are perhaps more practical reasons why some expatriates came to embrace the form. Most importantly, perhaps, autobiography provided opportunities for lesser-known writers through this period. With their vivid memories of life in Paris, a wide variety of expatriates received attention from publishers in England and the United States, providing an audience the size of which was unprecedented for many of them. "Autobiographers need and court readers," Stone argues further, "especially sympathetic ones who will generously confirm the identity of the self who writes and the self who lived."[50] Mortgaging one's creative ambitions to the baser curiosities of readers interested in gossip held obvious dangers, however. Emerging from the shadows cast by their more famous contemporaries, they might find that they had accomplished little more than to strengthen further the reputations of those writers whose fame they could never hope to emulate. One might cynically suggest that the works of expatriates largely forgotten found eventual influence because of their audience's perception of autobiography as a more accessible, an "easier" form that tantalizingly promised to elucidate modernism.

It is now well established that modern art had a fraught relationship with society at large. While clearly responding to the broad impulses of industrial culture, the elitist impulses of its artists separated modernism from its widest audience. Recently, John Carey has argued "that the principle around which modernist literature and culture fashioned themselves," in fact, "was the exclusion of the masses." In *The Intellectuals and the Masses* (1991), he makes the case that elitism was early twentieth-century art's "hostile reaction" to the "majority of people," a strategy intended to ensure the superiority of the artist.[51] This privileged position is perhaps best illustrated in the writings of Ezra Pound, whose 1916 article "The New Sculpture" established firmly the aristocracy of creative individuals:

> We turn back, we artists, to the powers of the air, to the djinns who were our allies aforetime, to the spirits of our ancestors. It is by them that we have ruled and shall rule, and by their connivance that we shall mount again into our hierarchy. The aristocracy of entail and of title has decayed, the aristocracy of commerce is decaying, the aristocracy of the arts is ready again for its service.[52]

The wider issue for contemporary readers may be the threat to the

very relevance of modernism as it developed. Its exclusionism, symbolized most potently by the romantic image of Charles-Augustin
Sainte-Beuve's "Ivory Tower," is what for some contemporary readers gave rise to postmodernism with its skepticism of all totalizing
narratives, but the immediate challenge Pound offered self-conscious,
aspiring modernists was securing for themselves a place within the
wider culture, a place that assured them the venerated position so
central to their definition as artists. The dilemma is obvious: while
equality between artists and their audience was undesirable, indeed
impossible, the widest possible audience must still be brought at least
to recognize and acknowledge the achievement of modern art. If
modernism was ever to be anything more than a minority protest
against prevalent artistic values, the key to its acceptance rested with
those who were least likely even to understand it. "The artist has no
longer any belief or suspicion that the mass, the half-educated sim-
pering general, the semi-connoisseur, the sometimes collector, and
still less the readers of the *Spectator* and the *English Review*," Pound
continued, "can in any way share his delights or understand his pleasure in forces."[53]

The romantic view had been that one of the tasks of criticism
is the popularization of literary works, "*creating* the taste by which"
a writer "is to be enjoyed."[54] As the reading public continued to
expand, however, the nature of the audience grew more heterogeneous, and the function of modern criticism inevitably changed
with it. "I consider criticism merely a preliminary excitement,"
Pound wrote of his own essays, "a statement of things a writer has
to clear up in his own head sometime or other."[55] Despite his out-
spoken support for a broad reform of education, his claim that "one
work of art is worth forty prefaces and as many apologiæ"[56] was
consistent with his position that it was actually the creative output
of "great writers" that best safeguarded "the whole machinery of
social and of individual thought."[57] Criticism, as traditionally conceived, could hardly be expected to illuminate masterpieces for a
presumptuous throng. So, too, for Eliot, creative works themselves
offered the best instruction to the truly sensitive, as a great "part of
creation is really criticism," after all. Criticism is not solely a private
matter for the artist, however; Eliot acknowledged, for example, that
some works of criticism "have been useful to other writers." But
because "the elucidation of works of art and the correction of taste"
endured as one function of criticism, he accepted that it might also
be "useful to those who were not writers."[58] If the consolidation of
a wider audience persisted in some quarters as one narrow function

of critical discourse for modern authors, might not autobiography, perceived after all as more accessible, be an ideal form to serve this modest purpose?

In the introduction to his *Autobiography* (1951), William Carlos Williams wondered whether readers would even be interested in such texts, comparing literary life stories to "rock candy," while "sweet-toothed" audiences might prefer "something richer and not so hard on the teeth."[59] But in discussing the overwhelming commercial popularity of autobiography, Albert Stone argues that a twentieth-century readership embraced the form precisely because it helped them "in bypassing the usual high-cultural institutions."[60] If modernism developed with elitist principles in ascendance, it was also forced to entertain broader, populist impulses in a desire to reach and influence an audience, even if these impulses might, at times, be rooted in narrow motives of commercial success and public esteem from which its most hallowed figures could not divorce themselves entirely. Upon the publication of *The Autobiography of Alice B. Toklas* (1934), Gertrude Stein found, after three decades of popular obscurity, that she had finally written something that would allow her to be recognized in her own time. Through autobiography, the infamously difficult author found the readers she believed she deserved all along:

> It can easily be realized that after these years of faith that there is and was a public and that som[e]time I would come in contact with that public, as I said in *The Making of Americans* which I wrote twenty-seven years ago, I write for myself and strangers, after these years to know that I have a public gives me what the French call a coeur léger, it makes me not light-hearted but it leaves me unburdened.
>
> And the readers of the autobiography will not only read the autobiography but they will read and see everything that has made the autobiography. And so all this which has pleased and contented me will please and content them.[61]

Through autobiography, modern authors thus found a way to communicate with a mass audience in an attempt to secure and improve their positions in the popular imagination. Despite the apparent simplicity of the narratives, autobiography allowed expatriate writers from the United States to shape perceptions of lives lived abroad. Thus, these narratives proved themselves to be far more complicated than they first appear.

This subsequent study will provide detailed readings of seventeen modern American autobiographies, using more than a dozen other such remembrances to further the social and literary context in which they were all written:

Chapter 1 examines the achievement of Alfred Kreymborg's *Troubadour* (1925), the autobiography that gave readers in the United States one of the earliest accounts of expatriate life for Americans in Paris. While Kreymborg was a little older than many of the young writers who traveled abroad in the early 1920s, his account of a fledgling American modernism, first in the bohemian neighborhoods of Manhattan and later among an international community gathered in Paris, furnishes a prescient overview of the developing movement. Kreymborg is certain that he is participating in the growth of important twentieth-century art, and while he is as yet unable to give the movement its name, the manner in which his narrative gathers together many of its central figures and their disparate aims mirrors the critical undertakings of more self-conscious modernists. By writing about himself in the third person, Kreymborg exhibits a characteristic skepticism about autobiography itself, and his text shows a movement beyond the sermonic tradition in its form. While he charts his own distinctive conversion from schoolboy to poet, his certainty that the artistic life is suitable only for a chosen few hints at a deeper elitism that comes to be a hallmark of modernism.

Chapter 2 explores the ways in which Gertrude Stein used autobiography to further her desire for literary acclaim. The acknowledged conceit at the heart of *The Autobiography of Alice B. Toklas*, writing her own story in the voice of her longtime companion, allows Stein to claim some degree of objectivity. Essentially, she seeks to write about her life without actually revealing too much about herself, and the care with which she refuses to discuss the nature of her lesbianism reminds readers how interpreting autobiography requires, in part, a deft reading of absences. By embracing autobiography, however, Stein concedes the interest readers have in the story of her life, even though she maintains consistently that an author's works themselves and not gossipy anecdotes are the only true embodiments of artistic essence. This is the sort of compromise she accepts reluctantly as the price of commercial success, though it reflects modernism's equivocal relationship with its audience. Stein undertakes a narrative strategy in both the Toklas book and the subsequent *Everybody's Autobiography* (1937) in which she seeks to distance herself from her contemporaries, and yet the texts work ultimately by contextualizing her achievement within that of the very people whom she hopes to deny. Her thoughts on expatriate Americans, her definition of the Lost Generation, are intended to differentiate her from them, but she succeeds only in connecting their lives with hers, writing records of life abroad that every remembrance of this period will have to answer.

Chapter 3 reviews Malcolm Cowley's detailed examination of the expatriate impulse in *Exile's Return* (1934/1951), the first text that invited a comprehensive discussion of the Lost Generation. Cowley's autobiography and its subsequent revision emphasize the diversity of the expatriate experience for Americans, but it is also noteworthy for its relative neglect of Cowley's own life story. By distancing himself from much of the central action of his narrative, Cowley also hopes to posit an objectivity that marks the early autobiographies of his contemporaries, but his text ultimately lacks a defining experience for lives lived abroad in the 1920s. Such a recognizable symbol of expatriation was provided by Harold Stearns, whose *The Street I Know* (1935) appeared soon after the first edition of Cowley's text. Stearns's disaffection with life in the United States was reflected in his early critical writings, and through them he encouraged a generation of young American writers to follow him abroad. While Stearns's dissipation in Paris offers Cowley the prohibitive example he requires, Stearns is virtually neglected in *Exile's Return*, so that its author can vindicate expatriates by stressing their timely reconciliation with their native land. Stearns's autobiography does chart his eventual return home, but his response to the hardships he encounters suggests that the self-discovery necessary for the writing of one's life can be as much a defining gesture as the reaffirmation of loyalty to country.

Chapter 4 emphasizes the importance of place in expatriate American autobiography. The example of Samuel Putnam's *Paris Was Our Mistress* (1947) and Bravig Imbs's *Confessions of Another Young Man* (1936) illustrates how less influential figures in American modernism use shared space to assert their position within the Lost Generation, how experience in Paris helps authors imagine a community to which they can connect themselves through the writing of their lives. Both these autobiographies thus emphasize diversity in portraying life abroad, and their authors resist exacting definitions and clear distinctions between expatriates of different nationalities. While modernism can be read, in part, as a reaction to industrialized space, Putnam and Imbs suggest that place itself plays an important role in defining one's life, and the former goes so far as to personify Paris to underline its influence on him. While the latter's text also presents vivid portraits of life outside the city, both expatriates see Paris as an important trigger to memory, and they search for the heart of modern American expatriation in specific locations along the Left Bank. For Putnam, it is the salon of Natalie Barney on the rue Jacob; for Imbs, it is Sylvia Beach's famous bookshop on the rue de l'Odéon. For many other expatriates, it must be said, expatriation is defined by the café culture that distinguishes the literary community of Paris from those of the American cities they leave behind.

Chapter 5 answers the gendering male of the Lost Generation. While American women played a crucial role in expatriate life in Paris, few records of their experience emerged before the 1950s, leaving uncontested the portrait of expatriate women that appeared in the stories written by men. That Sylvia Beach uses *Shakespeare and Company* (1956), the name of her bookshop, in titling her autobiography suggests that her life story understates her contribution to Left Bank life. But while expatriates from Malcolm Cowley to Samuel Putnam similarly emphasize community over individual in their remembrances, Beach's text has long been criticized for how she effaces her own experience. The challenges inherent to the reception of women's autobiographies remind readers that their authors embrace effectively a variety of different forms of life narrative, including letters, diaries, and journals. In fact, letters provided an important view of life abroad, and Janet Flanner's "Paris Letter," published in the *New Yorker* and anthologized as *Paris Was Yesterday* (1972), provides throughout the 1920s and 1930s a unique perspective on the Lost Generation, contrasting the experience of expatriate Americans with the lives of their French hosts. While the "Paris Letter" thus suggests that a genuine European life is beyond the reach of most American visitors, the fragmented mosaic of impressions Flanner creates reveals as much about her, and her impressions of life abroad, as any expatriate American autobiography of the period.

Chapter 6 surveys a number of revisions of the Lost Generation during the 1960s. Ernest Hemingway's *A Moveable Feast* (1964), perhaps the most famous expatriate American autobiography, can itself be seen as a revisionist work. Published posthumously by Mary Welsh Hemingway, his widow, the text follows nearly forty years of the remembrances of his contemporaries. Hemingway's autobiography is uncharitable to almost all those Americans with whom he spent time in Paris, as its author seeks to deny the influence of both mentors and friends. His desire to assert his superiority as an artist undermines even a loose sense of community among expatriate Americans. While other writers, like Matthew Josephson and Harold Loeb, brought forward their remembrances at this time, the most interesting view of life abroad is provided by Kay Boyle, who adds supplementary chapters to Robert McAlmon's autobiography to create a revised *Being Geniuses Together* (1968). By suggesting that there are many parallels to be drawn between the experiences of Americans abroad between the World Wars, Boyle hopes to connect herself to the Lost Generation, but the resulting text contradicts the antagonism at the heart of McAlmon's remembrances and, by doing so, it raises serious questions about textual authority and autobiographical voice.

Finally, chapter 7 considers the subsequent decades of expatriate American autobiography, as publishers continue to bring forward posthumously the remembrances of Lost Generation authors. As readings of modernism shift to answer claims of exclusion by pointing to the movement's diversity, these autobiographies serve to reinforce the full range of experiences Americans had abroad. Some texts, like Gorham Munson's *The Awakening Twenties* (1985), illustrate primarily how the revisionist impulse persisted in expatriates until the end of their lives. Other autobiographies, like Maria Jolas's *Woman of Action* (2004), add unique perspectives to the record of expatriation by exploring the different motivations people had in traveling to Europe after the war. But texts like Wambly Bald's *On the Left Bank* (1987), Eugene Jolas's *Man from Babel* (1998), and Waverley Root's *The Paris Edition* (1987) cut to the heart of established understandings of modernism by addressing directly charges of elitism in the modernist impulse. By emphasizing the connection between expatriate Americans and commercial newspapers, by examining the role of the Paris *Tribune* in supporting Americans abroad and fostering their creative ambitions, these texts reposition the Lost Generation by calling attention to its most populist impulses.

1

BEYOND THE
SERMONIC TRADITION

In *Educated Lives: The Rise of Modern Autobiography in America* (1976), Thomas Cooley outlines the importance of "religious narratives" in the development of American literature. More than one-third of all autobiographies that appeared in the United States before 1850 were remembrances of missionary work, spiritual autobiographies, and recollections of clergymen. Slave stories and captivity narratives became increasingly important to the developing form throughout the eighteenth and nineteenth centuries, and the "confessions" of criminals also began to assert popular appeal at this time as "unhappy examples" of lives lived. In all, early American autobiography performed an actively reformative function, instructing its readers in practical matters and providing what Cooley describes as "an aid to spiritual exercise."[1] Although religious texts have declined in relative importance in the canon of American autobiography over the past 150 years, Philip Abbott attempts to extend their rhetorical influence through a discussion of what he describes as "the sermonic tradition": finding even in secular narratives a reliance on the "conversion experience," a desire to contrast one's old self with a new, tracing one's development for the practical benefit of the reader by punctuating a decisive moment in life's progress. According to Abbott, "The life thus improved becomes a living model for others to imitate."[2]

Indeed, conversion is for some readers a useful trope for the understanding of all autobiography; conversion, as Peter Dorsey understands it, has been adopted consciously by authors as a narrative "model" to represent "many kinds of psychological change" in their respective lives.[3] From at least the end of the nineteenth century, such secular conversion has frequently involved, according to Philip Dodd, the discovery of one's "vocation" as the "resolution" of an individual's "self-determination and socialisation."[4] For the twentieth-century autobiographies with which we are concerned, the treatment of vocation took on a greater significance, of course. Asserting oneself as a writer was an important gesture in the emerging culture of modernism, a culture that extended without hesitation the romantic adulation of artists and their inherent gifts. But if the rhetoric of the conversion narrative seeks "to bind the life of the reader into its own pattern," as Geoffrey Harpham explains it, this process can be seen as attempting to normalize even the "extraordinary or unique" subject to make it relevant to its readers.[5] This is particularly important in writing about creative endeavors. While modernism sought to foster talent, it did not engage readers who could benefit from criticism by seeking to minimize the distinctiveness of creative aptitude. Modern criticism sought to familiarize an audience with its works without providing the comprehensive exegesis that might diminish the formidable achievement of its artists; therefore, if literary autobiography is to be successful in its own critical aims, it must never normalize artistry, despite the fact that its narratives are constructed to illustrate for their readers the development of artists themselves.

The first autobiography published by an American who spent time abroad between the World Wars was Alfred Kreymborg's *Troubadour*. Brought forward by Boni and Liveright in 1925, it tells the story of a minor poet and playwright best known at that time for his involvement with important little magazines like *Glebe* and *Others*. He distinguished himself through a variety of *vers libre* experiments, represented by the publication of volumes like *Mushrooms* (1915) and *Less Lonely* (1923), and he built a reputation through offbeat stage experiments in drama, music, and puppetry. His autobiography is important today primarily because of its distinctiveness as an expatriate artifact of the 1920s; after all, the text appeared almost a full decade before Gertrude Stein's *The Autobiography of Alice B. Toklas* (1934). But Kreymborg's text also follows what Philip Abbott would recognize as an archetypal conversion pattern to chart the emergence of one modern artist from the midst of a commercial American culture during the first years of the twentieth century, as its author moved from demonstrating musical instruments and selling popular sheet music in a Manhattan shop to writing poetry and performing fringe theater throughout the United States. Most critically, Kreymborg never attempts to use his own defining experience in *Troubadour* to shepherd others to the artist's life; he proselytizes here for acknowledgment alone. In doing so, this autobiography successfully establishes the presence of a critical self-consciousness we have been associating with the modern essay: justifying the experiments of what was, for Kreymborg, a contemporary art; reappropriating the derogatory term "modern"; taking first, tentative steps toward defining modernism as a movement; and asserting for this fledgling movement a privileged position within American culture. It also anticipates other autobiographies by providing readers in the United States an early glimpse of the lives lived by Americans in Paris and, indeed, throughout Europe, as Kreymborg tells stories of his travels in France, Italy, Austria, Germany, and England. The principal aim of this critical activity is clearly the fostering of an audience in the United States and abroad for a modern art Kreymborg himself had helped to nourish through the two decades preceding the appearance of this text.

Like many autobiographies, *Troubadour* underlines a number of difficulties in writing about the self. In an attempt to present "an impersonal picture of personal experience," Kreymborg tells the reader that "he tried to walk around himself, and to record what he found in the round on a flat surface."[6] This mapping trope is persuasive, but it is overshadowed by a more striking comparison between autobiography and necromancy. "Re-creating people is a process subject to tenacious resistance when you have less than dust to reanimate and only words for the chemicals," he observes. "Notwithstanding the most superhuman skill, brought to the service of the most passionate longing to give life to the past, images, composed of a few salient outlines and a modicum of harmonious tones, will be the sole semblance art is able to snatch from nature" (*T*18). In his hands, these fragments are brought back to life, but this understanding of life narrative is significantly different from our own, where selves are created, not recreated, in the discourse. What is more incisive is his apparent appreciation of memory as a process, what Sidonie Smith and Julia Watson see as "an interpretation of a past that can never be fully recovered," rather than the accessing of an assembled store of reminiscences.[7] "As he tried to touch the past," Kreymborg admits, "some of it responded and made what he was trying to do—he with his uncertain memory in the tumult of an ever-changing present—sharp enough for him to seize this or that particle in the round" (T414–15). In arranging these remnants, he slips—furtively at first—into the third person. As with *The Education of Henry Adams* (1918), the Pulitzer Prize–winning text that would almost certainly have been on his mind when he sat down to write, this manner of narration is the defining aesthetic feature of the autobiography. In his seminal reading of *Education*, Robert Sayre suggests that Adams adopted the strategy to create distance from his character in the narrative for the purpose of an "epic magnification and ennobling of the self."[8] While texts like Kreymborg's have an obvious interest in elevating and maintaining the social position of the artist, his reliance on the third-person narrator in *Troubadour* is probably best read as an extension of the skepticism he felt toward autobiographical writing itself. "Was it not an artist's duty, in so far as he could, to detach himself as observer from himself as an actor," he asks, "let the cooler of the two comment on the antics of the hotter as if the latter were a person totally foreign and curious?" (T143). In this regard, he claims to have "developed a spirit of detachment" (T212) that extended to his own reading practices. "He tried to walk around a book as one might around a sculpture, and constantly to examine himself as well as the object before him," Kreymborg claims (T147). By extension, in one of his first serious writing exercises, he experimented with trying to achieve a "strictly impersonal essay," an autobiography of sorts, to examine his life "all the way back to his boyhood" (T142). His discussion of this fragment of juvenilia is important, as he describes his subject as "a pathetically amusing stranger" to him, while the detached writer of the story functions as "an omniscient spirit containing one or two of the conscious attributes of a higher deity" (T144).

In discussing his formative years, Kreymborg notes that the medical attendant at his birth misspelled the name on his birth certificate, and because only someone named "Alfried F. Kreymburg" (T20) was officially fixed in language, he can justify his attempts to divorce himself from the autobiographical "I" throughout *Troubadour*. This apparent loophole to escape what we have seen as some of the persistent narrative problems that occupy readers of autobiography fails to simplify his own approach to subjectivity, however. While the text concedes that a definitive version of the self in the story is an impossibility, "a multiple being" appears, instead, with a young Kreymborg looking to a future that is remembered by another, older one (T14). This latter character, tied to constant reflection, is bound to the whims of memory. It is ironic, perhaps, that the

ability to forget was an early coping strategy for the young Kreymborg, as he admits that his childhood indiscretions, held back in
shame from Catholic confession, could be tamed in his conscience
only if he "forgot many of them, even most of them" (T27). As an
inquisitive adult, on the other hand, "beginning to look back in retrospect" (T28), Kreymborg's undependable recall presents genuine
impediments to the narrative. During a visit to California, he encountered "an old boyhood associate," for example, who "reminded
him of one of the things that had slipped his memory." This particular detail, revealed in the last quarter of *Troubadour*, turns out
to be a fact of great significance to the beginning of Kreymborg's
story: his earliest literary activity, writing as "chess editor" of the
grammar school paper *The Nonpareil*, had in fact been wiped from
his mind by a "freak of forgetfulness" (T297). Still, he compares the
emotional contact he has with his past with the physical contact he
once longed for from other writers. Accepting its capriciousness,
remembering allows Kreymborg to contextualize his own experience as an artist, as he imagines himself encountering his personi-
fied past:

> Your hands would greet each other as well—sometimes for the
> last time—though you never knew it then. It would be very hard
> to recall the precise variation of that pressure; the temperature
> of it; the mood of the moment which dictated it; and the im-
> mediate effect, or the effect long after, the effect right now, of
> the contact. Except to state that it drew you out of yourself for a
> while, and draws you out now, in the attempted re-creation of a
> past, almost the whole of which is out of sight, out of sound; and
> the residue, the wistful residue, a vague, though radiant recollec-
> tion, which has in it, however, somehow, somewhere, the intrin-
> sic power to help you along whenever you need it. (T13)

This more optimistic contemplation of remembering also carries
with it an acknowledgment of experience, notably unequivocal for
a modern writer putting pen to paper in the years after the First
World War. Despite Kreymborg's early struggles—his hunger, his
loneliness, his rejection—it is clear that he is grateful to have this
material upon which to reflect, grateful to have a past demonstrably
relevant to his present circumstances.

Ultimately, his strategy for illustrating the tensions between
memory and subjectivity is to persist in the characterization of
two Alfred Kreymborgs: child "Ollie" eventually gives way to adult

"Krimmie," though he admits that he cared little for either of these nicknames given him by others. While graduation from grammar school, confirmation in the church, and the adoption of "long trousers at the age of fourteen" represented significant rites of passage for other boys, none of these events facilitated Kreymborg's most significant change, a change that at first went virtually undetected among even his family members. Indeed, he writes that during his adolescence, his parents "never had the smallest suspicion that the idiosyncrasies of Ollie would ever develop or degenerate, as the case may be, into a profession so weird, so hopelessly impractical ...as poetry" (T25). While the passage of time carried Ollie toward adulthood physically, the advancing years alone did not come to define Krimmie as an artist. Kreymborg's portrait of Ollie as a sensitive, precocious youth suggests that his "conversion" to art was less a dramatic transformation than it was a manner of realization, the cultivation of his innate promise. He sees "growing up" as a mysterious process, in fact, an "education, or development, or whatever one chooses to call the factors" in a boy's progress (T47). His abilities as a fledgling writer, hidden though they may have been in the back room of his father's cigar shop in Manhattan and, later, the Bronx, were nourished by the environment that is Kreymborg's inheritance.

Throughout the text, he identifies himself consistently as a New Yorker. Born in 1883, he writes to chart the city's coming of age during the final years of the nineteenth century, and his narrative underlines the importance of Manhattan to the development of modern art in the United States, both as a fertile background for its artists and as a mercenary environment whose challenge is answered by their art. Kreymborg's story is also, in many ways, his coming to terms with the isolation of a modern metropolis, with the "tempestuous pace" of life in commercial New York. Young Ollie had little thought of "getting on in the world" (T76), of joining the "vigorous, live-wire groups known as corporations" asserting themselves at the time (T79), even though "such an attitude in such a town was suicidal" (T76). His creativity became a refuge for him, as he saw his position as more precarious than that of an immigrant first seeking his fortune on the streets of the city:

> He did not belong, and he felt he could never belong. No
> stranger, no matter how remote and primitive the background of
> the small town he hailed from, seemed as foreign to New York
> as this youngster who had been born there, who had never left

it and, as far as he could tell at the time, was never to leave it. Almost any outsider, after a short sojourn in town, knew more about it. Such a man entered it with zest, settled in it, made use of it, let it nurture him. Such a citizen progressed, prospered, and in plenty of instances, became a man of the realm, an example for other Americans to come and do likewise. Such folk brushed Ollie aside, figuratively spat on him. (*T76*)

Resigned to attempt some compromise with corporate America, Kreymborg took a job at Aeolian Hall on Fifth Avenue, for a starting salary of six dollars a week, demonstrating music rolls and trifling with the world of machines by playing "pianolas and orchestrelles" while dreaming "of writing books of his own" (*T85–86*). On the job, he jeopardized his sales average by investing "two or three precious hours converting" customers willing to listen to "better" music than they might have initially intended to purchase (*T97*). While he believed that it "was obvious enough" to most people "that hand-made things in general are more personal and precious than machine-made," he was also willing to acknowledge the role of machines in nation building, as "so vast a continent" as North America "required machines to conquer it." But out of his desire not "to build or work or become a machine" himself (*T80*), perhaps, he decided to quit this job after three years, a resolution that hastened the emergence of Krimmie. "He allowed himself to be lured away," as Kreymborg describes it, to take up residence in "a thing so quixotic as a studio—not even a studio, but a room, less than a room—up the stairs of a dismal, rickety building on West Fourteenth Street" (*T93–94*). By doing so, he attempted to separate himself from neophyte amateurs who talked "big about art" but practiced their craft only "on Sundays and holidays—when the offices they worked in closed for the day" (*T92*). He admits, "There was nothing now he wanted more than to start a literary career and no other way of starting it properly except in such a room" (*T99*). The nickname "Krimmie" was, in fact, given him at this time by Lance Hartpence, his "foremost crony in the [Aeolian] Hall" (*T97*) and a fellow hopeful artist who eventually got work at the Daniel Gallery on West Forty-Seventh Street. The "conversion" he helped Ollie realize was clearly not an evangelical experience, then, but as James Muldoon reads conversion, it may actually include "a range or spectrum of experiences," a "process of education and . . . development" rather than a "single moment," that might within a secular text signify progression within a vocation.[9] Kreymborg writes, for example, of his "apprenticeship to the great ones in literature," his voracious reading of international letters (*T*147). He endured long periods where he wondered

> how many more [rejections] would the postman bring, how many more would you walk to the bottom of four flights of stairs to remove from your black tin box in the vestibule and climb to the top of four flights of stairs to slit open and release, along with the rejected manuscript, the sheets you had typed so neatly, the white thing you had spent so many hours on, days on, weeks on, so much energy, blood, hope, despair, trying to make it speak, to fill it with you, cajoling it, imploring it, revising it, only to have it return, speechless, helpless, inanimate, folded where you had folded it, with the identical creases, and no sign to betray the thing had been touched at all, not even a smudge or a thumb print to prove the thing had ever left you. (*T*15–16)

Had he been hopelessly uncertain of his talent, however, no amount of apprenticeship would have allowed him to secure an audience. Casting forth in an uncertain manner allowed Kreymborg to follow a pattern Philip Abbott understands as a passage "from dependence to liberation"[10]; *Troubadour* sketches the writer's movement away from trust in the work-a-day commercial world of one New York to the artistic freedom granted by another. "Being an artist was clearly the most inexpensive profession one could possibly undertake," he enthuses. "And there was absolutely no joy like it—nothing like it. At times" (*T*100).

This autobiography is also the story of an American artist who ventured abroad, of course; the central trope in the text is that of the medieval troubadour carrying "the instrument of his expression," to use Kreymborg's favorite image, "from place to place" (*T*339). But the troubadour is a minstrel, not really a missionary, and by his itinerant ways he hoped only to familiarize as many people as possible with works rooted in the Little Renaissance of Greenwich Village. Initially, Kreymborg moved around the United States, traveling west, with this simple desire to bring more remote "centers into eventual communication with a more universal ideal" (*T*353). Rejecting the skepticism of small-town life expressed by contemporaries like Theodore Dreiser and Sinclair Lewis, he found outside New York finer and more hopeful aspects of American life, where the material ethos of a "dollar-ridden America" could be escaped (*T*339). If Kreymborg's dream was "the possibility of earn-ing one's livelihood on the road in the independent character of a troubadour," then, he hoped only to come "into more varied contact with the people of a polyglot nation" (*T*292). Thoughts of seeing Europe came relatively late. It was not until 1921 that he first ventured abroad, though it is with tales of his eighteen months in Europe that he begins and ends his autobiography, pages that occupy approximately one-quarter of the text.

John Dos Passos later wrote that college men like himself and e. e. cummings, who had been pretending "to live in the eighteen-nineties" rather than concern themselves with "the massacres round Verdun," were by 1916 "breaking off from the esthetes." The value these young men placed upon the legitimacy of genuine experience, "real life" as Dos Passos described it, put them at odds with their upwardly mobile contemporaries who were "getting ready to go out into the world to sell bonds." He maintained that after his graduation he was "dying to get to Belgium to exhaust surplus energy by going to and fro in the earth and walking up and down in it."[11] It was this sentiment that first brought some young Americans abroad in pursuit of a "romantic dream," as Arlen Hansen describes it in his study *Gentlemen Volunteers* (1996), of enlisting for ambulance duty even before the United States entered the First World War. Thus, an early "automobile craze" in the United States fueled the ambitions of individuals from Harry Crosby to Ernest Hemingway, Slater Brown to Archibald MacLeish, and this tentative awakening to Europe led to longer personal engagements through the 1920s.[12] But before hostilities began, Kreymborg had already celebrated his thirtieth birthday, and he spent the period of which Dos Passos writes so vividly composing "impassioned songs against war and death" that "even radical journals rejected." Although "he imagined that love songs could put an end to war," Kreymborg was disillusioned to find that such protests "might as well have been written in water" (*T*233). Once Woodrow Wilson committed American troops to the enterprise, Kreymborg could not avoid indefinitely the draft board's desire to make him "cannon fodder," as he viewed it, though once they discovered that "his pulse beat a little too fast, that he was troubled with astigmatism and was considerably below the required weight for a man five feet eight inches tall," he was exempted from military service (*T*323).

For this reason, it was not until 1920, immediately after the completion of a tour of California with his wife, Dorothy, that he thought about "trying a trip to Europe" (*T*340), but at the time he concluded that even "a short trip" was impractical because of the exhaustion he felt (*T*359). Within months, however, he was recruited by Harold Loeb to help launch the little magazine *Broom* and, owing in part to the international strength of the American dollar, the two men "talked about Europe as the continent from which to publish their venture" (*T*362). What attracted Kreymborg to this scheme, personally, was that establishing a magazine in Europe offered "an enticing opportunity to introduce lesser known American artists abroad" (*T*20). Because European literary magazines imported to the United States at that time, according to Kreymborg at least, "already gave evidences of a rapidly growing interest in" American art, he was optimistic about a venture that could publish his contemporaries in "European circles" (*T*362–63). This attitude separated him from expatriates who sought to escape a moribund cultural scene in the United States.

At some basic level, the adjective "expatriate" is valuable simply for allowing us to imagine American writers abroad, in a physical sense. But beyond the realities of absence and presence, Donald Pizer reminds us that expatriation involves a complex emotional process that at "its most fundamental level" implicates both "the rejection of a homeland and the desire for and acceptance of an alternative place."[13] Kreymborg, writing in the 1920s when the best of both his contemporaries and a younger group of writers ventured abroad for at least some period of time, understands an expatriate as someone who had permanently abandoned the United States. T. S. Eliot and Ezra Pound, for example, were expatriates because they left forever an America they viewed as "inhospitable" to art (*T*127). Kreymborg "rather dreaded Eliot might grow subservient to the dominant influence, however laudable, of his flawless scholarship" developed in Europe. "It might eventually thwart instead of nourish his originality," he cautions (*T*397). While he had great personal affection for Pound, he viewed him as "more Parisian than the Parisians" in his "velveteens, wide-open collar and flowing tie," and Kreymborg dismissed his critical judgments because despite the poet's declared faith in an American Risorgimento, Kreymborg believed that at heart he "hated all things American" (*T*369). On the other hand, neither Conrad Aiken nor John Gould Fletcher, living in London, should be considered expatriates because they remained committed to "the battles of American poetry" (*T*395). In this regard, Kreymborg's views had much in common with those of his friend William Carlos Williams, with whom he had frequently collaborated. In his *Autobiography*, Williams repeated his familiar complaint that Eliot's *The Waste Land* (1922) was "a sardonic bullet" that distracted young writers from availing themselves "of a new art form" that must be "rooted in the locality which should give it fruit,"[14] encouraging them instead to abandon the "local conditions" of American art.[15] Still, Williams resolved to visit Europe himself during the mid-1920s, at which time he continued to work on *In The American Grain* (1925), a study intended "to get inside the heads of some of the American founders" to assess the creative heritage of the United States.[16] That trip was neither his first nor his last journey abroad, but it illustrated the ways in which a strong-minded American writer could immerse himself in a foreign culture without being saturated by it.

Similarly, Kreymborg maintains that "no one surpassed him in his love of great foreign literature," but he too went to Europe with a defiant attitude. While this "great foreign literature has a superlative following in the past, present and future all over the world," he worried that "what there might be of great American literature has comparatively few readers anywhere." His artistic ideal is international, ultimately. "A man was an artist by virtue of being an artist and not because he had been born here, there or elsewhere," he believes most fervently (*T*130). But he still ventured abroad with some uncertainty, as his experience in the United States suggested that "worship of things overseas was so indiscriminate in most instances that the poorest European products, or even those which the old countries had found antiquated and had discarded, were accepted by the cognoscenti in preference to some of the fresh, crude, vital products of the native soil" (*T*406). He was wary of this manner of Europhilia to be encountered in New York, where "the prominent foreign visitor infested every lecture platform," and where "in the absence of any deep-rooted self-respect on the part of his hearers, was engaged and ogled indiscriminately" (*T*295). His own acquaintances had been to Europe where they "had been in touch with the latest art movements," and when they returned to the United States, the "stay-at-homes" they encountered "revelled in their stories and pantomime and plied them for more" (*T*240). On this point, visual artists provided Kreymborg with a hopeful paradigm, as Samuel Halpert and Man Ray possessed artistic "tools" of a "Parisian character" that still showed "the influence of the American scene," reflecting well "the architecture and machinery of" their native land (*T*199). But with fewer so-called "stay-at-homes" left by the 1920s, the dangers of immersion seem more pressing to Alfred Kreymborg.

Because his autobiography was published a year before the appearance of *The Sun Also Rises*, Kreymborg does not make use of the Lost Generation phrase, of course. But the enthusiasm with which the phrase was embraced to discuss Americans abroad was evidenced in his 1932 collection of verse entitled *The Little World: 1914 and After*, where Kreymborg titled a poem with those contentious words:

> Whether
> the apple
> Adam ate
> was green or
> ripe or rotten,
> some of
> his sons
> are very ill
> from being
> ill-begotten.[17]

"The Lost Generation," and other poems like it in a section entitled "Paris in 1930," was clearly inspired by a later trip to France. Kreymborg was willing, by that time, to recognize writers who came of age before 1920 as "an older generation" of American artists,[18] but when writing *Troubadour* he drew no such distinctions between Americans abroad, save criticizing as expatriates those who turned their backs on the United States. "Americans were hurrying back to Europe," he reports simply of what he saw in 1921, "or coming over for the first time." Kreymborg separates himself from many of the younger writers he encountered simply because of his age, but he was also marginalized by the limitations of his experience. He acknowledges that while "every foreigner spoke French of a sort," he had none, and "few Frenchmen ever descended to another language." If he does see himself as a man apart, though, this realization also allows him to take comfort in the fact that he was heading abroad only after he had "crystallized as an artist," so he, for one, could never lose sight of his American roots (*T*364–65).

While a muted portrait of life in Paris belies here sensational accounts of a bohemian expatriate colony, and it stands in contrast to more spirited records that brighten later autobiographies, Kreymborg's narrative makes the argument that Americans are blossoming amid a receptive audience abroad, just as he had hoped. Arriving in Paris, he asserts that "a number of contemporary American writers and painters were being hailed as they have never been hailed before and receiving for the first time the benefits of a so-phisticated criticism." Indeed, he claims to have encountered Euro-peans who openly acknowledged "that the art of the morrow must come from the States" (*T*372). While *Troubadour* recognizes the en-during influence of a range of Europeans encountered in Paris, including Jean Cocteau, Marcel Duchamp, Valery Larbaud, Francis Picabia, and Tristan Tzara, Kreymborg found there few Americans who could be described as "diluted Germans, Frenchmen or Brit-ishers." Instead, the Americans in Paris whose descriptions enliven this text were of a more defiant stripe: Djuna Barnes, Sylvia Beach, and Robert McAlmon, for example. Their antithesis, writers who "rushed abroad during the formative period of life and returned to the States with influence, however benign, which submerged their independence ever after," are never singled out by name (*T*364). But surely this relinquished sense of self informed the Lost Gen-eration that Kreymborg comes to write about, a cohort still ill-defined for him by the middle of the 1920s. Beyond these details of Parisian life, there are a number of additional ways in which the discussion of Europe in *Troubadour* fleshes out our understanding of Americans abroad. First, while Kreymborg was in Europe to take advantage of the favorable exchange on the dollar, he also reveals that "the rate of living in Paris was, for one who did not know Paris, higher than the rate at home." Survival as a writer in the city required some luck and considerable skill, especially when "French landlords, restaurants, taxis and shopkeepers were after the wealth Americans had made out of the war" (*T*372). Second, while writers from the United States are shown to congregate around the cafés of Montparnasse, Kreymborg found Americans scattered throughout Europe. While in London, he encountered the aforementioned Ai-ken, Fletcher, and Eliot; in Rome, he saw Sinclair Lewis and Edna St. Vincent Millay. "Munich," he claims with surprise, "was crowded with Americans," including Scofield Thayer and H. L. Mencken (*T*390).

The art on whose behalf Kreymborg was working during this period, the art on which he himself was laboring, was undoubt-edly experimental in form. He "had no argument against metre and rhyme," he attests, "but he had an impulse or intuition, which he expressed rather vaguely, that there was something he had to say which it was his business to find his own form for" (*T*155). The poet's solution to these matters was interdisciplinary in na-ture, encompassing his own musical proclivities. As a boy, he was introduced to music by his Aunt Isabelle, teasing melodies out of

"an antique piano" (*T*57); he discovered through his own first experiences with the instrument that he could "play by ear," and that
this knack "came more naturally" than the study of musical theory
(*T*38). Among his first writing exercises were his so-called "apos-
trophes," described as "prose poems to composers" based on their
own works; he gradually came to write longer pieces to which he
referred as "symphonies," featuring "four different movements with
words—an allegro, largo, scherzo, allegro" (*T*86). As he continued
writing, he maintained what he understands as a "compositional
kinship" (*T*189) between words and music, though he was careful
as a declared poet "to resist a slavish imitation of music" so that he
did "not fall" into further obscurity "between the stools of music
and literature" (*T*155). Once he began to spend time with visual
artists, he realized that their experiments also shared a great deal of
affinity with his work. His developing critical acumen expanded
to accommodate the spirit of inquiry emerging across the arts. As
Kreymborg explains it:

> He gradually learned that the lines of painting and sculpture
> complemented the lines of music and poetry; that, without
> drawing needless parallels, one could readily trace a relationship
> proving that many artists of the age, no matter what their me-
> dium, were seeking fundamentals and evolving individual forms.
> (*T*165–66)

While Allen Tate's assessment of him in the 1940s was that his
"poetry," in the final analysis, "was not impressive," he did single out
Kreymborg's promotional activities on behalf of the "new poetry"
as one of its enthusiastic critics.[19] Indeed, his editing work with
little magazines, "to publish the work of men and women who
had, as yet, no audience of their own" (*T*129), led by the end of
the 1920s to his involvement with the *American Caravan* anthology
series. His ruminations in *Troubadour* anticipate the publication in
1929 of his comprehensive history of American poetry entitled *Our
Singing Strength*, a study that featured prominently the contributions of his contemporaries and was accompanied by a collection
of works called *Lyric America, 1630–1930*. By that time, he was able
to write confidently that "there are values to be extracted" from
the poetry of the previous thirty years, and while claiming not to
be "an historian by temperament,"[20] Kreymborg establishes in his
autobiography the critical context used in his analysis of American
verse. He describes the manner of the endeavor he is undertaking

as "creative criticism" (*T*132), the kind of inquiry that blurs the distinction between the writing he had been doing and the "sharp division of men into classics and romantics" that he believed to be going on in universities, relying on such "terms he often discovered to be interchangeable" (*T*149). All around him, in fact, he saw examples of how effective a self-conscious criticism might be, a criticism taken up by writers themselves. During visits to Chicago, he marveled at the activities of established figures like Sherwood Anderson, Frank Norris, and Carl Sandburg; younger insurgents like James Cabell, Ben Hecht, and Burton Rascoe; and Harriet Monroe's *Poetry* magazine, all participating in an admirable "log-rolling" of "their friends across to the public" (*T*282).

Before Laura Riding and Edmund Wilson published their early considerations of modernism, Alfred Kreymborg's pronouncements took on their own historical implications. To begin, any sense of what he and his contemporaries were attempting had to be understood in terms of its continuity with the past. "He felt the deepest admiration and awe in the presence of the eternal past, and it gave him indubitable landmarks for studying the present in a superb perspective," he claims. "At the same time, the future tugged at him most of all, a period that had to be served if one intended to go on living" (*T*377). Still, the problem, as Kreymborg understood it, was that the American artistic establishment refused to accept him and his contemporaries as its heirs. He talks of how poets he knew and respected were sneered at in the years before the war by Joyce Kilmer, William Dean Howells, and the Poetry Society of America. Kreymborg showed a particularly fervent, early appreciation of the work of Walter Arnsberg, Vachel Lindsay, and Wallace Stevens, but he also acknowledges that "if he showed a persistent predilection for 'these moderns,' a silent ostracism would operate against him mechanically" (*T*162). He complained "that the Broadway theatres, Carnegie Hall, the Metropolitan Opera House . . . were rigidly blocked against experiment" (*T*167). Even a growing sense among readers that there might be some coherence to be found among "these moderns" failed to open the doors of the educational establishment. From his childhood, Kreymborg claimed to have "already formed a pernicious habit—a lifelong habit of teaching himself what he could not learn otherwise" (*T*33). His aversion to formal education led him to personify school as an "ogre" from which he should flee (*T*35), and he saw himself as "a prisoner" in his time under its influence (*T*69). While a talented writer might be able to polish "good form" through "intensive training" at a university, he still doubted that "the special instruction one deserves as a separate being" could be secured there (*T*273). He was not surprised when "academic graybeards," therefore, rejected his verse with gestures that betrayed their "arid self-importance" (*T*157). While he did eventually get opportunities to speak at universities in both the United States and abroad, and he recognized the efforts of poet-teachers like Robert Frost who introduced contemporary verse to their classrooms, the cool reception he received at the University of California at Berkeley after the war illustrated a far more typical interaction for Kreymborg. Members of the English department "snubbed him or treated him with a type of superior tolerance" during his visit there, and unable to imagine the role of the university in legitimizing modernism in the decades ahead, he remained skeptical of its value for twentieth-century artists.

> He did not envy the thousands of students—as he might have some years before—striding back and forth and imbibing so many different things in so many different lecture halls. Life had brought him things he would have lost in classrooms, and the books he had read he had opened only as he needed them. So little did he find of contemporary affairs in the . . . curriculum, he reached the hypothesis that the future of the country, the ideal he and his fellows felt so profoundly and worked so industriously for, had no place in the present museum. (*T*298)

How these new endeavors might negotiate their places among the museum pieces of artistic tradition is a recurring concern of *Troubadour*. As a child, Kreymborg revered Mozart, Beethoven, and Bach, while making room in his affections for "moderns" like Debussy and Strauss, for example, even while the musical establishment cast them as "excruciating cacophonists" (*T*87). Now that these mavericks had been accepted on their own terms, there was hope that perhaps contemporary poetry might, too, someday achieve the same standing without compromising its principles. In one telling episode, Kreymborg illustrates the manner by which he and Lance Hartpence, flushed with the success of a couple of modest poetry collections they published themselves in the first years of the century, hoped to position themselves, literally, within a broad literary tradition.

> And, on one side of the shelves in Lance's room and one of the shelves in Krimmie's, they stood, side by side, supporting and

almost embracing each other—*The Poisoned Lake* and *Love and Life*. To keep them from falling off the shelves, the new authors had carelessly surrounded their volumes with works by older authors, looking like so many colophons. Casually walking by the shelves and running one's eye along the list of authors, one might have discovered two queer names right in the more or less chronological or alphabetical midst of Chaucer, Shakespeare, Milton; Byron, Shelley, Keats; Emerson, Poe, Whitman. (*T*120)

While individual writers may well have been imagining their place in literary history, Kreymborg struggles to describe the network of artists that had emerged by the middle of the 1920s. "What were we seeking?" William Carlos Williams wonders years later of the writers during this period. "No one knew consistently enough to formulate a 'movement.' We were restless and constrained."[21] In *Our Singing Strength*, Kreymborg himself cautioned the reader, in his view of what we now identify as American modernism, that "it is necessary to use the term, group, advisedly,"[22] while his work with Van Wyck Brooks, Lewis Mumford, and Paul Rosenfeld on *The American Caravan* at that time was also an acknowledgment of both "the individual and the related qualities" of the writers anthologized.[23] Kreymborg's early experience with conservative literary clubs introduced him to "the type of literary politics" he claimed "to encounter and flee from over and over again" (*T*156). He was also involved with the Provincetown Players and its splinter faction, the Others group, in Greenwich Village, itself a location that attracted "a heterogeneous host of men and women from all over the country pointing their hobby-horses in the direction of Washington Square" (*T*208). But while contemporary art promised an opportunity to bring together writers in concerted efforts, as with "the birth of Imagism" in London (*T*240), such efforts must not sacrifice creative individualism. "He did not delude himself into supposing that creative work is produced as a result of the congregation of men in sympathetic groups or cliques spouting mutual admiration," Kreymborg suggests. "History had taught him that your true artist is a hermit; works his way out of the self in an active solitude." But he also believes that an artist needs to know "that what he is attempting in the dark has in it the power of communication," so the writer seeks out "the response of a number of intelligent recipients" (*T*166). For this reason, perhaps, "getting in touch with other writers" was an obvious goal for Kreymborg (*T*126), so that individuals might always have someone "to share things with" (T77). For much of *Troubadour*, though, it appears that he was living in "a generation without leaders, and, in the absence of a close-knitting commonality of inheritance," he complains bitterly, "it did not seem able to substitute anything apprehending a group spirit" (T150).

The first recognizable model for a self-conscious grouping of young artists in the United States was, for him, Alfred Stieglitz's 291 on Fifth Avenue. "One did not have to be a painter to feel at home in the gallery," Kreymborg asserts. "To Krimmie, among others, the gallery appealed as the one place in town for the study of the birth, development and tendencies of modern art." If the developments in visual art were applicable across disciplines, perhaps the experience of the Little Galleries of the Photo-Secession might, too, hold lessons for writers. "Krimmie was often assailed with the wistful notion that if the young literary men of the town had a haunt like this one," he suggests, "something in the nature of a concerted movement might at last be born among them, in the course of whose development each man would find himself" (T165–66). He hoped that such a modern art might be saved "from degenerating into groupism" but should, instead, be true to "a growing eclecticism in America." He held an ideal whereby an individual artist need not "sacrifice a particle of his own expression" within a community (T403). The best example he saw of this group spirit exhibited among writers, to this point, was among the Americans he encountered on the café terraces of Paris. "Had there been such resorts over here," he writes of New York, "Krimmie could have met many more men of his craft than he did" (T134).

In the meantime, the need to respond to the commercial culture that had come to define life in the United States was what for Kreymborg holds the greatest promise for the eventual drawing together of artists in a meaningful fashion. "Somewhere in the dark, in a hole, in solitude," he imagines, "one had to plan the manufacture of new weapons for the overthrow of this new tyranny" (T151). But because "under the commercial régime, there was little or no outlet for a man who had many a reason to fear he was nothing but a valueless entity dabbling with solitaire" (T166), concerted group action became increasingly necessary. As popular culture was doing nothing more than providing commodity artifacts for American business, in Kreymborg's view, contemporary art had to make its own opportunities to reach an audience. "That business enterprise should have permeated and directed material America was natural and wholesome, no doubt," he concedes with a touch of bitterness and more than a hint of sarcasm, "but that it should have stolen into spiritual America and contaminated everyone with creative expression—this was loathsome" (T162). His wariness of popular culture, however, betrays on his part an elitism that would emerge, as we have seen, as a hallmark of modernism. He chafed at having "to peddle popular airs, yards of comic operas and, still worse, the lighter classics" when selling rolls at Aeolian Hall (T85). Facing a struggle to get his earliest writings published, he was forced to compete with what he calls a "cheap, noisy chorus of happy-enders, optimists, uplifters, prettifiers and puritans" (T123). While even from his childhood, he remembered that he should not appear to be "a little snob" (T38), his early decision to involve himself with the little magazine movement was motivated by the desire to escape completely the commercial imperative of appealing to a large, lucrative readership. "There was to be no concern with the public taste—whatever that abstract term might mean," he writes of one of these publishing endeavors, "and no thought in the direction of advertisers, since there was to be no advertising" (T129). His fear was that by pandering to a larger audience, artists would themselves be "broken on the wheel of popularity" (T306).

One of Kreymborg's experiences with the theater illustrated the dangers of courting wide appeal. Believing that not even the Provincetown group was "sufficiently daring and elastic" in the productions they staged, Kreymborg successfully arranged to produce "poetic plays" (T312–13) himself on MacDougall Street. After a week of sold-out performances, the Other Players brought their production uptown to within "three or four blocks east of Broadway" (T320). What Kreymborg characterizes as a "high brow" bill (T315) drew "barely one hundred people" to its eight performances at the Bramhall Playhouse, and "the company quietly disbanded" (T320–21), he laments, after losing all its money. Such experiences made him sorry to have been born in "the New York of Pierpont Morgan" and not "the Florence of the Medicis, the London of Elizabeth, the Paris of Louis Quatorze" (T152). Away from New York, perhaps, Americans might get another opportunity to come together to answer the conditions of the modern world.

> But he had begun to find intermittent signs, however slight, of
> a groping dissatisfaction with materialism as an end in itself on
> the part of enough malcontents to encourage the belief that, in
> the course of time, such people would seize the leadership of

their communities and develop cultural centres. Despite tragic evidences that the very great majority of Americans were still devoted to the cult of speed and ugliness and the conventions of Main Street, he was passionately aware that a new era lay beyond the horizon. (T292)

This desire for escape, this longing for some new perspective on the burgeoning commercial culture of the United States was, of course, a strong motivation behind the decision other artists made to travel abroad, as Kreymborg had done. Contemporaneous motivations were perhaps best illustrated in the responses to a questionnaire entitled "Why Do Americans Live in Europe?" published in the expatriate American magazine *transition* in Paris in 1928. "I do not prefer to live outside America," wrote Kreymborg's friend Kathleen Cannell, defiantly. "I would prefer to live in America if I could make enough money to do so." Indeed, according to newspaperman Leigh Hoffman, the United States was "a land where the people are dominated by a single and basic idea—that of making a living." This "struggle for existence" stood in stark contrast to life abroad, where the artist could enjoy "the maximum of pleasure" with the "minimum of friction." While the photographer Berenice Abbott similarly hoped not to have to stay "indefinitely" in Europe, she consoled herself with the knowledge that "the very complex nature of America is, if possible, better understood from a distance than at close range."[24]

There is little evidence that Alfred Kreymborg had ambitions on an epic scale when he sat down to write *Troubadour* in a moment of "respite and tranquility" with the simple desire of "taking a bit of stock of the past" (T412). But there is also little doubt that something in which he had been participating, something he calls at times here "the modern art movement" (T200), required further delineation in "an era of a more concerted consciousness" (T208). As Kreymborg describes it:

> An invisible curtain had descended on the first scene—or what people like to fancy the first scene—of the birth or the renaissance of America in poetry, the novel, the short story, the theatre, music, painting, sculpture and architecture—and not only critics, but men and women who had been engaged, consciously or unconsciously in the movement, stood off for a while in perspective before plunging into action again. It might have been called an occupation with "theories after the performance," a

sitting down of an evening following a hard day's work at desk, easel or keyboard, for a discussion, not so much of what one had done, but of what one had tried to do. The critical weighed the creative for the first time, so it seemed, dispassionately. Many a moment was spent in the consideration of what-have-I-done, what-have-I-still-to-do. (*T*412)

American modernism was coming of age by the middle of the 1920s. "Many of the tragic material problems confronting the artists of former generations had been solved or nearly solved for artists of the present generation," Kreymborg reports. "There was now that quintessential medium, a background and an audience. No longer did a man have to wait year upon year for a hearing" (*T*406). Responding to the conditions of the modern world, artists of many disciplines had adopted experimental forms against the tendencies of an existing tradition. What contemporary artists hoped to continue was the search for a place within this tradition while not sacrificing their individuality, a struggle that continued to preoccupy Alfred Kreymborg. What place expatriate Americans might have within this movement was still a contentious issue for him, but his modernism was already distinguishing itself by its catholicism, its heterogeneity. Contemporary reviews of *Troubadour*, written by figures as diverse as Mark Van Doren and Gertrude Stein, commented on the effectiveness of Kreymborg's outline of the context in which American modernism was developing. "In this history of us of himself and us Kreymborg makes us makes himself and each one of us different enough so that some one can know us," Stein observed. "A history of himself and of each one of us and connections of more than one of us is a very sensitive thing. . . . Always this is a good thing."[25] In the meantime, as Dorothy Kreymborg watched her husband's manuscript as it "grew stouter and stouter," she asked him, "Is there no end to this thing?" While its author "could only sigh, smile and shake his head" (*T*415), in part acknowledging the open-endedness of autobiography, he could hardly know that writing the experience of modern Americans in Europe was only beginning. In fact, Gertrude Stein herself would soon weigh in with her own autobiography in an attempt to provide what she believed to be a more authoritative history "of each one of us" abroad.

2

SELF-AGGRANDIZEMENT AND EXPATRIATE REPUTATION

From her autumn 1903 arrival at the rue de Fleurus premises first secured by her brother Leo in his short-lived pursuit of a career as a painter, Gertrude Stein set out to establish herself as an American of prominence in Paris, continuing a tradition of intellectual investigation and bourgeois living abroad, a tradition older than the United States itself. Within a year, drawing on an unexpected dividend from the family income managed by their brother Michael, the two younger Steins augmented their small art collection, a collection that soon grew so extensive that the canvases were hung one above the other to the ceiling of their atelier. The strange compositions of Cézanne, Matisse, and Picasso attracted wide attention. So while this was the period in which Stein completed and published her *Three Lives* (1909), now acknowledged as a landmark of American modernism, the regular Saturday night gatherings at the rue de Fleurus drew artists in Paris not because of her writings but because of this art collection—and Stein's willingness to discuss art. What American reputation she had established in the years before the war was based in large part on the publicity afforded her verbal "portraits," newspaper coverage that coincided with the uproar caused by the Armory Show. But while she remained a recognized figure among both Europeans and her countrymen who ventured to France after the First World War, her more substantial work continued to be ignored, even as these younger writers earned their own acclaim. "Miss Stein, outside the circles in which she moved and a few devotees at home, had virtually no recognition," Alfred Kreymborg wrote after meeting her in 1922.[1] Within a decade, she had begun the book that redressed this situation.

Most of the renown she enjoyed by the early 1930s was still as a salonist and collector of modern painting; she remained known only obliquely as a coterie writer, and as such only among a select readership, for few people who did know her writing had read a representative sample of what she had written. The magazine *transition* published about a dozen of her works for its readership in Paris and the United States between 1927 and 1932, but these had only attracted the scorn of the press back home. It would be *The Autobiography of Alice B. Toklas* that became known as her most approachable work, an "open and public" book described subsequently by critics like Ulla Dydo, for example, as "easy reading."[2] At the time of its publication, it was a selection of the Book-of-the-Month Club, appealed to a wide audience, and became a bestseller. But the resulting, long-sought attention it brought elicited an equivocal response from Stein, herself. She craved the *gloire* that she felt would inevitably result from her autobiography, but she had continually dismissed with a "not possibly" any suggestion from the "many people, and publishers," as she describes them, who wanted her to write such a text.[3] The "writer's block" she experienced "for the first and apparently the only time in her life" after the publication of the Toklas book betrayed her continuing anxiety, according to Catherine Parke, about "how to tell something to others in a way that does not betray the teller."[4]

This betrayal was a sense of disloyalty to the part of Stein that equated popularity with compromise, a compromise that threatened to break nearly three decades of certainty in her own artistic principles, certainty that answered the incomprehension and hostility that met her work. And with this persistent caveat, this almost perverse fear of acceptance on anything other than her own terms, Stein well represented the ambivalent relationship modern art developed with the cultural hierarchy, "neither a straightforward resistance nor an outright capitulation to commodification," as Lawrence Rainey understands it.[5] Recognition still held value for all but the most radical artists in this period, as we have seen, so their insistence on the revision of the cultural establishment was imperative for them: not just because the fluid artistic values of the time demanded it, but because their success could only be assured once the paradigm shifted to afford them the acknowledgment that remained the only standard of achievement. Hence, while critics like Constance Pierce might read *The Autobiography of Alice B. Toklas* as "gossipy,"[6] Stein seeks to use the book to place herself at the head of what she maintained to be a dynamic cultural establishment that was made all the more relevant by her inclusion, and by the acceptance of the unconventional autobiography through which, in part, she accomplished this feat. Recognizing a unique opportunity, she instructed her agent not to place the *Autobiography* with "any publisher not willing to publish other books of mine already written."[7] Indeed, through the Toklas book, and in the subsequent *Everybody's Autobiography* (1937), Stein attempts with mixed results to exert control over the emerging critical discourse by framing elements of her personal and professional life to shape her own reputation. While her subsequent commercial success convinced her to begin to accept speaking engagements, leading to the publication of a series of her critical "lectures," her practice from the very beginning of her career of talking about the composition of her work in the work itself shows that she was always aware of the wider critical implications of her writing. Shirley Neuman points out that because Stein was "highly conscious of the process of both reading and writing," in fact, the interplay between author and audience was intrinsic to "her whole approach to narration."[8] It is likely, therefore, that Stein was keenly aware that the image of herself to emerge from the Toklas book would reshape public perceptions of her. This possibility, auguring both good and ill, born of unprecedented public scrutiny, was what haunted Stein through this period.

In a wider sense, as Joseph Fichtelberg argues, the reception of Stein's autobiographical writing illustrated to her and to her self-conscious contemporaries that writing about the self "confers glory" on the writer.[9] The reception granted *The Autobiography of Alice B. Toklas* and the increasing interest in the 1930s in American lives lived abroad helped inspire some of the figures in her life to write down their own remembrances over the subsequent decades, hoping ever to associate themselves with her in an evolving understanding of modernism. The irony is that while Stein saw herself at the head of an international movement of the arts, she attempts to use the *Autobiography*, ultimately, to distance herself from many of her contemporaries. Her self-consciousness locates her blossoming as a writer in a Paris where art dealers offered to cut up Picasso's canvases, where Matisse lived in a small room with his wife, and where under a portrait by Cézanne, Gertrude Stein began *Three Lives*. This was a city in which she had no peer as a writer, and as she traces forward the subsequent years, young writers came to sit at her feet. Indeed, *The Autobiography of Alice B. Toklas* establishes Stein as an *habitué* of a *belle époque* Paris shared with Natalie Barney, though neither woman would grant the achievement of the other. But because the Toklas book also gives shape to the Lost Generation of Americans abroad, and because her narrative strategy places her among them under the gaze of Alice B. Toklas, Stein conflates subject and object and ties her own reputation unalterably to theirs.

Toklas herself later described the *Autobiography* as "the history" of Stein's "friends and time."[10] The conceit at the heart of the text, of course, is that it is Gertrude Stein who writes as her longtime lover and loyal companion. But this "secret" of what turns out to be a carefully constructed, third-person account of Stein's life is not finally revealed to the reader until the last lines of the book:

> About six weeks ago, Gertrude Stein said, it does not look to me as if you were ever going to write that autobiography. You know what I am going to do. I am going to write it as simply as Defoe did the autobiography of Robinson Crusoe. And she has and this is it. (*AA*252)

The comparison between the writing of the *Autobiography* and the telling of the fictional life of Robinson Crusoe, itself a book that challenged in its own time the boundaries of genre, is an important one, as Toklas emerges here as much Stein's creation as the protagonist of Daniel Defoe's book was his. In this way, Stein betrays her own skepticism of authenticity in life-writing, connecting her approach to that of Alfred Kreymborg in *Troubadour* and anticipating earnest academic interrogations of the topic by as much as three decades. The fundamental "untruth" of this fictional Toklas, if you will, problematizes fidelity in autobiographical discourse, not the least in this case because Stein willfully encroaches on any autobiographical pact; as the possibility of fidelity is further dismantled under this kind of scrutiny, a text like *The Autobiography of Alice B. Toklas* questions the very viability of autobiography as a genre. Beyond these ways in which Stein manages to threaten the status of a discourse about which she seems perceptively leery, her reference to Defoe's novel suggests an even more pointed conclusion to be drawn by an audience who looks askance upon her work. She is, in fact, maintaining that something in *Robinson Crusoe* testifies to the truest nature of its author, just as something—perhaps everything of any true relevance—is best revealed of all authors through their writings. In this way, she chides people who seem persistently curious about the details of her life while showing little interest in her writings themselves, even as she reluctantly accedes to their wishes.

While much of the significance of Stein's authorship rests on the dramatic resolution of the *Autobiography*—how better could Stein have concluded a text that is, by definition, open-ended?—there are hints about her authorship scattered throughout. Why should readers be surprised that Stein has assumed Toklas's voice when Toklas herself pretended to be Stein while seeking to procure gasoline from the French government during the war? This practice is revealed under the scrutiny of an army officer:

> I was very confused. I hesitated. But I am not Mademoiselle Stein, I said. He almost jumped out of his chair. What, he shouted, not Mademoiselle Stein. Then who are you. It must be remembered this was war time and Perpignan almost at the Spanish frontier. Well, said I, you see Mademoiselle Stein. Where is Mademoiselle Stein, he said. She is downstairs, I said feebly, in the automobile. Well what does all this mean, he said. Well, I said, you see Mademoiselle Stein is the driver and I am the delegate and Mademoiselle Stein has not patience she will not go into offices and wait and interview people and explain, so I do it for her while she sits in the automobile. (*AA*177–78)

While Toklas was supposed to have told the officer that she would never have agreed to sign any legal document in Stein's name, Stein has no hesitation in assuming Toklas's identity in print here, of course. As is the case during the relief work they carried out in their old Ford during the war, Stein remains the "driver" here, quite firmly, and it is her story, ultimately, that is told through her "delegate." In the *Autobiography*, she does not need patience to explain herself to anyone: Toklas again does it for her. But this does not mean that the narrative fails to reflect some of Stein's signature impatience; showing little willingness to dwell too long upon past events, the story has a tendency always to run ahead, constantly anticipating a future that is the writer's present. Phrases like "but to come back" and "but to return" are repeated throughout the text, and at one point, Stein has Toklas upbraid herself pointedly: "But I am once more running far ahead . . . " (*AA*92).

All of this detail represents more than narrative idiosyncrasy, however. Gertrude Stein here seems genuinely concerned with the vagaries of memory, and by establishing Toklas as the narrator, she manages to spread around some of the responsibility for the things she cannot remember, and presumably for the things she would just as soon forget. "It is a confused memory those first years after the war and very difficult to think back and remember what happened before or after something else," Stein writes (*AA*193). She requires Toklas to think back a further decade in some passages, and because in these cases she has not yet arrived in Paris, Stein has to arrange for her to be privy to conversations of which she could have no firsthand knowledge. At one point, she overhears Stein discussing with Matisse a luncheon that has become celebrated for her having seated her painter acquaintances opposite their own works, an appeal to their vanity "to make them happy" when the success of the gathering had been in doubt. Because Toklas was still living with her father in San Francisco in 1906 or 1907, she naturally has difficulty following what the conversation is "all about," though Stein allows her to piece together enough of the event to record it for posterity. "But gradually I knew and later on I will tell the story of the pictures," Stein has her promise, "their painters and their followers and what this conversation meant" (*AA*15).

Gertrude Stein was notorious for her desire to avoid direct confrontation, and as characterized by biographer James Mellow, she "was inclined to let Alice dispose of sticky personal problems."[11] It is not surprising, then, that Stein uses Toklas's voice to lessen the discomfort of some of her more contentious statements in the *Autobiography*. She sidesteps the possibility of conflict with Picasso's remembrances of their early friendship by getting Toklas to acknowledge, "When Gertrude Stein and Picasso tell about those days they are not always in agreement as to what happened" (*AA*43). While she and Ernest Hemingway were no longer on friendly terms by the time the Toklas book was published, Stein appears to strike a conciliatory note here. "Later on when things were difficult between Gertrude Stein and Hemingway," Toklas contends, "she always remembered with gratitude that after all it was Hemingway who first caused to be printed a piece of The Making of Americans." But in the same breath, Toklas questions this very kindness: "I myself have not so much confidence that Hemingway did do this. I have never known what the story is but I have always been certain that there was some other story behind it all." More often, however, Stein uses Toklas simply to reveal the most unflattering things about others. When Hemingway parodies Sherwood Anderson's *Dark Laughter* (1925) with *The Torrents of Spring* (1926), Toklas steps forward to confess that both Stein and Anderson are "a little ashamed" of him; in fact, they consider him "yellow" for the way he treats his midwestern mentor, surely the worst insult the manly Hemingway can be expected to endure (*AA*215–16). Much more decisive is the way in which Stein has Toklas ridicule entirely more sporadic visitors to the rue de Fleurus and their summer home in Bilignin. In a drunken state, poet André Salmon was supposed to have "half chewed" one of Toklas's hats (*AA*107). Russian artist Genia Berman "was a very good painter," but "he was too bad a painter to have been the creator of an idea" (*AA*230). Of the painter André Derain, with whom Stein shared what Mellow describes as "a mutual though civil dislike,"[12] Toklas says, "Gertrude Stein was never interested in his work" (*AA*42).

This is not to suggest that Gertrude Stein was not frank in her own assessments, but she anticipates possible repercussions to what she says in *The Autobiography of Alice B. Toklas* by relating an incident in the early 1920s during which she was forced to placate sculptor Jacques Lipschitz when he did not like what she is supposed to have said about him.

> Oh hell, she said, listen I am fairly well known for saying things about any one and anything, I say them about people, I say them to people, I say them when I please and how I please but as I mostly I say what I think, the least that you or anybody else can do is to rest content with what I say to you. (*AA*203)

Other contemporaries would not be so easily pacified after the Toklas book was published, and she was answered vociferously. Eugene Jolas published a *Testimony against Gertrude Stein* in 1935 as a supplement to a later incarnation of *transition* magazine. Beginning with what was surely understatement in his view, Jolas suggested that the *Autobiography* "often lacks accuracy." But his tone quickly turned. "There is a unanimity of opinion that she had no understanding of what really was happening around her," he asserted, "that the mutation of ideas beneath the surface of the more obvious contacts and clashes of personalities during that period escaped her entirely." For this reason, *transition* was putting forward this pamphlet before Stein's text had the chance "to assume the character of historical authenticity." The Toklas book was Stein's "final capitulation to a Barnumesque publicity," according to Maria Jolas.[13] The familiar self-aggrandizement that characterized Stein's work had never before sought such wholesale disparagement of those around her, and the tone of this reaction illustrated how persuasive they suspected this work could be. "The fact that they respond to her book with testimony," Timothy Dow Adams asserts, "as if she were a criminal on trial, and the fact that their responses became known as a manifesto suggest more than the usual anger at being misquoted or misrepresented."[14] Eugene Jolas feared the text's "hollow, tinsel bohemianism and egocentric deformations" might become "the symbol of the decadence that hovers over contemporary literature."[15] In a letter to Carl Van Vechten, Alice Toklas commented that the *transition* supplement was "a scream" and that all it seemed to do was drum up media attention for a tour Stein and Toklas were undertaking in the United States. "The press came up in hordes," she reports gleefully.[16] *Testimony against Gertrude Stein* circulated primarily among English-speaking magazine subscribers in France, and after the initial publicity, readers in the United States were unmoved by arguments they had received largely secondhand. In any case, they were by this time enthralled with Stein's account of expatriate experience.

For this furthering of her reputation, Gertrude Stein makes greatest use of Toklas's voice to assert the importance of Gertrude Stein while appearing to assume some modicum of objectivity. Unlike Alfred Kreymborg's choice of third-person narration largely to underline personal change in his life, Stein's use of Toklas is meant to justify her most excessive claims. Shirley Neuman, who wrote some of the more insightful appreciations of the Toklas book in the 1970s and 1980s, acknowledges that approaching the subject matter of autobiography from this perceived distance, as if one were "a biographer," is a viable strategy for convincing readers of "the truth of an experience so subjective that the autobiographer alone can attest to its veracity."[17] While it is true that readers learn some unflattering things about Stein, like the fact that she "has an explosive temper" (*AA*11), was "bored" as a medical student at Johns Hopkins (*AA*82), and "has a reprehensible habit of swearing whenever anything unexpected happens" (*AA*87), Toklas's impressions of her leave an overwhelmingly sycophantic impression. Toklas's early, definitive claim echoes through much of the book.

> I may say that only three times in my life have I met a genius and each time a bell within me rang and I was not mistaken, and I may say in each case it was before there was any general recognition of the quality of genius in them. The three geniuses

of whom I wish to speak are Gertrude Stein, Pablo Picasso and Alfred Whitehead. I have met many important people, I have met several great people but I have only known three first class geniuses and in each case on sight within me something rang. In not one of the three cases have I been mistaken. (*AA*5)

This strategy of drawing out an impression of herself carries myriad implications. As Laurel Bollinger has pointed out, for example, Stein's success in mimicking Toklas's voice in the text is interpreted by some readers as evidence of "collaborative effort," and the possibility of a "fused self" emerging from the *Autobiography* threatens any claim of "genius."[18] But for other critics like Susan Schultz, Toklas acts as a rather unconventional muse. Whereas the traditional muse inspires the text and acts as its "best audience," Toklas is set out by Stein in this text to "advertise her work" to a potential new audience, no matter how hostile they might turn out to be.[19] In this way, Carolyn Barros sees the work as a performance of Gertrude Stein, "a chorus of ventriloquist voices" that simultaneously reveal "what she does and what she says, and what others say about her."[20] This very public Stein thus comprises different layers, collapsed together, obliging her in part to read herself through the eyes of others. As Toklas tells her story, Stein is drawn increasingly by contrasts with those from whom she would wish to be differentiated. Instead of defying comparisons, then, the narrative relies upon them for its effect; instead of defining the terms of the discourse, it relies on the critical language that had already begun to grow up around the discussion of modern art.

Alice Toklas's appreciation of Stein is realized, in part, by connecting the writer's experience with that of modern painters who overcame the early slights of an inhospitable public to gain their own positions of renown. While Stein admits that she had read widely as a child, reading "anything that was printed that came her way and a great deal came her way" (*AA*74), she had long connected her own writing technique with the elemental abstraction that characterized the painting she first sought to collect. She emphasizes here yet again how it was by "looking and looking" at Cézanne's portrait of his wife that she was moved to begin *Three Lives* (*AA*34), but she claims never to have "been able or have had any desire to indulge in" visual art herself (*AA*76). Instead, *The Autobiography of Alice B. Toklas* seeks to measure Stein's lack of recognition against the early plight of Matisse and Picasso, the two painters discussed most painstakingly throughout the text. Picasso's early, unappreciated brilliance was best represented by his 1905–1906 portrait of Stein herself, a painting "which nobody at that time liked except the painter and the painted and which is now so famous" (*AA*6). Stein does not restrict Toklas to a discussion of specific canvasses, however. There was a broad range of works on the walls of the atelier, and few people appreciated in the years before the war just how famous their artists would become and what prices their efforts would fetch. "It is very difficult now that everybody is accustomed to everything to give some idea of the kind of uneasiness one felt when one first looked at all these pictures on these walls," Stein has Toklas observe (*AA*10). But Matisse's early work "seemed perfectly natural" to Stein all along, repeating in the early 1930s a defense with which she had long countered claims of incomprehensibility in her own work. Because "she could not understand why" Matisse's technique "infuriated everybody," she leaves no doubt that she was equally frustrated with critics of her own work, over whom she wished eventually to have the last laugh. Not surprisingly, as she has Toklas describe it, "she did not understand why since the writing was all so clear and natural they mocked at and were enraged by her work," as well (*AA*35).

The most concrete example of how she hopes the reception of her writing might eventually follow the response given the paintings on the walls at 27 rue de Fleurus is represented by her experience publishing *Three Lives* in the United States. She completed the manuscript in the spring of 1906, but her "attempt to find a publisher lasted some time," she has Toklas exclaim ruefully. While Stein maintains that she was not "really discouraged" by rejections from houses like Duffield and Macmillan in New York (*AA*67), she eventually went ahead and allowed May Knoblauch, a former lover, to place the book with the Grafton Press, a vanity publisher that offered to bring out an edition for $660.[21] Alvin Sanborn, an editor in Paris who had been employed by Grafton director F. H. Hitchcock, soon arrived to work with Stein on the manuscript's many "errors." Toklas records their awkward exchange:

> You see, he said, slightly hesitant, the director of the Grafton
> Press is under the impression that perhaps your knowledge of
> english. But I am an american, said Gertrude Stein indignantly.
> Yes yes I understand that perfectly now, he said, but perhaps you
> have not had much experience in writing. I suppose, said she
> laughing, you were under the impression that I was imperfectly
> educated. He blushed, well no, he said, but you might not have

had much experience in writing. Oh yes, she said, oh yes. Well it's alright. I will write to the director and you might as well tell him also that everything that is written with the intention of its being so written and all he had to do is to print it and I will take the responsibility. (*AA*68)

While the book was a qualified critical success, it failed commercially, and it did little to further Stein's ambitions with other publishers. The irony, of course, is that while the paintings she had collected eventually found their acceptance, "everybody" was in fact not yet accustomed to "everything" in art, even by the 1930s, especially in regard to her writing. Instead, she feels she has endured a "long campaign of ridicule" undertaken by American newspapers against her writing (*AA*156). But on the heels of the success of the Toklas book, as Stein reports in *Everybody's Autobiography*, Bennett Cerf sought to add *Three Lives* to his Modern Library, "and that was pleasing."[22] Inclusion in a reprint series Cerf had struggled to increase in prestige was a belated acknowledgment of the book that, in Stein's opinion, marked the beginning of literary modernism. Her ambitious *The Making of Americans*, a book that Robert McAlmon published in Paris in his Contact Editions in 1926, also attracted fresh attention from publishers in the United States after her breakthrough. But Stein still continued to measure success by her own, more idiosyncratic standards. That *The Autobiography of Alice B. Toklas* had been serialized in the *Atlantic Monthly*, for example, was a tremendous achievement in her mind. Her old friend Mildred Aldrich, who had died in 1928, held out an appearance in that magazine to be the epitome of critical success, but editor Ellery Sedgwick rejected Stein's work for more than a decade. As Catherine Turner argues, however, publisher Alfred Harcourt recognized the vast "commercial potential" of the Toklas book, a work that could counter the overwhelming "public perception" that modern writers were irretrievably "highbrow," and he arranged the serialization of 60 percent of the text to further publicize the appearance of the published edition.[23] "There has been a lot of pother about this book of yours, but what a delightful book it is, and how glad I am to publish four installments of it!" Sedgwick enthused to the author. "During our long correspondence, I think you felt my constant hope that the time would come when the real Miss Stein would pierce the smokescreen with which she has always so mischievously surrounded herself."[24] To read her work of thirty years characterized as a stunt, even in private correspondence, must have been as much as Stein could bear; her willingness to endure such an assessment underscores the importance she continued to put in the *Atlantic Monthly* as a place to publish her work.

Although she may have loved to gossip about others, Stein scorned any discussion of her life that distracted from serious consideration of her writing. It is ironic, then, that it was a work about her life that brought attention to her writing. "It always did bother me that the American public were more interested in me than in my work," she laments in *Everybody's Autobiography*. "After all, there is no sense in it because if it were not for my work they would not be interested in me so why should they not be more interested in my work than in me" (*EA* 51). But while the Toklas book does discuss many of her ideas about art, it willfully plays up details of her life that define her as an eccentric personality. Indeed, many shining details of Stein lore that persist are first revealed in *The Autobiography of Alice B. Toklas*. She claims here, for example, that William James awarded her "the highest mark in his course" at Radcliffe College, supposedly for writing across the top of her examination sheet, "I am so sorry but really I do not feel a bit like an examination paper in philosophy to-day" (*AA* 79). So, too, do we read that Picasso responded to complaints that Stein did not resemble his now-famous portrait of her by claiming, "She will" (*AA* 12). Her phrase "a rose is a rose is a rose," taken from "Sacred Emily" published a decade earlier, is put in Toklas's hands to find its place "as a device on the letter paper, on the table linen" at the rue de Fleurus, and anywhere else Stein would allow it (*AA* 137–38). The skepticism toward her work betrayed by T. S. Eliot, who professed to want but ultimately delayed publishing "her very latest thing" in *The Criterion*, is framed by his pronouncement that "the work of Gertrude Stein was very fine but not for us" (*AA* 201–2).

In these cases, it is clear that Stein is drawing on the kinds of anecdotes that anchor weightier reputations. She had long before reprimanded Hemingway for what she saw as his reliance on similar gossip in his fiction, but the "series of remarks" dotted through her autobiography, as Lawrence Raab has characterized them, the stories that supplemented her notoriety and made her "famous," are not thoughtlessly or randomly chosen.[25] To appreciate the care with which Stein includes certain details of her life as she remembers them, readers need only remind themselves of what she chooses, carefully, to exclude. The nature of the relationship between Stein and Toklas is left obscured throughout the text, for example. Donald Pizer sees the book devoid entirely of "any hint of passion or sexuality,"[26] and this description is consistent with the guarded discussion of Stein's sexuality in many of the memoirs of contemporaries and critical studies published subsequently by a range of scholars. Indeed, readers have noted the contrast between Stein's discretion in the representation of her sexuality and the frankness of Natalie Barney's writing through this period. For Barney biographer Suzanne Rodriguez, for example, this underlines the difference in how each woman "experienced her lesbianism."[27] There certainly was no expectation that Stein would discuss these issues openly in the 1930s, even in a book that purported to furnish through its surface narrative an accurate reflection of deeper realities. But such facts can never be realized fully in the truth framed on the page, as the issue of sexuality well illustrates. It may be that Stein and Toklas were naturally private people in this regard, and as readers like Catherine Stimpson argue, the treatment of lesbianism in the *Autobiography* may simply be a good example of "giving the public what she calculates it can take."[28] But other critics like Leigh Gilmore have added that because "heterosexuality has been an unwritten context of the autobiographical subject," readers simply impose on Stein's domesticity their understanding of her arrangement with Toklas as a "simple miming of heterosexual domestic relations."[29] Should this in fact be the case, this truth is likely far from the nature of their union: if Stein and Toklas are read as heterosexuals, their relationship is atypical; to understand their domestic arrangement as an emulation of a heterosexual coupling is to assume something that is simply not discussed in the text. The nature of their living arrangement remains just beyond the reader's interpretative grasp, underlining again that truth in autobiography relies as much on what is omitted as what is frankly discussed. The anecdotes she chooses to include acknowledge the narrow curiosity readers have in her life, certainly, but whereas she had in frustration seen her public persona shaped for her in the past, she here takes charge of her image and attempts to use it to further her professional ambitions.

While interest in her work did increase through the 1930s, the reception of the *Autobiography* failed, ultimately, to earn for her the liberty with publishers she most craved. "I can be accepted more than I was but I can be refused almost as often," she complains in a discussion of the period immediately after the Toklas book became a bestseller (*EA*47). Indeed, this experience kindled in her a new equivocation about the nature of success. Though she claims in *The Autobiography of Alice B. Toklas* that she could never "have enough of glory" (AA235), and she equates such achievement, at least in part, with commercial success, influential friends are quoted as warning her about the perils of wide acceptance. As she has Toklas tell it, Picasso agrees "about young painters, about everything" that "once everybody knows they are good the adventure is over" (AA88). While she denies Henry McBride's belief that "worldly success . . . ruins you" by reaffirming that she "would like to have a little" (AA121), she revisits the words of the American art critic after she judges that she "was having some." The acclaim "did not spoil" her, she maintains, though it "did change" her, a clear allusion to the writer's block she suffered (EA48). Shirley Neuman has examined the manner in which success affected Stein's view of identity, as she came to terms with the response of her "audience" to only a "self it recognizes" in the autobiographical subject,[30] but this peculiar reaction to fame belies the influence of the audience on the artist, herself. In an interview published in the *New York World* in May 1930, Stein said, "Lack of popular success in America is the least of my worries. I am working for what will endure, not a public."[31] Meanwhile, she consistently returned to her more commonplace measurements of achievement: while she was more affluent than most of her countrymen abroad, she was always meticulous in securing payment for her writing. In *Everybody's Autobiography*, she is even more explicit in equating pay with status as an artist, even though valuing herself in this way troubles her.

> Before one is successful that is before any one is ready to pay money for anything you do then you are certain that every word you have written is an important word to have written and that any word you have written is as important as any other word and you keep everything you have written with great care. And then it happens sometimes sooner and sometimes later that it has a money value I had mine very much later and it is upsetting because when nothing had any commercial value everything was important and when something began having a commercial value it was upsetting. (EA40)

It is telling that she here equates success with commercial achievement: the writer is truly "successful" when "one is ready to pay money for anything you do." On the other hand, writing only for public approval, measured in part by sales figures, is a trap for the writer. For despite her talk of working independently of audience approval, she is unable to distance herself from such a mercenary conception of *gloire*, one that requires brokering with the commercial concerns of publishing houses. "One writes for oneself and strangers but with no adventurous publishers how can one come in contact with those same strangers," she muses in the Toklas book (*AA*240). By her own admission, her audience to that point had been "writers, university students, librarians and young people who have very little money" (*AA*244–45). Self-publishing brought her the satisfaction of seeing her work in print, but it had not helped her achieve widespread sales. With *The Autobiography of Alice B. Toklas* selling out its first printing of 5,400 copies more than a week before its official date of publication,[32] however, she expanded her fan base considerably. With an English, a French, and even an Italian edition planned, she was promised new "circulation of her work," in Catherine Turner's assessment, to "confirm her quality and spread her ideas."[33] This opportunity was reinforced, as she was persuaded to undertake what turned out to be that wildly successful lecture tour of the United States in 1934–1935. In Beverly Hills, a group of motion picture luminaries marveled at how she had "succeeded in getting so much publicity" (*EA*292). Before she left Paris, she had some indication of her new acclaim, in fact. "Well anyway when I wrote The Autobiography of Alice B. Toklas for the first time I received really a quantity of fan letters," she enthuses. "I was always reading something and I never wrote any fan letter to any one why should I have been so pleased when they wrote to me but I was" (*EA*159).

Gertrude Stein was undoubtedly flattered by the attention that came through fan mail, but her acknowledged inability to empathize with admirers whom she either inspired or awed hints at the extent of her condescension. Indeed, Stein not only placed herself with Picasso and Whitehead as "geniuses," she assumed an unrivaled position at the head of a literary tradition that culminated with modernism. She has Toklas conclude that in the early years of the twentieth century, Gertrude and Leo Stein found themselves "in the heart of an art movement of which the outside world at that time knew nothing" (*AA*28). Now that her taste in modern painting had been vindicated, having spent nearly two decades distancing herself from the influence of her brother, she could discuss her own writing among works she claimed to have had the foresight to recognize as important artifacts of a modern vanguard. Moreover, she maintains an abiding faith in literary tradition: she knew writers "from the Elizabethans to the moderns" (*AA*56) and asserts "that in English literature in her time she is the only one."

By using autobiography to situate herself at a moment that signifies the culmination of centuries of artistic ferment, she can thus dismiss a personal influence like Henry James as "quite definitely . . . her forerunner" (*AA*77–78). She scrupulously categorizes artistic movements within an evolving modernism, carefully (if controversially) attributing the origin of the term "cubist" to Guillaume Apollinaire, who "wrote the first little pamphlet about them," for example (*AA*62). She discerns between many of the experiments undertaken by her contemporaries; she rejects "automatic writing" (*AA*77) and a reliance on coinages, "an escape into imitative emotionalism" intended to rejuvenate letters. "She tried a bit inventing words but soon gave that up," she claims. "The english language was her medium and with the english language the task was to be achieved, the problem solved" (*AA*119). Eventually moving beyond mere anecdote, *The Autobiography of Alice B. Toklas* reconciles the aesthetic foundations of Stein's writings with the broader aims of modern art.

> Gertrude Stein, in her work, has always been possessed by the intellectual passion for exactitude in the description of inner and outer reality. She has produced a simplification by this concentration, and as a result the destruction of associational emotion in poetry and prose. She knows that beauty, music, decoration, the result of emotion should never be the cause, even events should not be the cause of emotion nor should they be the material of poetry and prose. Nor should emotion itself be the cause of poetry or prose. They should consist of an exact reproduction of either an outer or an inner reality. (*AA*211)

When Alvin Langdon Coburn came to capture her likeness before the beginning of the First World War, he was lauded as "the first photographer to come and photograph her as a celebrity." She admits to having been "nicely gratified" by the attention of callers (*AA*140), and the importance she placed on gestures of respect from those whom she might herself revere was already established as a pattern in her life. But while her early years in Paris were dominated by the presence of European contemporaries, her social situation soon changed. "The old crowd had disappeared," she finds, in describing her postwar salon (*AA*193). And this "old crowd" was replaced, increasingly, by younger expatriates from the United States. "When I first came to Paris there was a very small sprinkling of americans Saturday evenings," she explains, "this sprinkling grew gradually more abundant" (AA102–3). While working with the American Fund for French Wounded during the war, she and Toklas often befriended young soldiers, her beloved "doughboys" who distilled the best features of Americans and made her feel "with America in a kind of way that if you only went to America you could not possibly be" (AA184). William Rogers, in his 1948 remembrance of meeting Stein and Toklas at Nîmes, described their curiosity about soldiers as a "police grilling," albeit a friendly one. "They pumped me, however, for all they were worth," the man known to them as "the kiddie" recalled. "Where I was born, who were my parents, what did my father do, where did I go to college, who were my professors, how did I happen to be in the army, was this my first visit to France, what would I do when the war ended?"[34] She remained quite interested in these soldiers, maintaining correspondence in some cases for years afterward, as these men were to her the type of individuals "that would not naturally ever have come to Europe" (AA180). If, because of the war, the "old life" enjoyed by Stein and Toklas truly "was over" (AA142), the doughboys too came to be replaced in her affections by young writers and friends of writers who showered her with the attention fitting a mentor through the 1920s. She refers to them in *The Autobiography of Alice B. Toklas* as a "young generation" (AA8) who overwhelmed her adopted city:

> It was a changed Paris. . . . We saw a tremendous number of people but none of them as far as I can remember that we had ever known before. Paris was crowded. As Clive Bell remarked, they say that an awful lot of people were killed in the war but it seems to me that an extraordinary large number of grown men and women have suddenly been born. (AA190)

Caught up in this enthusiasm were ambitious young artists who had simply "heard of 27 rue de Fleurus," and one measure of their initial success was whether or not they were admitted there (AA13). By the early 1930s, Gertrude Stein is able to say that "geniuses, near geniuses and might be geniuses" came to her salon (AA87). Older writers like Sherwood Anderson, T. S. Eliot, Ezra Pound, and Alfred Kreymborg are discussed in the pages of the *Autobiography*; young Americans like e. e. cummings, John Dos Passos, and Ernest Hemingway who first came to Europe to volunteer with the ambulance service are also mentioned. Robert Coates, Harold Loeb, Robert McAlmon, Ernest Walsh, and Glenway Wescott appear,

but it is largely the friends and acquaintances of American composer Virgil Thomson who became known as her "young men."
While this "neo-Romantic circle" included "less than a dozen poets, painters, and musicians," more and more expatriates identified
themselves with Stein by the end of the 1920s. One member of this
expanded clique, the novelist Bravig Imbs, described by Thomson
as "serviceable as an extra" to Stein,[35] was inspired to entitle his
1936 autobiography *Confessions of Another Young Man.* "For we were
a coterie and most of us young enough to think it very important,"
he reflected. "We were all going to be great artists and we had all
sat with Alice and we had all given our homage to Gertrude."[36]
But it is the fiction of F. Scott Fitzgerald that "really created for the
public" a sense of this young generation of Americans, according to
Stein. Struggling as he was by the time of her writing to finish his
own *Tender Is the Night* (1934), an extensive portrait of Americans
abroad, and in the midst of a period of relative critical and commercial obscurity that would extend a decade beyond his death in
1940, the novelist benefited from Stein's considerable prescience
as she proclaims, "Fitzgerald will be read when many of his well
known contemporaries are forgotten" (*AA*218).

It is in the subsequent *Everybody's Autobiography,* however, that
she gives her clearest account of how "the war generation," this
"young generation," came to be known as the Lost Generation.
Here she attributes those words to the proprietor of the Hotel
Pernollet, who is supposed to have claimed that because the First
World War deprived young men of the socialization they should
have had in their late teens and early twenties, they "missed the
period of civilizing, and they could never be civilized" in any conventional manner. "They were a lost generation," she elaborates.
"Naturally if they are at war they do not have the influences of
women of parents and of preparation" (*EA*53). Her willingness to
engage these ideas in the mid-1930s testifies to the efficacy of that
phrase; her explanation belies how elusive her connection with it
would be throughout the rest of the century. Virgil Thomson himself later wrote, for example, that Stein actually meant that young
soldiers were "lost to a chosen profession."[37] It is not surprising that
Ernest Hemingway, who we know to have made his own extensive
use of the phrase, remembered differently Stein's explanation of its
inception. In *A Moveable Feast,* Stein adapts the phrase from a garage
owner who employs it to reprimand his shiftless, young mechanic.
As Hemingway understood it, she used the words specifically to
dismiss his contemporaries "who served in the war" and had "no

respect for anything." He thus rejected her "dirty, easy labels,"[38] offended certainly by her inevitable emphasis on the word *lost*.

Both Gertrude Stein and Ernest Hemingway shared the belief that Lost Generation characters must at least participate in an environment created by wartime experience. Stein's sixty-page chapter "After the War" gives much less sense of the dynamic between men and women than does Hemingway's fiction, however. Among the lists of figures who visit Stein, there were women like Margaret Anderson, Sylvia Beach, Djuna Barnes, Jane Heap, and Janet Scudder. But her sense of this milieu is defined by the influx of American men to Paris. Some critics, like Cynthia Secor, for example, argue that the key to Gertrude Stein's representation of women is that she sees gender categorization as "meaningless," creating a "truly radical" element in her writing.[39] She maintained at roughly the same time as she took up the writing of autobiography, "I think nothing about men and women because that has nothing to do with anything."[40] But she also commented privately on the possible "maleness" of her "genius,"[41] and even Sandra Gilbert and Susan Gubar acknowledge that it was only Stein's final texts that escape a "masculinity complex" to work "toward the recognition of female autonomy that has been perhaps most crucial for twentieth-century women artists."[42] Indeed, Gertrude Stein's portrait of her salon in the 1920s has played an important role in gendering male the Lost Generation. For while it is clear from *The Autobiography of Alice B. Toklas* that important American women artists and intellectuals were in Paris at the same time as Gertrude Stein, and their achievement could hardly be seen as being diminished by the fact that Stein writes extensively about men in the text, it is also clear that recognition of the achievement of these women through subsequent decades was not helped by Stein's lack of attention here.

The many men in her life sustained her curiosity through these years. "It did not take me long to understand that while I had her personal sympathy, I existed primarily for Gertrude Stein as a sociological exhibit," reflected the writer Paul Bowles.

> I provided her initial encounter with a species then rare, now the commonest of contemporary phenomena, the American suburban child with its unrelenting spleen. She wanted to hear every detail of life at home.... After a week or so Gertrude Stein pronounced her verdict: I was the most spoiled, insensitive, and self-indulgent young man she had ever seen, and my

colossal complacency in rejecting all values appalled her. But she said it beaming with pleasure, so that I did not take it as adverse criticism.[43]

While Stein had an uncanny ability to secure this kind of forbearance from a range of individuals, she returns again and again to Hemingway to illustrate the reverence she comes to expect from one who, as described by Ford Madox Ford, "sits at my feet and praises me" (*AA*220). In the *Autobiography*, she claims to have "found wanting" his early prose, but she "liked the poems, they were direct, Kiplingesque" (*AA*213). It is not surprising that she admires his verse above all else, a form in which she and Hemingway were unlikely to be viewed as competitors. As Hemingway was willing to grant in his own autobiography, Stein had by the time he met her "discovered many truths about rhythms and the uses of words in repetition that were valid and valuable and she talked well about them," but her willingness to talk became a problem in developing relationships with healthy balance, for Hemingway claimed that "it was much more interesting to listen" to her than to engage her in debate.[44] Although Hemingway was unable to gather together the generosity of spirit necessary to credit her as a mentor in his autobiography, his treatment of her sexuality in *A Moveable Feast* may not be part of "the most vicious slander" that critics like Marianne DeKoven have long seen.[45] Its uncharitable portrait of Stein and Toklas does include a discussion of the former's defense of lesbians who, unlike male homosexuals, "do nothing that they are disgusted by and nothing that is repulsive,"[46] and Timothy Dow Adams claims that Hemingway was here breaking "an unwritten taboo against mentioning in print that Stein and Toklas were lesbians."[47] But while such passages did stray from familiar, coded references to "friendship," they were really only shocking in their flirtation with crudity. Bravig Imbs had raised the same issue three decades earlier by seeking to soften perceptions of a brusque Stein. "We must be getting back to Alice," he remembered her saying as they drove through the countryside. "If I am away from her long I get low in my mind."[48]

Ultimately, Gertrude Stein maintains that the attention of younger writers through the 1920s made her "nervous," but it is clear that it provided her ultimately with much of her sense of well-being during a difficult period, professionally. While she sat apart from her young men, she saw herself as their mentor, unwilling to correct specifically the "detail of anybody's writing," but reinforcing "principles, the way of seeing what the writer chooses to see, and the relation between that vision and the way it gets down" (*AA*214). In this way, she claims to have "taught many young writers" that "observation and construction make imagination" (*AA*76). But in return for this advice, she expected that her young charges would "devote their lives" to further her career (*AA*217). She brokered no conflict with these writers, maintaining that "no artist needs criticism, he only needs appreciation" (*AA*235). So while she claims that "a sense of equality" is "the deepest thing" she possesses, her judgment that "one person was as good as another" becomes little more than a method to ingratiate herself with others. "If you are like that, anybody will do anything for you," she claims (*AA*174).

Into the 1930s, however, it was also clear that she had grown resentful of the attention paid her protégés. "I used to tell all the men who were being successful young how bad this was for them," she claims in *Everybody's Autobiography* (*EA*48), using Henry McBride's words now to suggest something of her own ironic bitterness. While the Toklas book reprimands expatriates like Hemingway and McAlmon whose willingness to defer to her had faded, its publication followed an even more dramatic purging of her salon. "It was amazing how rapidly the little court was dispersed," Bravig Imbs mourned, though he blamed Alice Toklas's jealousy for the "destruction."[49] Indeed, one of the purposes of *The Autobiography of Alice B. Toklas* is to try to differentiate Stein from the circle of admirers whose success, whose very presence, threatened to overshadow her. What may be ironic is that those individuals from whom she seeks distance made up much of her traditional audience. And in the same way that Alice Toklas, as speaker, also assumes the role as the text's first reader, Gertrude Stein as subject dissolves into the broader portrait of life in the rue de Fleurus. Evidence of this unintended consequence is affirmed by Cynthia Secor, who laments that Stein remains in the popular imagination "a writer of the 1920s."[50] Of all her autobiographical texts, the Toklas book relies most heavily on placing Stein in her social and artistic context, and while she seeks to affirm her place at its head, she can never effectively transcend it. Still, one can argue that with her commercial success in the 1930s, she had less need for the adulation she had gleaned from her circle a decade before. She speaks subsequently of developing "a tendency to go out more and see different kinds of people" in a social setting. "In the older days mostly they came to see me but then we began to go out and see them," she admits. "I had never been to any literary salons in Paris, and now well I did not go to many of them but I did go to some" (*EA*33).

As artifacts of a life abroad, Stein's two 1930s autobiographies may be most notable for the manner in which she discusses the United States itself and the implications this discussion holds for the international aspirations of modernism. One gets little sense of the breadth of Paris life here, and in subsequent books like *Paris France* (1940) and *Wars I Have Seen* (1945), Stein describes a city and countryside colored by conflict. *The Autobiography of Alice B. Toklas* discusses instead generalizations based on the traits of her international friends. She asserts that "the psychology of americans," for example, is fundamentally different "from the psychology of the english" (*AA*152). London was "infinitely depressing and dismal" (*AA*84). Americans had an affinity with Spaniards as they were citizens of "the only two western nations that can realize abstraction" (*AA*91). Still, the United States had much in common with France, politically, as both were "profoundly intensely . . . a republic" (*AA*153). Perhaps this is why "all roads lead to Paris," especially for young Americans (*AA*86). While Stein here establishes what Phoebe Davis describes as an "essentialist view of nationality," the *Autobiography* also suggests that affinities with others can "be adopted and performed."[51] This equivocal view of personality can be traced back as far as *Three Lives*, but in this context it suggests the inherent value of living abroad, stretching oneself beyond narrow allegiances. Stein, ultimately, rejects the term "expatriate" to describe her relationship with her country of birth, though. She maintains that she is "completely and entirely american" (*AA*16). Like those who had ventured abroad after the war, she bristles at the negative connotation that word had taken, but the circumstances of her departure from the United States could not have been more different from theirs. She muses, "Imagine how horrible to have been brought up in New York" (*AA*73), gainsaying any connection to the intellectual ferment of Greenwich Village. And unlike those who had come to Europe as adults with strongly held opinions, she had experienced life abroad as a child. Indeed, her view of being an American among French speakers hearkens back to the linguistic aptitudes of a child, though her exposure to French serves only to strengthen her attachment to her mother tongue:

> I feel with my eyes and it does not make any difference to me what language I hear, I don't hear a language, I hear tones of voice and rhythms, but with my eyes I see words and sentences

and there is for me only one language and that is english. One of
the things that I have liked all these years is to be surrounded by
people who know no english. It has left me more intensely alone
with my eyes and my english. (*AA*70)

She had been asked in-depth questions in the late 1920s about
her long estrangement from the United States, and she claimed at
that time rather cryptically that she had been escaping an older
culture by fleeing to Europe. While many of the Americans who
came abroad after the war were attempting to make sense of a
heritage they believed to have been shattered by the conflict, Stein
had long ago abandoned pretense to a salvage expedition, putting
herself at least a decade ahead of the young writers with whom
she is associated in our minds, and separating herself from her true
contemporaries like Pound and Eliot. The Toklas book gives her a
further opportunity to explain why America, to her, is older than
Europe.

> Gertrude Stein always speaks of America as being now the old-
> est country in the world because by the methods of the civil war
> and the commercial conceptions that followed it America cre-
> ated the twentieth century, and since all the other countries are
> now either living or commencing to be living a twentieth cen-
> tury of life, America having begun the creation of the twentieth
> century in the sixties of the nineteenth century is now the oldest
> country in the world. (*AA*78)

In this sense of a modern world shaped by the progress of the
industrial revolution, she was correct in suggesting that the innovations of the nineteenth century found full bloom in the United
States. But it is only in *Everybody's Autobiography* that she hints at
the implications for her art. In a country with its modern character
already determined, she feels that she would be at a disadvantage
in exercising her creative genius, for "the minute you or anybody
else knows what you are you are not it." If development as a person,
or an artist, or indeed as a nation is a journey, as Stein suggests, if
"everything in living is made up of finding out what you are," then
France, which she believes to be "forming itself to be what it is,"
provides the best environment where Stein's "genius" could truly
be "made" (*EA*94). The impulse to seek out such an environment,
a desire perhaps understood across a broader spectrum of young
Americans as a desire to escape conditions in the United States,

would soon be examined in other life narratives. But the greatest legacy of *The Autobiography of Alice B. Toklas*, in particular, is that virtually every expatriate autobiography after it, every remembrance that dealt with the interwar period and the flowering of high modernism among Americans abroad, would have to come to terms with its story. Perhaps Stein knew this when she risked writing such a document over six weeks in 1932. For while defining herself in this way, she was clearly drawing a line under a major part of her career, as evidenced by her desire to separate herself from many of those by whom she had been surrounded. But after explaining to the world what she was, she was losing control of that part of herself forever. And in light of the influence of the Toklas book, how it has forced everyone else to define themselves in part by their relationship to her story, one can see both Stein's greatest success and most substantial failure.

3

SEARCHING FOR A
REPRESENTATIVE EXPATRIATE

"I want to set down the story of this Lost Generation while its adventures are fresh in my mind," Malcolm Cowley writes in the prologue to his 1934 "Narrative of Ideas" entitled *Exile's Return.* "I want to tell how it earned its name (and tried to live up to it) and then how it ceased to be lost, how, in a sense, it found itself."[1] He is here acknowledging the potent currency of Gertrude Stein's "famous remark" among those Americans who wished self-consciously "to express their feeling that youth had a different outlook" in the years after the First World War (*EN*7), an outlook represented most clearly by "a whole world of people with and without talent," in Cowley's assessment, who "deserted the homeland" for Europe (*EN*233). From June 1921 to August 1923 he himself was abroad, participating in the record of American expatriation by his own actions, but a decade later his study of that time gives him a comparatively small role in the very record he presents. In revising *Exile's Return* in 1951 as "A Literary Odyssey of the 1920s," he explains that because he "had shared in many of the adventures" of that decade, he set out originally "to tell a little" of what had happened to him "but only as illustration of what had happened to others."[2] The result, in either edition, is a "collective autobiography," as John Hazlett understands it,[3] a book that "privileges a 'we' over an 'I' in a work primarily concerned with American selfhood."[4] While Cowley's waning commitment to communism through the 1930s and 1940s might have diminished one justification for a narrative approach that emphasized a collective understanding of young American intellectuals, preserving the appearance of critical detachment in this account of what Hazlett describes as a genuinely identifiable "literary coterie" persists as an effective rhetorical strategy. Cowley shows himself and his contemporaries "at odds with the dominant culture" in the United States, but they are also portrayed as possessing the "cultural power" to make them the likely inheritors of a literary tradition of which they are still wary.[5] After all, Cowley judges his generation as "probably the first real one in the history of American letters" (*EN*7), and he is sure they "will hold an important place in the history" of art in the United States (*EN*10). Though the first edition of *Exile's Return* was as much a commercial failure as *The Autobiography of Alice B. Toklas* was a commercial success, Cowley, like Stein, harbored his own desires to reach a wide enough audience to help mediate the reception of modern American literature. In fact, the project began in late 1931 as a series of five critical articles in the *New Republic*, whose literary section had become by that time the responsibility of Malcolm Cowley himself.

Despite the "enthusiasm for generationalist ideas" that he helped to instigate and to which he gave voice,[6] Malcolm Cowley was still uncomfortable seeing the Americans at the heart of his narrative as a single group. He admits that "the young men and women who were graduated from college, or might have been graduated, between 1916, roughly, and 1922" actually "include several loosely defined groups that are not always friendly with one another" and even "many individuals who differ with every group among their contemporaries" (*EN*9). But it was because "they differ even more with writers older or younger than themselves" that Cowley accepts with some reluctance and propagates the idea of a "literary generation" as an organizational strategy for his analysis of expatriation. John Hazlett is left with no doubt that *Exile's Return* must still be read as an autobiography, presenting the reader with "a significant portion of the writer's life story" that provides "a first-person retrospective construction of the writer's identity," even if Cowley emerges only within his wider social context.[7] Hazlett is untroubled, ultimately, by a work that privileges "the group rather than the individual," though it allows Cowley to attribute to historical forces rather than personal initiative events that shaped American culture after the war.[8] Fusing his personal story with that of his contemporaries also allows Cowley to downplay the ways in which his own experience might contradict the wider pattern on which the narrative comes to rely, of course, but by doing so he risks jeopardizing the foundation of his own story. Reflecting on a time in which prose forms were notoriously fluid, Donald Faulkner is happy to read *Exile's Return* as representing "a new medium" that seeks both to frame and to "be a part of American literature itself."[9] But, for Marc Dolan, precisely because Cowley gathers himself "into the narrative's unified plural subject," the work "almost compulsively effaces its central narrator and protagonist." Dolan's reading fails to identify "any meaningful impressions of either the narrating or the acting Malcolm Cowley."[10]

If, as Hazlett implies, Cowley genuinely wishes to depersonalize the expatriate impulse, the uneasy feeling of absence that readers like Dolan take away from *Exile's Return* is consistent with the disillusion that sent Americans abroad in the first place. The fact remains that Cowley still places great value on individual stories, if not necessarily his own, going so far as to identify figures representative of the expatriate experience. In the first edition, he focuses on Harry Crosby, whose spectacular suicide in 1929 we know to have been seen as most meaningful in the popular press. "It happens that his brief and not particularly distinguished literary life of seven years included practically all the theses I have been trying to develop," Cowley concludes near the end of his text (*EN*243). This assessment of how Crosby illustrated experiences like "the separation from home," "bohemianism," and a "final period of demoralization" is carefully preserved in the later edition. In fact, a tale that had been told in two long sections—"The Story of a Suicide" and "To Die at the Right Time"—within a chapter called "No Escape" is later given its own chapter entitled "Echoes of a Suicide." Cowley reads Crosby's life, and especially the end of it, as crucial to an understanding of the American experience abroad. "His death, which had seemed an act of isolated and crazy violence," he argues, "began to have a new meaning, began to symbolize the decay from within and the suicide of a whole order with whom he had been identified" (*EN*284). Crosby thus "becomes a symbol" by a death that "carries us outside his own story, that of a minor poet, into the vaster story of an era about to end" (*EN*272). But such decoration was too much for the socialite's widow. In her autobiography *The Passionate Years* (1953), Caresse Crosby described as "fiction" these "imaginative remarks" of Cowley's. "We never knew him in those days," she maintained, "nor he us."[11]

It is important to Cowley that the end of *Exile's Return* be punctuated with a prohibitive tale. While older writers who had gone abroad before the war might stay in Europe, he believed that disillusioned young Americans had, as early as the middle of the 1920s, only two choices remaining: return to the United States and participate in the reinvigoration of American intellectual life or remain abroad and forfeit their cultural relevance and renounce their right to be heard, an invalidation of their influence represented in his mind by the image of premature death. While Edward Germain, in an edition of Harry Crosby's diaries, argues that having experienced all the expatriate "rites of passage," Crosby had a "special place" in the Lost Generation,[12] readers would not be faulted for concluding that he did not represent the most effective symbol for Cowley's purposes. Crosby's ideas, including a pagan devotion to sun worship, seem too bizarre to be representative; his salacious death seems unnecessarily wanton, even in an era that prided itself on challenging sexual mores. While including his story, Cowley is still conscious of how newspapers had pointed to Crosby in dismissing outright the expatriate impulse. In fact, *Exile's Return* ultimately relies on an example of someone whose experience could embody the legitimacy of time abroad while underlining the necessity of reembracing one's homeland. In the revised edition, certainly, Cowley reveals some second thoughts about investing Crosby with the full weight of this symbolic burden, while still preserving and even enhancing his story. "I had written at length about the life of Harry Crosby, whom I scarcely knew," he admits, "in order to avoid discussing the more recent death of Hart Crane, whom I knew so well that I couldn't bear to write about him" (*EO*11). In a section of the 1951 edition called "The Roaring Boy," Cowley turns his attention to his talented friend, who took his own life in 1932 by jumping from the ship *Orizaba* on his return to New York from a stay as a Guggenheim Fellow in Mexico. While there, the normally homosexual Crane had fallen in love with Peggy Baird, whose divorce from Malcolm Cowley was not yet final. Although Crane's main vice, drink, is perhaps more accessible to the public imagination than some of the demons that haunted Crosby, the poet appears here larger than life, perhaps too large, laughing "twice as hard as the rest of us" and drinking "at least twice as much" as his friends (*EO*228). "He was more lost and driven than the others," Cowley observes further, "and although he kept fleeing toward distant havens of refuge he felt in his heart that he could not escape himself" (*EO*234). Still, one must keep in mind that Hart Crane spent but six months in Paris in 1929, an experience hardly representative of interwar expatriation.

Perhaps if Malcolm Cowley had not been so certain of the

need to represent expatriate deterioration through actual death, if he had not feared investing the symbolic weight of the expatriate experience in a rival who had a legitimate claim to having personally precipitated it, he might himself here make more use of the story of a broken man who returned to the United States at about the time of Hart Crane's suicide, a man who described himself in the 1930s as "a ghost of a generation that has gone."[13] Critic Hugh Ford has subsequently called Harold Stearns "the quintessential expatriate,"[14] and with the publication of Stearns's autobiography *The Street I Know* (1935) within months of the appearance of the first edition of *Exile's Return*, readers in the United States had the opportunity to hear from one who had, more than a decade before, challenged the best and brightest of his contemporaries to follow his example and go abroad. But if it is true that his life in Paris illustrated the furthest limits of that experience, Stearns differed from Cowley in his view of American life in the first half of the twentieth century. While Stearns was consistently appalled by the industrial expansion he saw redefining the country, for example, the other man saw opportunity. Like most American Marxists in the 1930s, Cowley hoped that the machines that fueled industry in the United States could be harnessed to overthrow capitalism; while he had abandoned class struggle by the 1950s, Cowley never softened his position that his contemporaries abroad should have come home in a timely fashion to help their country realize the vast potential of the interwar years. Harold Stearns lingered in Europe, of course, though his attempt to reconcile with his country after more than a decade abroad stood in stark contrast to the failures of both Harry Crosby and Hart Crane.

In any case, Cowley's skepticism of Stearns clearly went beyond the length of his protracted time abroad. "Young Mr. Elkins," the title character in a 1,500-word prose work published by Cowley in the December 1922 issue of the expatriate literary magazine *Broom*, offered a thinly veiled denunciation of Stearns's reactionary politics. Cowley points out, first of all, that Elkins, like all Americans, owes an underacknowledged debt to a burgeoning industrialization in the United States. "To make the factory wheels revolve," he writes, "eternal hills squeezed minerals from their bowels and prairies co[st]umed themselves in wheat." The resulting "civilization," itself then one of the country's natural gifts, "laboured in its turn and brought forth Mr. Elkins." In fact, Cowley wonders sardonically whether "it was only to produce young Mr. Elkins that American civilization existed" at all. But if a dynamic, modern United States is a "volcano" responsible for this little "pea" of a man, Elkins shows effrontery incommensurate with his stature by being nothing but "critical" of his country. Not only "the milk-and-honey" but "even the rye whiskey of America" goes "bitter in his mouth."[15]

Cowley thus read Stearns's expatriation not as a gesture of youthful defiance but as an out-and-out renunciation of the United States. Even if this was the case, Stearns's autobiography is still a genuine act of repentance, and his reasons for leaving his homeland are overshadowed here by a desire to reconcile himself with American life. While he maintains that he was by no means "a natural story-teller," and he doubts that autobiography offers us an opportunity "to analyze ourselves . . . with any degree of accuracy," his account of life abroad is still a most potent illustration of American expatriation.[16] *The Street I Know* is thus an important supplement to *Exile's Return*, though Malcolm Cowley would never admit as much, as Stearns provides both illuminating examples of tendencies Cowley identifies and useful counterpoints to some of Cowley's fundamental ideas. While Stearns spends little time ruminating self-consciously on the concept of the Lost Generation, and he pays little heed to how his prolonged experience in Paris might be reconciled with that of other young intellectuals who had indeed come home to assume the inheritance of a tradition of American letters, *The Street I Know* expands our understanding of intellectual history in the United States by challenging a narrower pattern of expatriate life established so authoritatively in *Exile's Return*. To bestow upon him too much symbolic significance would be as arbitrary as any strategy undertaken by Cowley, but to ignore Stearns is clearly to leave incomplete any comprehensive reading of life abroad.

It should come as no surprise that charged political issues relevant in the second decade of the twentieth century continue to preoccupy Cowley as he reflects on this time. For him and for his classmates at Harvard, the years from the beginning of the war until the United States entered the conflict changed the world as they knew it. Initially, university insulated them from their wider surroundings. While students may have been looking for "a key to unlock the world," Cowley reveals that their professors offered only "the special world of scholarship—timeless, placeless, elaborate, incomplete, and bearing only the vaguest relationship to that other world in which fortunes were made" (*EN*33). He confirms Alfred Kreymborg's worst fear that, sheltered safely in their ivory towers, young people like Cowley's Mr. Elkins took for granted the country that sustained them in their obliviousness.

Those salesrooms and fitting rooms of culture where we would spend four years were not ground-floor shops, open to the life of the street. They existed, as it were, at the top of very high buildings, looking down at a far panorama of boulevards and Georgian houses and Greek temples of banking—with people outside them the size of gnats—and, vague in the distance, the fields, mines, factories that labored unobtrusively to support us. We never glanced out at them. (*EN36*)

But reality changed for Cowley, as outside forces imposed themselves even on Cambridge, Massachusetts. "During the winter of 1916–17," he admits, "our professors stopped talking about the international republic of letters and began preaching patriotism." This patriotism, needless to say, was unlike "that of French peasants, a matter of saving one's own fields from an invader." Instead, there developed a brand of "abstract patriotism" among young Americans, and it never had anything to do with conditions in the heartland of the United States, concerning itself instead with issues as conceptual as "world democracy and the right to self-determination of small nations" (*EN45*). Young men already raised with ideas about "escape" to Europe found no reason to abandon them now (*EN17*). Cowley himself hoped to get "abroad with the least delay." He was one of the many young men, "the young writers then in college," as he describes them, who found themselves "attracted by the idea of enlisting in one of the ambulance corps attached to a foreign army" (*EN45*). These men made the French ambulance corps "the most literary branch of the army" (*EN46*), and the resulting experience served them in turn as "college-extension courses for a generation of writers" (*EN47*).

Still, the war effected in Cowley and his comrades "a spectatorial attitude" (*EN47*); at some level, it was viewed simply as "a great show" (*EN49*). But if they truly felt a "monumental indifference," it was only "toward the cause for which young Americans were risking their lives" (*EN52*). No one was left unmoved by their actual experiences, of course, touched as they were by the real danger in which they found themselves, even in the ambulance service. For writers like e. e. cummings and Ernest Hemingway, and a great number of their lesser-known contemporaries, their work was changed by it. One of the perceived crises of modern letters as they developed was the malaise felt by artists about traditional "subjects that had seemed forbidden because they were soiled by many hands and robbed of meaning" (*EN*51). Moreover, as Cowley understands it, "young writers were especially tempted to regard their own experience as something negligible, not worth the trouble of recording in the sort of verse or prose they were taught to imitate from the English masters" (*EN*33). But, after the war, it was readily apparent that "danger" had effectively "revivified" these very subjects, even for artists not touched directly by this conflict, and this "made it possible to write once more about love, adventure, death" (*EN*51). The actual war experiences of expatriate Americans were captured more vividly in fiction, in works like *The Enormous Room* (1922) and *A Farewell to Arms* (1929), than they are in *Exile's Return*, a text more concerned with an analysis of experience abroad. But Cowley is still capable of arguing that the price of this experience was considerable. While "school and college had uprooted us in spirit," he observes, it was more significant that the war left young people "physically uprooted." The resulting "rolling and drifting" over the world transformed a group of individuals distinguished by their youth, gave them a sense of collective identity, and rendered them "lost," in Cowley's understanding of the word at least (*EN*39).

While Harold Stearns was seven years older than the author of *Exile's Return*, he also felt a sense of rootlessness as he grew up. Because his father died before he was born, Stearns's mother was forced to move from community to community seeking employment as a nurse. "I never remained long enough in one place to get in with the right crowd," he remembers, "indeed, seldom long enough in one place to get in with any crowd" (*SK*40). He attended high school just outside Boston, and he graduated with the class of 1913 from Harvard, where he savored the protected environment Cowley would watch crumble. He finished his examinations months before his classmates, and he decided to move to New York to continue his newspaper work before he had even received his degree. "Instinctively, I wanted to get to New York," he claims. "I felt that New York was the only place for me—it was the magnet, as I suppose it still is to all young writers and newspapermen in other cities" (*SK*86–87). He sees this wanderlust, and that which followed, as the inevitable extension of his upbringing. "Perhaps it is because I had no genuine 'roots' up there, in the sense of a steady home, a town, a street, a crowd I grew up with," he explains. "Perhaps it is because I am just naturally one of those unfortunate people who really are homeless and spiritual vagabonds" (*SK*88). Indeed, after a little more than a year in the city, his "determination to go abroad became almost an obsession." Much like Cowley, he claims to have "read so much about Europe, thought so much about England and London and Paris" (*SK*107) that he possessed "merely a natural desire to go abroad" (*SK*105). His impulsive decision to travel overseas in 1914 had nothing to do with political events; it was a "compromise with the spirit of 'flaming youth' of" what he recognized as a distinctive age.

> To people a generation younger than I am it may seem incredible, the easy-come, easy-go fashion in which people went abroad in those mythical pre-war days. No red-blooded American citizen ever bothered with such nonsense as a passport; that was for diplomats and big-wigs. Your face—and your pocketbook—were what constituted sufficient passport in any country. And usually, too, you didn't decide on what boat you were going—until the last minute. It was considered quite "chic," if you had a few hundred dollars in your pocket, or had a checkbook that really warranted that amount, to step into a taxicab in front of the bar where you had been garnering Dutch courage, and say to the driver, "Pier So-and-So," and to your admiring friends, "See you in Paris next month." (*SK*109)

Stearns was not disappointed by his first experiences in France. "It is difficult for one of us," he acknowledges, "who afterwards has lived for a long time in Paris, to recall exactly one's first impression of the city, especially if we make its acquaintance when we have grown up" (*SK*116). If he was not possessed of a childlike enthusiasm for life abroad, and even if he was fated to augment this visit with a longer trip in the 1920s, Stearns still explains here what the city meant to him as a younger man. He was most impressed by the "animation" of Paris, "its life and color and stridency." He explains, "The bells on the buses have a gayer sound, the toots of the taxicabs are shriller and more cheerful, less menacing even if they ought to be more, considering the way Paris drivers dart their cars in and out of traffic." He sensed always "an undertone of people walking, doors slamming, little bells ringing, laughter, bits of music from the cafés, saucers being slapped down on tables, as the faithful customers pile up their drink reckoning" (*SK*118).

It was ironic that Stearns's first journey to Europe was as colored by the war as those of the men of the ambulance corps would later be: while the hostilities did not bring him abroad, they did drive him home. He was in Paris when war was declared, and he saw for himself doomed soldiers heading for the front. "Everywhere you saw men hurrying to railway stations with bags," he remembers. "On almost every street-corner you saw women kissing their men goodby, as you saw sons kissing their fathers and brothers kissing brothers goodby; you saw tears and heartache" (*SK*121). But unlike Cowley and his classmates, Stearns claims to have been instinctively appalled by an enterprise he saw as reckless waste. "Politically," he asserts, "I really didn't give a damn about Europe then" (*SK*99). He returned to New York, naïvely certain in his heart that the United States would never be dragged into "any such mass-murder as this European war might well turn out to be" (*SK*123). But it was, of course, its doughboys following the young ambulance drivers who left from, among other safe havens, a Harvard University that by that time would have been unrecognizable to Harold Stearns.

In the wake of the armistice, Malcolm Cowley also found himself back in the United States, while some of his comrades stayed abroad. He "drifted to Manhattan, to the crooked streets south of Fourteenth" to take refuge in Greenwich Village where it was possible to "rent a furnished hall-bedroom for two or three dollars weekly or the top floor of a rickety house for thirty dollars a month" (*EN*57). By this time, the so-called "Seventh Village," the "bohemian enclave" identified by radical journalist Floyd Dell, had only "strengthened and extended" its artistic character. But Gerald McFarlane has argued that "ethnic, class, and cultural diversity" was by the end of the war challenging "neighborhood-wide social intimacy,"[17] so if there were like-minded people with whom to associate, there was little sense of a formal movement remaining to which the dispossessed might belong. While young artists continued to take up residence in New York, Cowley describes the return there of those who had been abroad as, primarily, an arrangement of convenience.

> We came to the village without any intention of becoming Villagers. We came because the living was cheap, because friends of ours had come already (and written us letters full of enchantment), because it seemed that New York was the only city where a young writer could be published. There were some who stayed in Europe after the War and others who carried their college diplomas straight to Paris: they had money. But the rest of us belonged to the proletariat of the arts; we had been uprooted from our own soil; we came to Greenwich Village because there was nowhere else to go. (*EN*57)

Though inexpensive rents and agreeable neighbors may have confirmed the Village as a destination for all manner of American artists and agitators, newspapers were bestowing on the neighborhood a more sinister identity "as the chief of the aggressor nations," as Cowley remembers it (*EN*62). "Revolution was in the air that summer," he acknowledges. "The general strike had failed in Seattle, but a steel strike was being prepared, and a coal strike, and the railroad men were demanding government ownership" (*EN*60). Magazines like the *Saturday Evening Post* claimed "that the Village was the haunt of affectation; that it was inhabited by fools and fakers; that the fakers hid Moscow heresies under the disguise of cubism and free verse." But, as Cowley recalls, these commentators were also certain "that the fools would eventually be cured of their folly." Coming to terms with the reality of a postwar America, "they would forget this funny business about art and return to domesticity"; they would reembrace life "in South Bend, Indiana, and sell motor cars, and in the evenings sit with slippered feet while their children romped about them." Lampooned mercilessly as "longhaired men and short-haired women," the Villagers rejected this way of life with a concerted "campaign of their own against the culture of which the *Post* was the final expression" (*EN*62).

In its discussion of New York, *Exile's Return* hopes to place postwar Greenwich Village in historical perspective. While its idealism may have been blunted, it was still a kind of "Bohemia" that had, elsewhere, represented "revolt against certain features of industrial capitalism" (*EN*64). But Cowley points out that "New York bohemians, the Greenwich Villagers ... came from exactly the same social class as the readers of the *Saturday Evening Post*" (*EN*67–68). In his discussion of the political character of the Village in these years, Ross Wetzsteon acknowledges that radical ideals could often be distorted into "frivolity," "self-indulgence," "grunginess and sloth" by dilettantes.[18] Rather than coming together as a coherent political force, then, nonconformists in New York grew disillusioned by the American experience in a European war and an aftermath to that involvement that Cowley thinks "destroyed their belief in political action." So, he concludes, most people spent their time "trying to get ahead, and the proletariat be damned" (*EN*68). To draw together some of the ideals that were demonstrably at work in the Village, Cowley identifies eight fundamental points that might be understood as an informal "doctrine." Some of its principles seem to have universal applicability. "The idea of living for the moment" pursued by Cowley and his contemporaries, for example, resulted from a desire for profligacy in the face of postwar uncertainty (EN70); "the idea of salvation by child," on the other hand, reaffirmed faith not only in youth but also in the "special potentialities" of all individuals threatened "by a standardized society" (EN69). "The idea of paganism" was, perhaps, inevitably carnal, the desire to emphasize one's physical appearance and to give free rein to one's sexual appetite. Because of the importance of "the idea of liberty" to Villagers, anything that prevented "self-expression or the full enjoyment of the moment" had to be opposed. But some of the other beliefs Cowley discusses seem peculiar to the experience of artists: "the idea of self-expression," for example, suggests that the objective of creative individuals was only to achieve "full individuality" through their art. Still other principles were firmly rooted in the twentieth-century experience. "The idea of female equality," for example, extended beyond the workplace to ensure that women had "the same opportunity for drinking, smoking, taking or dismissing lovers" (EN70). "The idea of psychological adjustment" reflected a growing interest in Freudian psychoanalysis in America, but Cowley here applies its implications only to life in Greenwich Village: because Villagers concentrated on coming to terms with their reaction to the social conditions they encountered, they developed a sense that their "environment itself need not be altered" (EN71). Indeed, rather than agitating for social change in the United States, many of them put their faith in "the idea of changing place" and heeded their impulse to travel abroad.

Ironically, Cowley believes that all of these principles, viewed so skeptically by the American establishment, were actually compatible with the "consumption ethic" that arose among more conventional Americans after the war. "Thus, self-expression and paganism encouraged a demand for all sorts of products, modern furniture, beach pajamas, cosmetics, colored bathrooms with toilet paper to match," he explains by way of example. "Living for the moment meant buying an automobile, radio, or house, using it now and paying for it tomorrow" (EN72). Because the related "production ethic" of "industry, foresight, thrift and personal initiative" so important to capitalism was not to be found among Villagers, however, their demand for goods and services did little ultimately to endear them to their elders (EN71). Still, the American establishment was wrong to fear a unified movement in an increasingly fractious Village. While strains of both "bohemianism" and "radicalism" had labored together before the war, "the esthetic and the political" conspiring with each other, Cowley also concludes that the conflict and its aftermath convinced "political rebels" that they had "no place" in New York. Once "talk about revolution gave way to talk about psychoanalysis," agitators felt out of place in a society "going Greenwich Village," an America whose imitation of the Village lifestyle diluted radical ideals (*EN*76–77). "If, however, the Village was really dying," Cowley argues, "it was dying of success. It was dying because it became so popular that too many people insisted on living there" (*EN*75–76). Indeed, tensions in the Village were aggravated further by divisions based upon age and tenure. Men and women "who had just arrived from France or college" grew ever more distinct from residents "who had lived in the Village before 1917" (*EN*80). It became increasingly difficult to reconcile Cowley and his friends with their "fresh faces and a fresh store of jokes and filthy songs" with those people for whom Mabel Dodge's salon had served as an introduction to New York intellectual life (*EN*81).

Harold Stearns had himself grown restless and dissatisfied in Greenwich Village, where he too had taken refuge, but his discontent was sown in the reality of the home front, while the war still raged in Europe. Before 1914, as he interprets it, the United States was in "a mood of goodnature, a mood of feeling secure, a mood of tolerance toward other countries, other people, and even other people's ideas" (*SK*101). New York, itself, "was colorful, interesting, full of life and hope" (*SK*104). But when the world teetered on the verge of change, when he returned from Europe to find the war's influence already being felt on the other side of the Atlantic, Stearns embraced the only lifestyle he saw at the time as embodying the freedoms he had once taken for granted. "I decided to become a Bohemian," he remembers two decades later. "I didn't have a job; I didn't have any money; I didn't have a girl. What ought one to do in a melancholy situation like that?" (*SK*125). He spent most of the war years in the Village, following what he describes as a "typical bohemian existence" (*SK*126). While his memories of this time, he claims, have "the merit of being extensive" (*SK*127), he provides few details in *The Street I Know*. Instead, he claims only that artistic conviviality provided "happy days," although he was aware that he and his contemporaries "were all under the uneasy shadow of the war" (*SK*137–38). Of his "truly Bohemian days," as he describes them, he observes, "I suppose they were wasted; I suppose I was 'getting nowhere.' But I'll be damned, if I am sorry for them" (*SK*131). Although he dislikes the label "pacifist" (*SK*123), he admits that he resisted American involvement in the war, even as the country was "being dragged in" (*SK*141). In his work reviewing books, for example, he wrote only about texts "not concerned immediately with the war," and he strove to carry "over this self-imposed attitude to the daily business of life" (*SK*144).

Eventually, Stearns decided to leave the Village, to accept a job editing the *Dial* in Chicago in the months before it was, ultimately, transplanted to New York, making enough money to help support his mother and giving him an opportunity to "claim exemption from the draft" if he was ever called to service (*SK*146). But wherever he traveled in the months after the United States entered the conflict, he found "the social atmosphere was becoming impossible." He wonders, "How could one work at intellectual things, when young men were dying in France?" (*SK*159). What seemed to disillusion Stearns most profoundly was the attitude taken by other Americans toward the war. He believed that "mass public opinion," a fear of what "other fellows would say," was what ultimately took men "to the recruiting office first, when war breaks out" (*SK*18). The legacy of this attitude was not felt until the 1920s and 1930s, Stearns maintains, when readers in the United States were forced to confront this "false and overemphasized masculinity," as revealed in the war fiction of Americans like Ernest Hemingway, expatriate writers who set their sights on those who had said nothing about "the slaughter of the world's youth in a senseless war" (*SK*164). In the meantime, Villagers did not have to wait to be disillusioned, overtaken by the cynicism of returning soldiers that confirmed the hollowness of Woodrow Wilson's "verbal gymnastics" (*SK*175).

In such an environment, Malcolm Cowley agrees, plans for escape were rife. Because everyone in Greenwich Village supposedly "held in common" a belief in "exile," a certainty that "they do things better in Europe," expatriation remained an attractive option. Young Americans of Cowley's age had been "uprooted" before, after all; they had been "wrenched away" from any "attachment to any region or tradition" (*EN*11). Their schooling "was involuntarily directed toward destroying whatever roots we had in the soil," he claims (*EN*29). Moreover, the world for which their schooling had prepared them had been ruined by conflict, and so "the war prepared them," in Cowley's estimation, "for nothing." He sees the early 1920s in the United States as "a period of confused transition from values already fixed to values that had to be created." So if, as he believes, young Americans "had no trustworthy guides" among their elders (*EN*11), it should come as little surprise that they turned to a contemporary figure to lead an escape from the Palmer Raids and prohibition. Through both *America and the Young Intellec-*

tual (1921) and an anthology entitled *Civilization in the United States* (1922), Harold Stearns asked one prevailing question, according to Cowley's paraphrase, that prompted a widespread exodus: "Why was there, in America, no satisfying career open to talent?" (*EN*85). Rather than addressing this question in any meaningful, practical fashion, many people simply deferred their answer. Cowley believes that most of his contemporaries held that "a young man had no future in this country of hypocrisy and repression. He should take a ship for Europe, where people know how to live" (*EN*89). By thus discussing the many "obituaries on civilization in the United States," there can be little doubt that Cowley is referring primarily to Stearns, though the latter certainly would have had his imitators (*EN*62). It was more than Stearns's willingness to speak aloud his discontent that was influential, however: his own departure for France provided a reassuring illustration of how escape was possible. Cowley writes, "His was no ordinary departure: he was Alexander marching into Persia and Byron shaking the dust of England from his feet." And "everywhere," as he remembers it, "young men were preparing to follow his example" (*EN*89–90). While Cowley later told his friend Kenneth Burke that "the chiefest benefit" of traveling to Europe was that he escaped "the prejudices" against America provoked by Stearns's work and discussed by its citizens in its wake,[19] by following him within weeks of his departure, Cowley actually gave credence to much that Stearns said.

In fact, evidence of Stearns's disaffection was scattered throughout the writing he published during this time. "We do not want to cut ourselves off from our national life," he wrote of "young intellectuals" in the United States, as he described them in the *Bookman* magazine in March 1921, "but we are inexorably being forced to do it." Stearns experienced a "hollowness and hypocrisy" in American life, a condition that still prevented "honest work, serious work, intelligent work" of the mind, two years after the armistice.[20] He was wary of a "new world" he feared was "coming into being right before our eyes" because of a war fought with the assistance of, and ultimately in service to, American industry. As a child, he was appalled by his first "little taste of the horrors of industrialism," a summer job that illustrated "the monotony and stupidity of piece work on machines" (*SK*43). Looking back in the mid-1930s, he sees as profoundly ironic that a time when "mechanical and technical innovations" offered "so many new and wonderful things," the war claimed the most "inventive people," young innovators "who would most have appreciated and enjoyed" the opportunities of the modern world (*SK*165). Because he does not share the faith Cowley harbored in material progress, therefore, "industrialism" cannot be tempered for Stearns by anything "more gracious than a desire for all the profits going" (*SK*134).

In *America and the Young Intellectual*, Stearns had attempted to explain why "the young men we should do our best to keep with us are leaving on every boat." The establishment in the United States was intent only on "blackjacking" youth into furthering conventional interests.

> Something must be radically wrong with a culture and a civilisation when its youth begins to desert it. Youth is the natural time for revolt, for experiment, for a generous idealism that is eager for action. Any civilisation which has the wisdom of self-preservation will allow a certain margin of freedom for the expression of this youthful mood. But the plain, unpalatable fact is that in America to-day that margin of freedom has been reduced to the vanishing point. Rebellious youth is not wanted here. In our environment there is nothing to challenge young men; there is no flexibility, no colour, no possibility for adventure, no chance to shape events more generously than is permitted under the rules of highly organised looting.[21]

Years later, Stearns still maintained that "the shadows of prohibition and intolerance, all the unlovely aftermath of the great Wilsonian crusade were closing in" by the summer of 1921, though it was also apparent through more than a decade's hindsight that an idiosyncratic "old restlessness" was partially responsible for his decision to flee (*SK*202–3). *The Street I Know* thus exhibits a depth of personal despair unmatched in expatriate American autobiography through the 1930s.

In 1919 Stearns had married Alice Macdougal, a woman from California who worked in New York for the publisher Horace Liveright, and at the time he determined that "vagabondia was over with" for him. "I could—and would—do what every man in his heart at some time or other believes he wants to do," he remembers, "that is, settle down" (*SK*182–83). But his wife died in childbirth the following January when visiting her parents in San Francisco, while Stearns remained in New York. "There was no faith for me, as for many people, to fall back on in a crisis like this," he laments. "There was just emptiness, blank, loss of all feeling" (*SK*187). He had been writing *Liberalism in America* (1919), but he questions whether "any young author has ever been less interested—fundamentally and really less interested" in the reception of his work (*SK*189). He published *America and the Young Intellectual* in 1921, but this influential volume could not compare with the sheer scale of another project that year, keeping him "busy and occupied" through his grief (*SK*192). *Civilization in the United States* brought together more than thirty original essays devoted to topics ranging from "Art" to "Advertising" to "The Alien," "Politics" to "Philosophy" to "Poetry," "Science" to "Sex" to "Sport and Play." The collection, according to its editor, was intended as a "deliberate and organized outgrowth of the common efforts of like-minded men and women to see the problem of modern American civilization as a whole,"[22] and to do so Stearns drew on a host of experts including Van Wyck Brooks, Ring Lardner, H. L. Mencken, and Lewis Mumford. In "The Intellectual Life," his own essay, Stearns held out hope that "the America of our natural affections" would reassert itself over "those who to-day keep it a spiritual prison."[23] His actions, however, belied any optimism; as he remembers it, he dated the introduction to the book "Independence Day, 1921," stepped aboard the *Berengaria* in New York harbor, and sailed to Le Havre. "I had only envisaged a short summer trip to Europe," he reflects. "I did not realize, though I think I had a sort of dim, subconscious feeling that it was going to be longer than just a summer trip, that I was going to stay in France for almost thirteen years" (*SK*203).

It is left to Malcolm Cowley to draw more cynical conclusions. "The exiles of 1921 came to Europe seeking one thing and found another," he writes. "They came to recover the good life and the traditions of art, to free themselves from organized stupidity, to win their deserved place in the hierarchy of the intellect." Instead, he argues, "they found valuta." By so saying, he acknowledges the vagaries of the currency exchange rate that so affected American journeys through Europe in the 1920s and 1930s. He observes wryly that "the continent of immemorial standards . . . had lost them all" (*EN*91). With considerable savvy of his own, Cowley made the best of his money, voyaging widely to surrounding countries. "I wrote in the brief mornings, studied Molière and Racine, sat in cafés playing dominos," he remembers, "and traveled—there was always a new city where life was more agreeable or cheaper" (*EN*141). But, without exception, he returned always to Paris, expressing his affection for the city by making comparisons with the industrial shrines that continued to hearten him and promise a brighter future.

Paris was a great machine for stimulating the nerves and sharpening the senses. Paintings and music, street noises, shops, flower markets, modes, fabrics, poems, ideas, everything seemed to lean toward a half-sensual, half-intellectual swoon. Inside the cafés, color, perfume, taste and delirium could be poured together from one bottle or many bottles, from square, cylindrical, conical, tall, squat, brown, green or crimson bottles—but you drank black coffee by choice, believing that Paris itself was sufficient alcohol. (*EN*143–44)

He was influenced by his contact with the Dadaists, a group that represented for him "the very essence of Paris" (*EN*145), and especially French writer Louis Aragon. Aragon and his co-conspirators embraced the effects of the modern world with a "childishness and audacity" that "suited the temper of a world disorganized by the War" (*EN*147). Cowley also attempts to place both the avant-garde and the experience of expatriate Americans in historical perspective. His cohort, for example, was descended from "younger Russians" who traveled across Europe "after the middle of the nineteenth century" (*EN*94) to "the source of literary fashions . . . in an atmosphere that seemed more favorable to art" (*EN*99). But his personal experiences abroad also convinced him that the United States, and its expatriates, did not suffer through any analogies made with their hosts. "Everywhere, after the War, one found unfavorable comparisons between the intellectual life of America and that of Europe," he acknowledges. But within the decade, "this feeling had gone and even its memory was fading" (*EN*104–5). The time Cowley and his contemporaries spent abroad was crucial to shaking any feelings of inadequacy that might have remained from their experiences in the United States. "They had merely to travel, compare, evaluate and honestly record what they saw," he maintains of expatriates. "In the midst of this process the burden of inferiority somehow disappeared—it was not so much dropped as it leaked away like sand from a bag carried on the shoulder—suddenly it was gone and nobody noticed the difference." With their burden thus lifted, Americans abroad began to accept that "their own nation had every attribute they had been taught to admire in those of Europe." With the things that interested Americans thus suddenly relevant everywhere, Cowley discovered a new challenge. "American themes, like other themes, had exactly the dignity that talent could lend them," he maintains, and as a way to represent their new status, Cowley's cohort "invented" what he characterizes as "the international myth of the Lost Generation," a process culminating with the publication of *The Sun Also Rises* (*EN*106–7).

Harold Stearns also reads advantages in his early experiences abroad. "Life really *can* go by like a dream in Paris—it so often has for me. It did then," he remembers wistfully. The early 1920s in France had "a genuine gaiety," long before "the tourist flocks . . . swooped down on the place." In his remembrances, at least, this was a time when visitors from both the United States and England were "serious" about their intellectual pursuits, not simply seeking "an irresponsible sexual and alcoholic holiday," as he describes subsequent waves of expatriates (*SK*208–9). If, unrealistically, he recalls his first years abroad as unsullied by decadent impulse, he also imbues them with nostalgia for a Europe untouched by industrial expansion. "I want France to be France—to be local, provincial, narrow-minded, split-up heterogeneous," he complains. "After all, if I want standardization and uniformity and all the lovely by-products of large-scale production, coupled with 'national' distribution, I can get them at home. I don't have to go to France for them" (*SK*231). Because he had been in Europe when war broke out, Stearns should not have been thus surprised as nineteenth-century cultural ideals began to shatter. But if expatriation was really about reaffirming the values of American life, as Malcolm Cowley concluded, Stearns was slow to draw this conclusion, and by the mid-1920s he showed a real desire to adopt Paris as his permanent home. "I spent some of the best years of my life there," he maintains (*SK*238). While earlier expatriates like Natalie Barney, Ezra Pound, and Gertrude Stein illustrated the manner by which Americans could willingly adapt to European life, Stearns's heart-wrenching 1924 trip to California to visit his young son, Philip, illustrated an emotional destitution that left him with little choice but to try to re-embrace a life abroad:

> For as I look back on it now, I realize how deep and strong was the emotional conflict within me—I felt I was running away from America, this time really without good and sufficient reason; and yet I couldn't help running away. "Home" was not home to me any longer. But Paris was not my home either. I was just an uprooted, aimless wanderer on the face of the earth. And a lonely one, too. I didn't like that; I hated it. And, since there was nothing else to do, I would go into the bar and take another drink—and try to forget. (*SK*254)

This aimlessness and dissipation underlined both the geographical and moral bewilderment for which the Lost Generation had to account. William Shirer, who found fame as the author of *The Rise and Fall of the Third Reich* (1960), was working on the Paris *Tribune* by the mid-1920s, and he later remembered vividly his first sight of a disoriented Harold Stearns. "He wore a soiled, beat-up felt hat, which seemed to be glued on his head, for he never removed it, though it was a rather warm evening. His melancholy face was unwashed, unshaved, and his hands and fingers were dirty," Shirer recalled. "I was taken aback by his shabbiness. This was not at all the Harold Stearns I had imagined from my college days, when he was one of my heroes."[24] After Stearns was seen to have turned his back on his country yet again, his image became a prohibitive warning for a life wasted abroad.

For Malcolm Cowley, expatriate Americans "were like colts who had jumped the fence without breaking their tethers" (*EN*107–8). The freedom they sought was thus, ironically, dependent on their return home. Cowley met Stearns in New York after the latter's failed attempt to reconcile with his son, an exchange added to the 1951 edition of *Exile's Return*. But he might just as well have had Stearns in mind as he looked to the precedent of nineteenth-century Russians in Paris who feared that if they stayed home, they would remain "provincials doomed to follow last year's Paris styles." If they stayed abroad, they risked the possibility of losing "contact with their own people" (*EN*99). At the end of Cowley's own time abroad, he claims to have been itching to get home.

> In Europe we were learning to regard the dragon of American industry as a picturesque and even noble monster; but our friends at home had not the advantage of perspective; for them the dragon blotted out the sky; they looked up and all they could see was the scales of its belly, freshly alemited and enameled with Duco. They dreamed of escaping into older lands which the dragon hadn't yet invaded—while we, in older lands, were already dreaming of a voyage home. Soon we began to argue back and forth across the water. (*EN*118)

Still, Cowley's strongest calls for repatriation came well after his own return to the United States. He and Slater Brown, Kenneth Burke, Robert Coates, and Matthew Josephson, for example, published a selection of letters, essays, and parodic poems taunting expatriates entitled "New York: 1928" in *transition*. But by this time,

Cowley had been home for five years. His own moment of reconciliation with his country had been clear, and he had needed little additional coaxing. On an early summer night in 1923, he got into a fight at the Rotonde and, in the midst of the melee, gave the proprietor what he describes as "a glancing blow in the jaw" (*EN*175). Cowley was amused that he had undertaken action to which the "favorite catchwords" of Dada could be applied (*EN*179). In fact, the matter was somewhat more serious, as described in other remembrances. Robert McAlmon suggested that any impromptu pugilist faced "a six month jail term, for they are strict about fisticuffing in France." Cowley was spared because of the intervention of some fifteen expatriates who swore to the police that he had been defending the honor of a woman. "We were all against the patron of the Rotonde," McAlmon admitted. "He disliked Americans, had become rich through them, and was sour-faced and mercenary at best."[25] In any event, with a degree in French studies in hand from the Université de Montpellier and having fully exhausted his investigation of European avant-gardism, Malcolm Cowley soon returned to the United States. In advance of his departure, he had begun to write "about America," about "movies and skyscrapers and machines, dwelling upon them with all the nostalgia derived from two long years of exile." He was "enthusiastic over America" for perhaps the first time in his life. He admits, "I had learned from a distance to admire its picturesque qualities" (*EN*179). In July 1923 he sailed from Normandy, but in New York he was "greeted by no official committee of welcome" (*EN*181).

For his part, Harold Stearns read no great significance into Cowley's gesture of violence. This descent "into violent fisticuffs" was simply an attempt to convince Europeans "that Americans were as up-to-date in literary fashions and absurdities as were the French themselves, if not more so" (*SK*298–99). If Stearns had ever been trying similarly to measure himself against French intellectuals, he had long since ceased doing so. Indeed, foreshadowing his spiral into alcoholism is his description of his first trip abroad, where he recalls his "first drink in Paris," a "vermouth-cassis" ordered "because it looked gay and because people were having the same thing" (*SK*117). More than a decade later, he was suffering through what he describes as "the summer and autumn of my discontent in Paris." He recognizes of his existence abroad that "the dream couldn't go on forever," but neither could he have foreseen "what the awakening would be." The last half of the 1920s saw him attempt to live "without regrets about the past or plans concerning the future" (*SK*258).

Looking back, he attempts to connect his physical decline with the waning of the expatriate impulse. "In Paris," he maintains, "the American will" grows "enfeebled," and Americans abroad inevitably "relapse into mere wishing and dreaming" (SK298). Of his legendary debts, for example, he tries to appear carefree. He acknowledges that the saucers from his drinks, representing his tab at a favored café, were piled up "sometimes until they almost touched the ceiling," but rather than shame, they provide Stearns with nothing more than "a painful visual reminder" of his poverty, as he resolves to scheme for more money (SK313). According to Kay Boyle, one of Stearns's most popular ruses was to raise money among Americans in Paris for a lame horse he was supposedly nursing back to health. "I'd like you to come and see him sometime," Stearns is supposed to have often said, cheekily.[26] His fascination with horse racing, beginning with a trip to the Grand Prix de Paris in June 1923, presented him with many opportunities to handle wagers for his friends: the lure of easy money was overwhelming.

> But towards the end I became reluctant to take bets for other people; I was always sailing too close to the wind myself. And I knew the dangers too well; I was tempted to take chances against myself, so to speak, that my horse would *not* win—and to keep the money in my pocket. And, of course, that was precisely the time he *would* come through it almost goes without saying, at odds that were ruinous to me, for it takes a braver man than I am to say, "I'm sorry, but I changed my mind when I got to the track and backed what I thought was the safer thing." Some people could say that—and get away with it, though not too often. But I could not. I had to tell the truth—and, when I couldn't pay, owe the money. (SK327)

He does acknowledge that he had run up debts in this way. But if he is grudgingly honest in such matters in *The Street I Know*, that does not mean that he is above shaping his tale carefully to present his vices in the best possible light. He claims at one point, for example, that one of his friends believed the root of Stearns's failing health was that he did not "drink enough" (SK353). There is no hint of irony in such a statement, no shame in his suggestion that others were thus more wanton, no sense that he believed himself anything but transparent in his suffering. He attempts to contextualize his bad behavior, but he struggles to find specific examples of depravity in others against which to balance his own conduct.

"I understand quite well how some people went morally to pieces during that time," he writes, "and, if I was saved, as naturally I flatter myself I was, it was simply by my work and my regular, even if absurd, hours and habits" (SK277). In fact, his writing assignments eventually dried up. While he had done foreign assignment work for the Baltimore *Sun* and *Town and Country*, and he had even worked on the copy desk of the Paris *Herald*, he finally could secure work only as "Peter Pickum," the horse racing correspondent for the Paris *Tribune*. While this gave him the opportunity to go to the track "professionally," and he claims that he wrote "from one o'clock in the afternoon until half past eight in the evening with no let up and at a high nervous tension" (SK359), he also describes this newspaper work as "a one-way ticket to the Never-Never-Land of male irresponsibility, absurdity, and entertainment, of which all men in their hearts forever dream—and so seldom ever reach" (SK335). It is perhaps merciful, if not inevitable, that these events are available to the reader through the fog of Stearns's memory. "There are periods in our life, I think—at least, I can only assume so, judging from my own experience," he maintains, "which stubbornly resist all efforts of our memory to recapture" (SK363).

Harold Stearns's inability to look clearly at his past has an interesting parallel in his failing health. As undiagnosed infections agonized him, his world was shaken. "Probably I had turned white—or green—or any other color. I shall never know," he suggests. "For what had taken place is something easy to write down in cold words, but the effect of which on anyone to whom it happens is likely to do more than merely change their color a little bit. In a word, I went blind" (SK342). With some residual ambition to fulfill his intellectual potential still flickering, these increasingly frequent episodes of temporary blindness gave him a sense of "how a man feels when he is sentenced to be executed" (SK348–49). Compounding "the most terrible months" of his life, he was homeless, wandering the streets of Paris in a wretched condition:

> Happiness, which meant nothing less than security, friends, an amusing and interesting life, comes to mean much simpler things. Things like warmth, a full stomach, a decent pair of shoes, a clean bed in which to sleep even up to noon undisturbed, if you wish. When it gets down to about its lowest terms—as it actually did with me—you can look no further ahead than a glass of water, and you think of all the possible cafés where you might go and not be refused that sort of elementary animal courtesy. (SK364)

He would occasionally "run into a friend or an acquaintance" who, being "shocked" at his appearance, would pay "for a night's rest and perhaps a meal." But, he also admits, "there were weeks at a time when, had you met me on the street and asked me where I spent the night, I could not have answered you truthfully." Certainly, fellow expatriates seemed more willing to respond to the promise of shared debauchery than the reality of private deprivation. Stearns reveals that it was easy to find someone who might part with "75 or 100 francs worth of drinks" but who "looked pained" with obvious embarrassment when asked for just a fraction of that amount "to get a cheap hotel room so that I might have a place to sleep" (SK365).

As his condition deteriorated, he could not work at all. "I had thought I was well enough to write articles, even a book possibly. But I wasn't," he admits. "I couldn't concentrate; I couldn't seem to remember anything . . . and what I did remember was as often as not wrong" (SK368). Ultimately, the only solution to his health problems was the extraction of all his teeth, a humiliating disfigurement that pointed him homeward:

> With no teeth, few friends, no job, and no money I naturally decided that all I could do was return to my own country—and try to start all over. Everything about Paris had suddenly become distasteful to me; I suppose because I felt so alien and alone. Something deep in me, however, kept saying, "Go home, go home, that is the place for you. Go home to America." But how? (SK370)

Eventually, the American Aid Society, an organization that helped people from the United States in difficult circumstances abroad, bought Stearns a ticket home. But instead of an ocean liner bound for Manhattan, the man who had left New York as the swaggering young intellectual returned to New Jersey on a freighter.

In *Exile's Return*, Malcolm Cowley is careful to acknowledge the sometimes-difficult plight of expatriates as they came home. He has, above all else, a self-conscious sense of his cohort and its place in American literary history, and he seeks to understand the depth of its experience. Even if, as he suspects, there was "no group" and there was "no solidarity" in the sense of a uniform movement, there were still "prevailing habits of thought" that tied together expatriates in the 1920s. There was an apparent pattern of migration, for example. If "hundreds and thousands" of young Americans, in Cowley's estimation, "became veritable exiles," it was also inevitable that "most of them didn't remain exiled forever," no matter when and

how they heeded the call to return. "One by one they came lingering back to New York," he observes, "even though they came there
as aliens, many of these holding ideas that would cause them a difficult period of readjustment" (EN215). America had changed, but
so had they. "New York, to one returning from Paris or London," as
he describes it, "seemed the least human of all babylons" (EN210).
Cowley puts a personal face on this upheaval, slipping into the first
person to discuss his own representative experience.

> Everything was strange to me: the exhausting and dispiriting
> heat, the colors of the houses, the straightaway vistas, the girls
> on the sidewalk in their bright frocks, so different from the drab
> ones that the French shopgirls wore, and most of all the lack
> of anything green to break the monotony of the square streets,
> the glass, brick and iron. The next year—the next three years, in
> fact—would be spent in readjusting myself to this once familiar
> environment. (EN182)

Returning to the United States, he was certainly looking for
"something," he acknowledges, that "was no longer there." While
he savored "a sense of belonging to something, of living in a country whose people spoke his language and shared his interests," he
recognizes that all expatriates effectively risked withdrawing from
American "society itself, from any society with purposes they could
share, toward which they could honestly contribute and from which
they could draw new strength" (EN222–23). Ironically, the practical
act of reconciliation was complicated by the prosperity to which
expatriates initially returned in the 1920s. Their outlooks had been
broadened, but their ambition "to be the guardians of intellectual
things" (EN218) had to be deferred as many were tempted by jobs
writing copy where, if they were not changing the world, there
were at least "abundant compensations for their lot" (EN213). Con-
sequently, they set to work "reproducing in New York the conditions that had seemed so congenial to life abroad" using their new
lucre (EN184).

> They were learning that New York had another life, too—
> subterranean, like almost everything that was human in the
> city—a life of writers meeting in restaurants at lunchtime or in
> coffee houses after business hours to talk of work just started
> or magazines unpublished, and even to lay modest plans for the
> future. Modestly they were beginning to write poems worth the

trouble of reading to their friends over coffee cups. Modestly they were rebelling once more.

In the meantime, their new dreams of escape were confined to the American "countryside" in upstate New York or "perhaps on a Connecticut farm" (EN214).

Despite the comfort of their bourgeois trappings, returning expatriates found an environment that was also more politically charged. "Once a writer had recognized that society contained hostile classes, that the result of their conflict was uncertain and would affect his own fortunes," Cowley points out, "then he ceased to believe that political action was silly." More and more artists thus found themselves "politicized." They became more "radical" when they recognized that "the working classes" was the group "whose interests lay closest" to theirs, after all (EN241). Cowley and his friends maintained their faith in "the rapid development of applied science, power machinery and mass production" to hasten "the decay of capitalism" (EN299). Unfortunately, the diversity of thought that often makes it difficult to recognize a single, discernable cohort throughout *Exile's Return* also hindered political action that might, itself, define the generation. "We should have realized that there was no chance of imposing our ideas on others when we couldn't agree among ourselves," he admits. In this, Cowley claims that he and his friends were "beaten almost before we began" (EN193). He hoped that perhaps the looming economic crisis in the late 1920s would finally shake remaining artists from their malaise. For then, he believed, "the artist and his art had once more become a part of the world, produced by and perhaps affecting it" (EN287). Even remaining expatriates seemed to have gotten the message:

> Everywhere was the atmosphere of a long debauch that had to end; the orchestras played too fast, the stakes were too high at the gambling tables, the players were so empty, so tired, secretly hoping to vanish together into sleep and . . . maybe wake on a very distant morning and hear nothing whatever, no shouting or crooning, find all things changed. (EN280)

Things moved quickly after the 1929 Wall Street crash. "The refugees from America often thought vaguely of coming home," he gloats. "Now the depression was forcing them home by cutting off their incomes" (EN240). Even the most recalcitrant stragglers were back "in a flood," and it was particularly significant for Cowley that "Harold Stearns, the Young Intellectual of 1922, was back in New York" (*EN*285).

Few struggled as publicly as did Stearns upon his return. "Anyway, I knew one thing then right away, and knew it clearly," he admits of his arrival. "One part of my life was over—forever" (*SK*373). He secured a commission to write an article on his repatriation for *Scribner's* magazine, and he began to review books for newspapers. Malcolm Cowley did not invite him to review for the *New Republic*, but he did loan him some money. In the meantime, Stearns shared a room with a friend in Newark, and there he wrote an article on horse racing that was eventually published by *Harper's*. Securing his own room in a house on Charles Street in Manhattan was an important "symbol" of his gathering "success" (*SK*395). He wrote a book called *Rediscovering America* (1934), but for an analysis of his expatriation and his return to the United States, he chose to embrace autobiography. He recognizes the limitations of a form that relies upon both "imagination and memory" (*SK*27), acknowledging that he might "remember some things and not others" (*SK*17). Because we all "romanticize the past" (*SK*101), he abandons any pretense to objectivity. "Most of us, after forty, tend to think we would have been a great deal better off, had we done something else than what we in fact did" (*SK*92). He substitutes meticulousness for detachment, claiming, "I have tried to tell the truth, and to tell it interestingly. As far as I can, I have avoided heroics, and I have tried not to sentimentalize about myself" (*SK*400). In the end, he realizes a "feeling of release and serenity that comes to any man when he makes an honest attempt to see things as they are rather than as he would like them to be" (*SK*411). He is proud of his effort to take stock, seeing as a testament to his rehabilitation that "every line of the book you are reading" was pounded out on a typewriter in his little room in Manhattan.

> It is not much, I know—a poor thing, but my own, if you wish
> to be cynical. When I think back, however, to some of those
> nights on the benches of the Boulevard Montparnasse, I am not
> wholly ashamed of what I have done. It is, say what you want,
> quite a distance to have come in so short a time. . . . It is easy
> enough to write that now, after the event. Remember there
> have been plenty of nervous, anxious moments during that
> period—moments when I have thought, in spite of everything,

that I simply could not, as the English put it, "carry on." But when I moved to Charles Street my faith in life was again restored. I had, I thought, done the impossible. (*SK*396)

Beyond the personal, Stearns is aware that he is writing about an extremely important time. Like other modern thinkers, he wonders if in the twentieth century "not merely our America, but the whole world of which it is now such an important part, have both changed more than has any time previously in two whole centuries" (*SK*46). But unlike many modern writers, he sees modern art not as the vanguard of a new movement, but as a harbinger of some movement's end. He feels fortunate, indeed, to have gotten to Harvard before the war, to have been a member of "the last class of the Victorian era" (*SK*69). Out of step with an interdisciplinary curiosity shared across a variety of forms, he confesses a "rather lamentable indifference" to visual art (*SK*198). He has an unquestioned respect for literary tradition, which he sees "as much a part of a writer's natural background as the way he hears words in the street" (*SK*86). While he helped popularize the idea of the "young intellectual" in 1920s America, he is skeptical of the concept of the Lost Generation, of which he writes, "During my first years in Paris I don't think I reflected much on the so-called expatriate problem, especially with respect to American writers" (*SK*301–2). He grants that "our youngsters used to come to Paris looking for culture," but he suggests wryly that "it was a mark of something or other in intellectual progress" that eventually "they came over looking for trouble" (*SK*299). Stearns argues that such a change in material circumstances is beside the point for the artistic temperament, however, and not likely to concern genuine artists:

> But it always impressed me as an irrelevant thing. Simply, I am trying to say, an imaginative writer's problems (critical as well as "creative") are so essentially and forever internal that I for my part have never thought of outer circumstances—whether of color, race, time in history, or even language—as anything but incidental and accidental. It is the *spiritual* struggle every writer—every real writer, of course—has to go through: It does not much matter, when he comes to go through with the struggle, where he is or even what language he speaks—and certainly not terribly much what the economic system is under which he lives and writes at all. (*SK*302)

About the only external influence he is willing to concede, ultimately, is the one he so carelessly abandoned in 1921: country. He feels a new affinity with his countrymen, Americans "without jobs and without hope" who thought, during the Depression, that "they didn't belong" (*SK*385). He can hardly believe "that men could have struggled and worked, dreamed dreams, had wars and revolutions for centuries" and ended up in the despair of the 1930s (*SK*389). But rather than once more turning his back on the United States, he asserts defiantly, "I myself discovered that I was an American after all." Hardship might be encountered anywhere, but he judges it "unnatural" to endure one's suffering abroad.

> When we leave our own country, it should be only for a pleasure trip or a relatively brief voyage of study—otherwise we shall not find even a fraction of what we have left behind. Prosperity and money may give us temporarily the illusion of not caring about being uprooted—but it *is* an illusion, nevertheless. We cannot escape a dim feeling of uneasiness and insecurity, just as we never are really certain how people, basically not like ourselves, will act in the emergencies of life—whatever the civilized veneer. I mean, simply, we are homeless enough in this world under the best of circumstances without going to any special effort to test our capacity to be more so. (*SK*409)

By thus invoking an Emersonian edict against wanderlust, the remorseful expatriate finds some measure of political engagement, though it is not an engagement the radical Cowley might have envisioned. In his reconsideration of "The Intellectual Life" for a new anthology of essays in 1938, Stearns equated communism with fascism, rejecting both as "anti-intellectual," "bitter," and "contemptuous of democracy" by eschewing "tolerance and reasonableness."[27] Unfortunately, his view of the world also exhibited a fair degree of naïveté. In *The Street I Know*, he maintains that he would "never live to see victorious German troops marching down the Boulevards of Paris" (*SK*124). Elsewhere, he claimed that "the war-like mind" is involved in "a bitter losing battle." While he was eventually willing to take a softer view of modern innovation, best represented "by science, by rapid communication and ease of travel, by commerce and productive industry," seeing these things as "powerful disinfectants" against military aggression, he little foresaw that they might still be harnessed by the greedy.[28]

Unlike Harold Stearns, who died in 1943, Malcolm Cowley

found many opportunities to reevaluate his thoughts about expatriation. "I hate to write and love to revise," he observes in thanking the Viking Press for an opportunity to refashion *Exile's Return* in the 1950s (*EO*10). While he was not the only expatriate who sought to correct the impression of expatriate life in Paris, his later text is most important for the influence it still wields. For Donald Faulkner, the 1951 edition "stands alone among the chronicles, memoirs, and remembrances of the making of American literature in the 1920s."[29] The changes between the two texts are, for John Hazlett, best explained as Cowley's reaction to being "embarrassed by his decade of Marxist enthusiasm"[30]: his decision to emphasize his generationalist narrative strategy to the detriment of his earlier political material, passages Cowley later believed "intruded into the narrative" (*EO*11). The 1951 edition thus becomes for Hazlett "a cautious literary reminiscence," that upon closer scrutiny sacrifices what had been "an excellent autobiographical narrative that followed Cowley and his friends on their ideological odyssey from bohemianism to Marxism."[31] As a record of expatriate experience, the 1951 edition does leave "untouched" (*EO*12), as Cowley describes it, much of the salient detail of the earlier text, though its changes seek to contextualize further his cohort within literary history. He now refers to "the lost generation" in the past tense and with lowercase letters, acknowledging that there was, indeed, an important group of American writers abroad in the 1920s while also suggesting, perhaps, that emphasis placed upon the decadence of that experience continues to miss the point.

Donald Faulkner thus argues that with the republication of *Exile's Return*, "public awareness" of American literary advancements and "the roles Cowley and his contemporaries played in extending it had been established."[32] But one can appreciate a more provisional sketch of modern American expatriation by juxtaposing the earlier edition of Cowley's text with Harold Stearns's remembrances of his time abroad, just as one might have done in the 1930s. Unfortunately, few did. Neither book was widely read at that time, and only by placing them side by side now can readers appreciate the kind of intellectual heterogeneity that always threatened Cowley's uneasy attempt to define his generation. In a footnote to his revision, Malcolm Cowley grants that Harold Stearns eventually "became a reformed character" (*EO*285n). But even as his own views shifted, Cowley was unable to acknowledge the extent of what he owed a fellow exile returned. Now only contemporary readings can begin to redress this debt.

4

PLACE AS A STRATEGY
OF ATTACHMENT

The engagement of modern writers with their urban surroundings is evident in many of their most notable works. Expatriate Americans during the first decades of the twentieth century also had strong reactions to the cities whose growth embodied the spirit of the industrialized world. J. Gerald Kennedy observes that "displaced writers of the modern age" turned their attention to "a half dozen great cities," responding to "the cosmopolitan density of experience and urban energy."[1] As evident in the narratives of expatriation examined thus far, the experience of American writers in the urban centers they inhabited played an important role in the life stories they tell. The cities of the American Midwest embodied the narrow provincialism from which expatriates fled; New York was not immune to the malaise and hypocrisy from which Europe promised escape. Once abroad, Americans traveled to Berlin, London, Rome, and Vienna, but Paris was most often their ultimate destination. Jerrold Seigel reads this congregation of Americans leading "sexually free and economically shaky lives in the name of art or literature" as a significant gesture reaffirming the city as "a center of Bohemia."[2] Paris, as Kennedy reminds us, had indeed been "a city of exile" since at least the middle of the nineteenth century,[3] and for Eric Cahm, its "long-standing reputation as a focus for European culture, and the earlier movements and bohemian tendencies it had sheltered," continued to make the city a focal point for expatriates of all nationalities in the years before the First World War.[4] The popularity of the city for expatriate Americans in the 1920s, according to Arlen Hansen, represented "a conscious surrender" to the "magnetism" of Paris.[5] But the central importance of Paris in the autobiographies of expatriate Americans cannot be accounted for simply, because their art may be read as a response to industrialization and, as Malcolm Bradbury describes it, "the modern artist" has thus "been caught up in the spirit of the modern city, which is itself the spirit of a modern technological society."[6] It is also unlikely that most Americans abroad would choose to render these surroundings with such careful detail in their narratives simply because Paris became their dwelling place. One might expect that by offering "a haven to the fleeing or seeking" writer in a deracinated "community of artists," as Noël Riley Fitch points out, the city might but kindle an "interest in homeland and a keen and objective perspective on place."[7] In fact, the meticulousness with which Paris appears in expatriate narrative reflects its writers' recognition of the developing importance modern art placed upon authenticity. The sheer experience of life abroad gave these Americans an insight that they believed their contemporaries back home simply did not possess, and preserving a convincing sense of place in their writings was the wage of that experience. But through the 1930s and 1940s, as the critical reputations of expatriates like Gertrude Stein and Ernest Hemingway began to grow, lesser writers also wrote about Paris, hoping through their autobiographies to shape readings of the Lost Generation. Indeed, expatriate Americans with little creative affiliation to developing appreciations of modernism forged their connections with the fledgling movement by emphasizing their proximity to its most storied European locus. In this way, marginal figures contributed to the importance of place in our understanding of modernism, and their response to place has endured subsequently as a defining feature of the movement.

Perhaps the most important text for considering place as a discursive strategy of attachment is Samuel Putnam's *Paris Was Our Mistress* (1947), where the American translator, biographer, and newspaperman personifies the city as "a wise and beautiful" woman at a time during which his home country "had turned a strumpet."[8] Putnam reflects upon "our Paris," the expatriate refuge of the late 1920s and early 1930s in this case, to provide a "report" to "supplement" examinations like Malcolm Cowley's *Exile's Return* (*PM*6). Gerald Kennedy's *Imagining Paris* (1994) argues of life writing, generally, that "it is difficult to imagine the recounting of a life story apart from the tangible, physical scenes where important episodes have occurred," and thus, for Kennedy, "place may be crucial to autobiography."[9] Paris is essential to both Putnam's book and his understanding of himself, however, as he situates his move to the city as central to his life: his early experiences pointed him toward Europe, and his experiences there facilitated his movement into an adulthood fully realized.

Indeed, in studies of expatriate place like *Imagining Paris* and Donald Pizer's *American Expatriate Writing and the Paris Moment* (1996), the city itself remains the real focus of the analysis, discussed as it appears in what Pizer describes as "felt responses to Paris and the expatriate experience."[10] In that both examinations look at fiction as well as autobiography, neither Kennedy nor Pizer has occasion to linger long upon the selves that emerge from expatriate life writing, providing us instead with readings of the subjective contours of the city. But more than his portrait of Paris, in fact, Putnam's examination of his perceptions of his life in a foreign city is what makes *Paris Was Our Mistress* interesting. To read the first edition of Malcolm Cowley's book does not lead one to believe that its author thought himself to have already participated in the activity that would best define him. But having returned to the United States to undertake translating work and organization of the artistic Left, Samuel Putnam had by the mid-1940s good reason to reflect most fondly on time spent in Europe between 1926 and 1933. It took other writers even less time to muse nostalgically on that time in Paris by attributing to the city a similarly essential role through the writing of their selves.

Following the commercial success of *The Autobiography of Alice B. Toklas*, for example, Bravig Imbs quickly published his own *Confessions of Another Young Man* (1936). Donald Pizer describes Imbs as one of "the now-forgotten or the distinctly third-rate" members of Gertrude Stein's circle, one whose claim to fame in Pizer's estimation lies in his "discipleship" to Stein.[11] But while only *Eden: Exit This Way* (1926), a book of poems, and the novel *The Professor's Wife* (1928) stand as a monument to Imbs's creative aptitude, he uses his autobiography to make a case for inclusion in the modernist enterprise on the basis of his residence in and around Paris and his shared intimacy with Gertrude Stein and the composer George Antheil. By his own admission, Imbs was "more than indolent," and from an expatriate who combined his desire to do "nothing at all" when abroad with "a glamorous idea" of his own potential as a writer,[12] *Confessions of Another Young Man* also grants its author a final opportunity to curry favor with influential friends who had found him wanting.

Using Paris to provoke recollection belies an attempt to disengage the urban from memory that David Gross dates from the middle of the nineteenth century. As city planners in the United States and Europe undertook "regulating and rationalizing the urban environment," they ordered massive demolitions, even though many of the sites they altered "had long served as markers of cultural and historical memory." The ideal of the modern urban environment might thus be read as a space recreated without any "traces of nostalgia," engineered "so that people would not be distracted from the practical affairs of everyday life."[13] But both Putnam and Imbs connect their experience to the landmarks of their adopted city, building their memories on their appreciations of a French past stamped on their surroundings during the middle of the nineteenth century. Putnam writes, for example, that "all these things take on in memory a nostalgic significance which would be hard to put into words but which is evoked by any good and honest set of photographs of Parisian street scenes" (*PM*52). Bravig Imbs similarly reflects, after returning to the city after an extended absence, on "how wonderful it was to be walking once more along the railing of the shadowy Luxembourg," and he discovers for himself how "a house here, a street corner there, a tree across the way" act as "touchstones to my memory" (*CM*194). For these two expatriates, the fantastic dreams of their own ambitions become for them integral to a dynamic history of Paris, and the glory of their experiences there appear to their readers as vividly as the exploits of the most renowned of expatriate Americans.

Born in the small midwestern town of Rossville, Illinois, Samuel Putnam found at an early age a love for languages, and his natural acuity would one day open up to him the world of international literature around him in Paris in the 1920s and 1930s. The subtitle of his autobiography encourages his readers to see his experience as representative "of a lost and found generation." Indeed, he positions his own life story as central to at least one wave of expatriation between the World Wars. He acknowledges in the early pages of his text that "the present work will of necessity be in good part autobiographical, reflecting the formative period of my life and the Paris I saw through my own eyes and those of my contemporaries" (*PM*7). That Putnam would suggest that he has seen as his contemporaries have seen is, itself, a narrative gesture of remarkable self-centeredness, an indication of how closely he wishes to associate himself with the better-known members of his cohort. Like Malcolm Cowley, he also claims that the specific details of his life are not "important in themselves," but rather he wishes to read them "as symptomatic of a certain revolt that was growing in the minds of the young" after the war (*PM*33–34). Putnam does devote significant sections of a book about his life to formal studies of more significant American and European artists. "From a Latin Quarter Sketchbook" examines Ford Madox Ford, Ernest Hemingway, Gertrude Stein, and Ezra Pound; "Continental Vignettes" looks at Jean Cocteau, Louis Aragon, Pablo Picasso, André Derain, Constantin Brancusi, Marc Chagall, and Luigi Pirandello. Putnam also devotes a section to a discussion of Dada and Surrealism, obscuring the distinction between the mainstream modernist enterprise and the historical avant-garde. In this way, his writing reflects the relentless aggregation of modern criticism in reappropriating artifacts that sought initially to resist works of American expatriation. To justify this catholic understanding of modernism, Putnam is careful to trace the nature and historical significance of Americans abroad. He acknowledges the skepticism at home of writers who wanted to spend time in Europe, and he concedes that the word "expatriation" still holds "a more or less unsavory connotation" in the country. Expatriates were seen to have "something wrong" with them, to be weak with "some hidden vice or other shameful secret to conceal" (*PM*8). But Putnam seeks to dissociate the expatriate impulse from any sense of selfish escape, arguing that American writers had long found themselves at odds with American society, and many of the most important figures of American letters could be read as expatriates emotionally, whether or not they ever left "native soil" to undertake their insurrections against the predominant wisdom of the United States (*PM*11). By the first decades of the twentieth century, young Americans encountered both "overwhelming material values enforced by a standardized and machine-made civilization" and "the hypocrisy, the repressions that go with such a civilization." To counteract these conditions, writers and artists determined that "life must somehow be spiritualized" once more, and "this could be done only in Europe" (*PM*27–28). While Putnam obviously acknowledges the long history of American expatriation, paying particular attention to a nineteenth-century legacy from Fenimore Cooper to Mark Twain, he argues that the scale of the interwar exodus was unprecedented. "Never before in history had there been such a mass migration of writers and artists from any land to a foreign shore," he claims. "For a decade and more, Paris was a good deal nearer than New York or Chicago to being the literary capital of the United States, as far as earnest and significant writing was concerned" (*PM*5). For himself, he suggested that, from childhood, he "wanted to get away" from "the prairies, that endless waving sea of green" (*PM*32–33).

Putnam is comfortable embracing the words "lost generation" in reference to expatriates of all nationalities in France between the World Wars, in compensation perhaps for a "group spirit" and "group loyalty" that he admits did not assert itself consistently among writers from the United States. He dedicates *Paris Was Our Mistress* to "the Nonexistent, Always Existing Left Bank Club" of that time (*PM*v). "This is . . . a book about a generation *in Paris*," Putnam attests. "That it would have been the same generation anywhere else is inconceivable" (*PM*6). Interestingly, he still acknowledges the distinction between Americans who traveled abroad in the early 1920s and those who came later, perhaps because he can speak with most authority about the latter group. Putnam read Hemingway's *The Sun Also Rises* as "a literary post-mortem" that succeeded in "embalming in a work of fiction . . . the spirit that animated those who came in 1921 or shortly after" (*PM*69). Putnam was among that later wave of expatriates, of course, and he claims in fact that while the earlier travelers received the most attention, "the bulk of migration came from 1925 to 1930" (*PM*67). Aboard the steamer *Rochambeau* in 1926, he encountered "a surprising number" of Americans who "were going to France with the idea of remaining there." This prompts him to conclude that "the expatriate movement of the early twenties had by no means spent itself as yet" (*PM*49). But the country from which these later Americans fled was vastly different from that rejected by Harold Stearns. In fact, these expatriates were "unscarred . . . by anything other than the prosperity-crazed America of Calvin Coolidge, the America that preceded the crash of 1929." The excess of a jazz age immortalized by F. Scott Fitzgerald in *The Great Gatsby* (1925) was their impetus, but having arrived safely in Europe, these men and women did not hesitate to connect themselves to the world described in *The Sun Also Rises*. By doing so, they "availed themselves of the Hemingway tradition, claiming a heritage that was not rightfully theirs" (*PM*69–70). Interestingly, these expatriates "of the second phase" also had a novel to summarize their experience: Henry Miller's *Tropic of Cancer* (1934) seemed best "to suit the temper of the times" (*PM*115). At no point in the text does Putnam make a value judgment when distinguishing between these groups of expatriates, however; the reader gets no sense of how the author views their different motives for escape, and he seems not to favor the creative contribution of one cohort over the other. In fact, this seminal distinction serves sometimes only to justify *Paris Was Our Mistress* as a supplement to earlier studies like Cowley's, while Putnam points out "that the scene was a decidedly mixed one" (*PM*70). Like the expatriate community in *Exile's Return*, the generation in Putnam's text is, upon closer inspection, made up of "little groups within the larger mass" (*PM*104), and the foreign urban environment provides a magnet that helps hold together the diversity of the expatriate experience. Putnam's community in Paris is heterogeneous, yet inward-looking and suspicious; it is tightly knit, yet loosely defined in any terms other than geographical. This eclectic rendering of the Lost Generation is reflected in his understanding of the city. "Two Parises exist side by side," he exclaims. "Did I say two Parises? There were many, any number of them" (*PM*57). But this shared experience, this search for spiritual renewal in Europe is not without its darker side. "One *can* starve in the Latin Quarter," he writes. "I've seen it happen." Despite "all the tales of the gay Bohemian life" his own story would help further embellish, Putnam hopes to emphasize "the dull grind of daily hardship, a strapping poverty and the suffering it entailed" (*PM*107).

Bravig Imbs dwells little on the hardships of expatriate living, although he undertook newspaper work, teaching assignments, and editing projects to supplement handouts from his midwestern parents. He was in Paris to escape the academic environment of the Ivy League, having abandoned the "elms and shutters" of Dartmouth College in the summer of 1925 (*CM*33). For himself, Imbs sought "immunity from professorship" and parole from his strict religious upbringing (*CM*51). In *Confessions of Another Young Man*, he takes a wry view of contemporaries who are skeptical of the value of expatriation; when he met Allen Tate in New York in the late 1920s, for example, Tate "launched bitterly against expatriates," but once he secured a Guggenheim Fellowship, he too "left straight for Paris where he spent a wonderful year" (*CM*191). Imbs saw little opportunity for creative endeavor in the United States, in fact. "America is a wonderfully deadly place to work in; the critical spirit which rules there, manifested so often in mere carping, is an unendurable force," he complains. "It has not the advantage of a frank obstacle, because it is too insidious to incite one to rebellion, but its chilling finger is on the creative pulse wherever it beats." He argues that "the major virtue" of a life abroad is the opportunity to undertake "almost ceaseless industry" in an atmosphere of "freedom" (*CM*52).

In this way, Imbs begins his analysis by marrying time and place in identifying what Donald Pizer has subsequently defined as the "Paris moment," an ability to imbue the city with the spirit of creativity. "Here, in this new and exhilarating world," as Pizer describes the reaction of expatriates, "the spirit and its attendant capacity to speak through art are reborn."[14]

Samuel Putnam similarly provides his readers with an idealized, subjective view of the city's promise for Americans abroad. He writes of a "sentimental beginning" to his time in Paris, suggesting in fact that it is "hard to write of Paris without being sentimental." Both he and his wife, Riva, had "an instinctive reaction to the physical beauty and ultimately unanalyzable psychic charm" of Paris, a city that "for centuries has been the refuge and the home of exiles, of lost souls and, yes, of lost generations as well." There is, however, no sense of disillusion reflected in this record of their first impressions. "Wandering down to the Seine, we crossed the pont du Carrousel and found ourselves in the garden of the Kings of France. The Tuileries with a moon above," Putnam remembers. "We stood there for a moment without saying a word, and then Riva burst into tears. Now, a woman's tears to me are as often as not a thing of mystery, but for once I understood. I felt that way myself" (*PM*50). Paris is thus an anchor for these expatriates, never shown as the site of their disenchantment.

> There are, of course, innumerable other aspects: the famed Paris in spring, the broad boulevards and the trees; Paris in the rain, Paris between showers—above all, Paris in the early hours of the morning, an awakening Paris, the honk of Parisian taxis which only Gershwin has captured, the rumble of carts and hoofs over the cobbles, the imperialism of small shopkeepers annexing the sidewalk for their displays, the little tobacco shops where one may purchase a single cigarette, the *bistros*, the chauffeurs and *ouvriers* stopping in for a morning drink on the way to work, the flower vendors, the kiosks with the world news flaming at one in headlines. (*PM*51–52)

And having recognized Paris as the center of expatriate life, Americans could travel confidently throughout Europe, sure that they would be welcomed in the city upon their return. "But it was Paris that was our home," Putnam writes with no hint of irony about the tendency to wander over the continent. "It was to Paris that, sooner or later, we never failed to return" (*PM*48).

Indeed, Bravig Imbs illustrates that while he too had experience with other European countries, he was most comfortable in France, and he truly cherished his time in its largest city. While he "loathed England" (*CM*137), for example, he exclaims upon arriving in Paris, "I determined that I had found my home, at last, and that I would never leave it." In this sense, his initial attitude toward the city was quite naïve. "Paris, I thought, would offer a welcome to one who so dearly loved and admired her," he maintains. Around him, he saw "every step" on the city's "pavement" as "an inspiration" (*CM*29–30). Certainly, he also describes his surroundings in lyrical terms:

> It is when the streets are empty that Paris is loveliest. In the late hours of the night, or in the early hours of the morning, Paris takes on an ethereal dreamlike aspect with the green quais all wreathed in fog, the vast deserted avenues stark and orderly and elegant, the golden glint of the Invalides dome, the innumerable spires and towers rising above the quiet grey masses of houses, and the dull brown Seine undulating between its stone embankments like some guardian serpent of the town. (*CM*69)

After time away from the city, "to return to Paris is a signal joy." He enthuses, "Paris is often sad, and sometimes grim, but it never becomes usual, never palls" (*CM*193). It had an almost narcotic effect on him. "Paris is the only city I know which acts like a drug," he writes. "Either Paris illuminates or excites you as it did me the first time I visited it, or it makes you incredibly drowsy, so that its streets seem like streets in a dream" (*CM*274). But this is not to suggest that Imbs is above grousing about the city, as did all expatriates from time to time. "I think it was the first experience with the Winter climate of Paris which so dislocated the tranquil routine of my life," he complains elsewhere. "I could not get used to the liquid cold of Paris rain, the damp which penetrated with the clammy finger to one's very marrow, the French idea that 60°F was an ideal temperature for an apartment, the almost total absence of sun" (*CM*84–85).

Samuel Putnam recognizes that the city he inhabited "has been the capital of the art world . . . ever since the middle of nineteenth century" (*PM*56). He makes the important distinction between the Rive Droite, the fashionable Right Bank of the Seine, and the Rive Gauche, the more spirited Left Bank. Noël Riley Fitch points out that even today the Right Bank has those things that "tie the foreigner to his material needs" in Paris.[15] Not surprisingly, therefore, Putnam speaks about having to visit the American Express there to cash a money order and pick up his mail, to visit a bank, to conduct his business at the American consulate, to undertake research at the Bibliothèque Nationale, or to shop at Brentano's bookstore. To wander over to "the other side," as he describes it, "was like making a journey into a foreign country" (*PM*58). Despite the fact that he often lived in Paris's suburbs, he has a special affection for Montparnasse, which he lovingly calls the "artists' quarter" (*PM*56). In fact, he makes no distinction between the historic "Latin Quarter" of the fifth arrondissement and the streets around the boulevard du Montparnasse to the west in the sixth. In this way, he creates the geographical flexibility to claim for modern expatriates the historical legacy of "la vie de Bohème," and he imparts to his own haunts an almost mythical standing.

> Such [was] the Montparnasse we knew: a weird little land crowded with artists, alcoholics, prostitutes, pimps, poseurs, college boys, tourists, society slummers, spendthrifts, beggars, homosexuals, drug addicts, nymphomaniacs, sadists, masochists, thieves, gamblers, confidence men, mystics, fakers, paranoiacs, political refugees, anarchists, "Dukes" and "Countesses," men and women without a country; a land filled with a gaiety sometimes real and often feigned, filled with sorrow, suffering, poverty, frustration, bitterness, tragedy, suicide. Not only was there never any place like it; Montparnasse itself had never been before and never will be again what it was in the 1920's. (*PM*116)

Still, Putnam wonders why it is to this quarter of Paris that Americans "seem to gravitate," and he admits that it is "a bit hard to explain" how a small corner of the city thus limited expatriate contact with a full range of continental experiences (*PM*65–66). "I will leave it to some future social-psychologist, who was not there, to explain just what the hold was that Montparnasse had on us: those two or three squares centering about the intersections of the boulevards," he asserts. "Why did the 'exiles' tend to gather here in this garish environment, with so much that was palpably false about it, to associate almost exclusively with other Americans and grow in upon themselves?" (*PM*68–69). In fact, this tendency toward blinkered thinking came about as "too many of the American artist colony . . . tended to associate more or less exclusively with other Americans or with the British." Because of these patterns of behavior, there was always the danger that the expatriate would learn "little more about the French, or France, or, for that matter, Paris, than if they had remained at home in Greenwich Village or one of its numerous counterparts" (*PM*53). Putnam, too, came first to Montparnasse, settling in "the Hôtel Raspail, opposite the café du Dôme" before venturing even as far as the suburbs (*PM*50).

The cafés of the arrondissement, in particular, had their own magnetism. After all, they had been granted "a dubious fame" by the success of *The Sun Also Rises* (*PM*127), and from the beginning of *Paris Was Our Mistress*, Samuel Putnam acknowledges that popular conceptions of life abroad in the 1920s had from those days included "lurid tales" repeated in the United States of expatriate exploits "in the general vicinity of the café du Dôme and the café Select, some of which were exaggerated while others fell far short of the truth" (*PM*6). It is the place where "discussions of art and America and the artist soul" were undertaken (*PM*100). Writing two decades after arriving in Paris, Putnam uses "the rapidly filling cafés and café terraces on the Left Bank" to give shape to his memories, but these places also allow him to invoke people (*PM*52). He thinks of painter Joseph Stella, whose duel with colleague Ary Stillman at the Dôme was a "battle of art with a walking stick" (*PM*252). The table held for Surrealists of various nationalities at the same establishment "was invariably the noisiest of all" (*PM*181). He pictures novelist Sinclair Lewis, ignored at the Dôme because of "the stenographic, Pullman-smoker school of writing" his *Main Street* (1920) and *Babbitt* (1922) represented for younger authors (*PM*101). Putnam encountered the "bitter old" anarchist Emma Goldman outside the Select (*PM*86–87), the café where Hart Crane undertook a "savage, furniture-smashing battle with police" (*PM*107). However, the success of these establishments was also, for Putnam, convincing evidence of a self-conscious "Bohemia made to order." The only exception seemed to be the Rotonde, a café that "clung persistently to the character it had won for itself where one could sit and think and be alone with his sorrows." Otherwise, the spirit of an "old Montparnasse" was sacrificed in the 1920s to a desire for profit, "a new form of commercialism" made from pandering to "the ever-increasing third-class-tourist trade and 'exiles' coming in by the boatload."

This is symbolized for Putnam by "the big and almost painfully modern Coupole," a large café opened on the boulevard du Montparnasse in December 1927 (*PM*66–67). He forever associates this establishment with the artist and model Kiki, well known as one of Man Ray's most famous muses, who took up her position there "at cocktail time" (*PM*80), and with Henry Miller, who "would expound his *Weltanschauung*, principally in words of four letters" as the sun came up (*PM*112). Remembering Harold Stearns, Putnam pictures him "wandering at night from bar to bar," often avoiding the larger establishments in the arrondissement to frequent "the little American bars" off the beaten track (*PM*28). Putnam encountered him "looking his seediest" at the café Flore one night, embodying the features both of "tramp" and "intellectual" (*PM*29–30). The Flore and the Deux Magots on the place Saint-Germain-des-Prés made up "neutral ground, a vague No Man's Land . . . between the Right Bank and the Left" (*PM*98) where feuding Surrealists met or where Putnam discussed "very amicably" his differences with *transition* editor Eugene Jolas (*PM*229). It was also a "tranquil . . . relief to Montparnassians who wanted to get away from it all" (*PM*98), where Putnam and Ernest Hemingway "sat over drinks" as the author of *The Sun Also Rises* admitted that "the war played hell" with him and his contemporaries while the success of his seminal work came as a result of "knocking around with the bunch" and seeking then to "put it down" on paper (*PM*127, 129). Indeed, while English author Ford Madox Ford "never came near the Dôme," he too could be found at the Deux Magots (*PM*125), as could "little crippled" Bernard Faÿ, who was so sympathetic to expatriate Americans (*PM*73).

Bravig Imbs "kept very much" to himself in the café scene of Montparnasse, according to Putnam (*PM*71), and so it is not surprising that the peculiarities of life along the boulevard play virtually no role in *Confessions of Another Young Man*. But for other contemporary references to Parisian nightlife, one need only look to the remembrances of its most beloved intimate. Samuel Putnam claims that "one of the best known and most popular" of the characters of the expatriate community was Jimmie Charters, the British barman whose autobiography was "ghost-written" by American newspaper journalist Morrill Cody (*PM*78–79). While Charters claims that he wishes "to leave it to the critics to add the theories," the stories he tells take an insider's view of Paris after dark.[16] Best known for working at the Dingo on the rue Delambre, Charters provides an intimate look at life along the Left Bank in his *This Must Be the Place* (1934), a work that also foregrounds its emphasis on geography. The title is inspired by the reported exclamation of two women tourists who were certain they had found the heart of the new bohemia when American chorus girl Flossie Martin sneered at them as they sized up the Dingo from the sidewalk outside. As Charters remembers another famous story, a young American girl was supposedly prevented from smoking on the *terrasse* of the Rotonde, and so she moved across the boulevard du Montparnasse to "a small bistro of working men." From that point onward, "the Dôme grew to international fame and became the symbol for all Montparnasse life," standing, in practical terms, as "the center around which everyone gravitated." Still, as he concedes, "the half mile which stretches from the Montparnasse station to the Place de l'Observatoire" held "more than thirty establishments" in addition to the "innumerable others" along the area's "side streets" where "one could slake his thirst" (*TP*5–6). There were tourists who were not only "curiosity seekers" but also would-be imbibers of the "bohemian life" (*TP*102). Ultimately, "sightseers, visiting firefighters, and tourists" forced out "the artists and writers" (*TP*197), so that serious workers made up only about "forty percent" of the expatriate community (*TP*209).

The establishments with which Jimmie Charters is most familiar remained crucially important to those who stayed and sought to refine their creative vision. "Those ideas were developed, not only in the attics and studios," he claims, "but also in the companionship and stimulation of the cafés and bars" (*TP*37). Names like Coupole, Falstaff, Jockey, Parnasse, and Sélect resonate again and again throughout the text, and the tales Charters tells of life behind the bar fill out the picture. "These smaller bars really took the place of the American living room," he argues further. "No one ever entertained at home, first because French housing laws do not permit *any* noise after ten o'clock, and secondly because it was so much more economical to meet your friends at a bar where each paid for his own drink" (*TP*8). The unassuming surroundings betrayed little hint of the hospitality afforded foreigners on the Left Bank, as Charters explains:

> Physically Montparnasse was little more than a gray and dull street holding a broken double row of cafés, but in spirit it was stronger than home or religion, the ultimate of the social reaction to the War. Whoever had troubles with his parents or his wife, whoever was bored with the conventions of stability, begged or borrowed the money to come to Montparnasse, led on by a promise of complete escape. Never has there been such an international gathering of more or less brainy excitement seekers. And excitement they found! But it was excitement with a purpose. It was organized rebellion against all in the world that is narrow and confining. (*TP*7)

One of the most interesting elements of *This Must Be the Place*, however, is the extent to which its story resists simplifications. Though from the time of Henry Murger, as Jerrold Seigel argues, the bohemian heart of Paris was fixed in the attitudes of youth and "not marked on any map,"[17] Charters questions the expatriate American connection with that legacy on grounds that are only geographical. "Montparnasse is well removed from the Latin Quarter," he points out, "though the two Quarters are often confused" (*TP*4). Charters claims that his customers were only about "seventy percent" Americans (*TP*16), and bar patrons, generally, made up a heterogeneous "mixture" of people that did "not separate into class or intellectual groups" (*TP*13–14). He rejects the characterization of the Left Bank as either shelter for "a band of drunks, perverts, degenerates" or as a "haven of intellectuals" (*TP*7). While he saw himself proudly "as a person rather than a servant," he also knew his "place" among expatriates in Paris (*TP*9). "I was unimpressed by the great names because most of them were unknown to me," Charters writes (*TP*11). But for critic Hugh Ford, the bartender became "something of a celebrity himself" (*TP*ix), his reputation also bolstered by the invocation of place.

It was, of course, more than cafés that nourished the expatriate community in Paris. One of the most important places on the Left Bank was Sylvia Beach's bookshop and lending library on the rue de l'Odeon, described by Putnam as the "shrine of literary pilgrims." It was here that a "true worshipper" could "revel in the thrill of propinquity" to James Joyce or Gertrude Stein (*PM*96-97). Indeed, Putnam refers derisively to Shakespeare and Company as "Miss Beach's incense-filled little chapel" (*PM*235). Bravig Imbs had a more intimate attachment to the place. Remembering one warm evening in particular when "the shop looked so cool and inviting" (*CM*78), he sees it as a refuge, above all else.

> Shakespeare & Co. was at that time and still is one of the most peaceful, pleasant spots in the world. It is a harbour of quietness with its rows and rows of orderly shelves and low tables laden with magazines. It is not too light and most of the time is softly illuminated by a yellow lamp. An atmosphere more conducive to browsing could not be found, and the clock that ticks on the wall seems only a jest. Time cannot exist where it is so easily forgotten. (*CM*38)

At the time of Imbs's arrival in Paris, George Antheil lived in what the composer described as an "impossibly small" apartment above the bookshop.[18] Imbs began an important friendship with Antheil upon his first visit to Shakespeare and Company, where Beach herself was "a sympathetic listener" to Imbs's ambitions as a writer (CM40). From the point of this first, tentative errand for paper on which he hoped to write a great novel, he thought the spot magical. "The longing I had felt so keenly at Dartmouth to be in Paris among artists who spoke my language was being satisfied at last," he enthuses, "and so perfectly that I bit my tongue to see if I could still feel" (CM42).

The real center of the city for Samuel Putnam was on the rue Jacob, where Natalie Barney hosted "the one real salon in all Paris, possibly in all the world." Invited often to "her afternoons," Putnam forged a connection to an old Parisian intellectual tradition. "There was the grace, the wit, the dignified *abandon*," he speculates, "which, so I imagined, must have characterized the salons of a former day" (PM73–74). Indeed, he saw the salon as a French phenomenon that appealed little to expatriate Americans, and thus Barney herself was of little interest to an "English-speaking colony" that wanted nothing to do with surroundings beyond "the *bistro*, the café, and the concierge, of their daily lives" (PM75). As Putnam was never counted, nor indeed did he ever count himself, as one of "Stein's devotees" (PM135), he was not invited to her rival gatherings on the rue de Fleurus. He claims, in fact, to have been "afraid of Gertrude," but he does admit to having accompanied the newspaperman Wambly Bald in an excursion to "go up and see Gertie" for an interview (PM136). His recorded impression of her famous atelier is not extensive. "Inside, we found the walls covered with Picassos," he sniffs. "Picasso, Picasso, and more Picasso" (PM137). While this meeting was unremarkable, he speculates as to whether there was another reason why he had few opportunities to consort with Gertrude Stein. "What moral there is to this, I am sure I do not know," Putnam writes in contemptuous reference to Stein's lesbianism, while avoiding any discussion of Barney's scandalous reputation, "but if one is to judge from the reports brought back, she appeared to get on better with the women" (PM135).

It is Putnam's contention that few Americans were personally acquainted with Stein's "studio" through the end of the 1920s, despite the attention it had received by then. While the rue de Fleurus "was not far removed from the roaring center of Montparnasse life," it might well have been "in Timbuktu" for most expatriates who spent their time on the café terraces. According to Putnam, Stein was viewed as "a cloistered being," and she remained "quite accessible to her admirers" alone through this period (*PM*134–35). Putnam identifies Bravig Imbs as an enthusiastic initiate, and so it is not surprising that *Confessions of Another Young Man* locates "Miss Stein's salon" at the heart of expatriate life. Imbs admits to "social climbing" at the rue de Fleurus, "a sport in which a great many young men indulged" (*CM*113). In fact, he reveals at the beginning of an autobiography whose very title makes reference to Stein's privileging of various "young men" as her protégés that his "great ambition" simply "was to meet Gertrude Stein" (*CM*15). In time, he attained a position of favor within the "little coterie" (*CM*171), a "little group" that "did constitute a court" with Stein as its unques-tioned "sovereign" (*CM*113). He succeeded, apparently, by showing promise as a writer; he claims that she judged him to "have the gift of true brilliancy" (*CM*171). Because his position was sustained through his willingness to heap constant praise on his mentor, how-ever, the atelier remained for him a "tangled . . . web" (*CM*113).

Not surprisingly, Imbs pays little attention to a description of the exterior of Stein's home, a "house" that "stood in a courtyard which always looked the same, summer and winter, paved in stone with an oval plot of evergreen plants in the center" (*CM*114). But the inside, with the atelier filled with art, remains vivid in his mind. It was, for Imbs, a "shrine" to modern art (*CM*113), and he de-scribes it with appropriate religious fervor:

> Every square inch in the room was interesting, but it was so very softly lit by low table lamps and four magnificent candles in or-nate silver sticks that I was hard put to make out certain objects, and the lovely blue Picassos, high on one wall, were all but invis-ible. Nevertheless, I was able to appreciate the perfect arrange-ment of the paintings—there must have been nearly a hundred of them—all hung close together and literally covering the walls. And yet no picture impinged on another, and each seemed in its proper place.

Still, this was no sterile place for Imbs. "There was no sensation of being in a museum either," he explains, as "the room had a distinc-tive life all its own." He speculates that Stein held "nothing sacro-sanct about the arrangement of the pictures," and she even "shifted them about a good deal" (*CM*117). Far from a serene environment, it became a vital and dangerous arena where even "degrees of intimacy were very carefully graded" (*CM*119). He reveals, for example, "To talk about James Joyce in Gertrude Stein's salon was rushing in where angels feared to tread" (*CM*154). In fact, Stein was always concerned "to shake loose the people who bored or annoyed her," and in this task she had the faithful assistance of Alice Toklas, who acted "as a sieve and a buckler" (*CM*116). Imbs, too, felt the couple's wrath. By the time he began writing his autobiography, he had been expelled from Stein's circle. "It was amazing how rapidly the little court was dispersed," he comments; he ends his text by lamenting, "I missed Gertrude and Alice very much for a year" (*CM*300–1). It is not clear whether he believes *Confessions of Another Young Man* might endear him again to Stein, in fact. While he had seen the banished Virgil Thomson return through the success of *Four Saints in Three Acts* (1934), an opera based upon Stein's works, it is unlikely that this effect could have ever been achieved simply by the gener- ally flattering portrait of her that emerges here. "She had the easiest, most engaging and infectious laugh I have ever heard," he reveals, explaining that "it was so straight from the heart, so human, so rich in sound" (*CM*118–19). He was moved to hear her read her own work. "Every once in a while she would produce a sentence so perfectly proportioned, so well sounding, so clear and spontaneous that it was joy to hear it," he remembers (*CM*286). Stein's critical judgment reflected her "unerring accuracy" in literary matters, and she was generous of spirit, as Imbs describes her. "Gertrude had the secret of imparting the enthusiasm to others," he reports, "for as an artist, she was sincere and she felt deeply and she was bound up in her own writing, an humble subject in the kingdom of words" (*CM*121–22). After the success of *The Autobiography of Alice B. Toklas*, he marvels, a little naïvely, that it is "strange to think her work ever needed defence!" He grants that she was "sensitive to appreciation," and he thus recognizes that his esteem in her eyes was connected to the fact that he genuinely likes her work (*CM*127). Perhaps it is out of sheer habit that Imbs ventures but cautiously into criticism of Stein. He doubts whether "Gertrude knew much about paint- ings at any time," for example, though because of her "flair . . . for people and particularly for genius," he believes that "she seldom erred" in any critical judgment (*CM*124). But it was her jealousy, in large part, that disrupted her coterie. "Although Gertrude had Alice," Imbs reflects, "she really could not bear any two people be- ing together for long." It is "undisputed homage" that she demands (*CM*250). Imbs's marriage to Valeska Balbarischky threatened the friendship with Stein, but it was the couple's pregnancy that precipitated the final break. When he suggested that Valeska might spend time in the countryside with Stein and Toklas in advance of her delivery, he was dismissed for his "colossal impertinence" (*CM*296). The boom was lowered by Toklas by telephone.

Both *Paris Was Our Mistress* and *Confessions of Another Young Man* are noteworthy for providing their readers with a sense of place outside Paris. For someone like Putnam, "who spoke French," and even for those Americans who "learned to speak it," there was the possibility of living "among the people of the country" so as to "discover many things" that most expatriates simply did not see (*PM*53). "Paris summed it all up; Paris was France," Putnam observes, "and yet, in a very real sense, Paris was not France at all" (*PM*55). His own decision to venture beyond the city was precipitated by its many distractions. "However much I liked Paris, just because I did like it so much," he admits, "I never found it a good place to work, any more than I do New York City" (*PM*59). Having ventured out into the countryside, most Americans encountered difficulties dealing with the locals. The average French citizen saw the United States as "the land of gold," as he explains it, and so they believed that the "writers and painters" they encountered, "being Americans so far from home and with nothing to do but paint or write, must be wealthy." In turn, the expatriate response to this attitude was, itself, "unbelievably callous." Putnam acknowledges, "We did not realize, we made no effort to realize, how hard life was for the average Frenchman." On the occasions when these cultural obstacles were overcome, the effect could be most beneficial. "When we did come to know each other, in regions unspoiled by the tourist and under conditions quite different from those that marked his intercourse with the inhabitants," he maintains, "we learned that the French were an altogether likable folk who could teach us much." It was also in this context that the French got to see that Americans were not all "Hollywood millionaires" but genuine "human beings" (*PM*53–54). Perhaps a more compelling reason Putnam had for venturing outside Paris, for escaping Montparnasse, specifically, was that expatriates found themselves "getting on one another's nerves." They chose, ultimately, "to live in solitude somewhere in the provinces" or fled to "runaway colonies" like Majorca or Cagnes-sur-Mer (*PM*247–48). Putnam took his own family to Mirmande, a little village with "a constantly diminishing population of 125 persons" (*PM*248). There, with "less than a dozen" Americans and French visitors composing a budding "art colony," Putnam found, instead of a pastoral idyll where "one could really think things out, keep his clarity and his balance, milk his goats of an evening, and be at peace," the familiar "clash of egos" and "petty squabbling and backbiting" (*PM*249).

On his most notable foray outside Paris, Imbs hiked to the head of the Vallée de la Chevreuse. What greeted him, in his description, was a vista of unimaginable pastoral loveliness.

> For a while the thick woods on either side prevented my see-
> ing anything but the road, and then, suddenly, the whole lovely
> pastoral scene opened to my sight: the rolling fields rising gently
> to the brim of the valley which was edged with thick copses
> and dark woods, the snug grey houses in the hollow, the delicate
> steeple of the church, the sturdy towers of the little chateau, the
> low stone bridge called, "le point hardi," and the winding stream
> it spanned called, l'Yvette—a fresh and exquisite picture, the
> outlines dimmed by the mist and falling night. (*CM*145)

Approaching "almost solemnly," enchanted by his surroundings, Imbs fell under the spell of the village of Garnes, and he took a room there at an establishment run by "Monsieur et Madame Sabin Luttenschlager" (*CM*146). Persuaded by the first meal he was served, "rosy-veined and aromatic" pâté, "thick and juicy and rare" steak, "crisp and salty and hot" potatoes served with "tender and delicate" cauliflower, and a pear "so fragrant that the room smelled like an orchard," Imbs decided on the spot to abandon life in the city. "As I sipped my brandy and tiny cup of black coffee," he remembers, "I felt I had made a great discovery, and that I should like to live for the rest of my life in this charming town of Garnes" (*CM*147). He convinced his father in the United States to send him ten dollars a week for six months, enough money for room and board, so he could continue work on a biography of Thomas Chatterton. With the promise that he would return to America after his sojourn, he was granted the money, but he found that with "so much leisure," he "could scarcely find a minute to write." He was lured into a sensual life of indolence:

> I would arise at ten or eleven, dress slowly, have a delicious
> breakfast of toast and eggs—eggs still warm from the nest—then,
> pipe alight, go off on a six-mile walk through the forest, return
> ravenously hungry to have an enormous and delicious French
> luncheon, followed by coffee and cognac and long mellow pipes;
> back to my room where I would have a nap until five, then play

a Mozart Sonata on my fiddle to sharpen my faculties, and finally
sit down and write until dinnertime. Dinner was always very
late—half past eight or nine, and quite as copious as luncheon.
I ate lunch alone, but dinner I always had in the cozy kitchen
with Sabin and Madame Sabin. (*CM*149)

This existence was further bolstered by the lady of the house, in
fact, who told neighbors that Imbs was a writer. He was "respected
everywhere" by young and old alike, "little boys and doddering old
men were quick to lift their caps," in fact. "Only in France could
one be a grand seigneur on ten dollars a week and an artificial reputation!" he exclaims (*CM*150). To his credit, Imbs saw the limita-
tion of this lifestyle, asserting that had he "lived in Garnes day in
and day out," he would "have become a vegetable very quickly."
Luckily, perhaps, Paris continued to entice him with "feverish
week-ends," and this allowed him to maintain contact with his
friends (*CM*151). While his country life threatened to estrange Imbs
from other expatriate American writers, the vividness with which
he imbues his description of the countryside with its dramatic
views and piquant tastes reflects the value placed on authenticity
that also defined many of their works. Some time later, in fact, Imbs
attempted to recreate the conditions of this pastoral retreat, but the
moment had passed. With his new wife, Valeska, he took up residence in Le Tremblay-sur-Mauldre; it could only ever be an "ap-
proximation" of Garnes, however, with its "spare and austere" surroundings (*CM*243–44).

These forays outside the city suggest that expatriates could escape Paris, heralding the real possibility of repatriation. Imbs thought
of returning to America as "an unpleasant subject," as he believed
that "it meant grinding routine in some cubicle and living in surroundings I had hated since childhood" (*CM*165). In fact, he died
abroad in 1946. But Samuel Putnam did return to the United States,
in 1933, and *Paris Was Our Mistress* also reflects on the challenges of
that journey. Putnam had brought a wife and young son to Europe,
and he originally thought of France, too, as "the home of our off-
spring, the generation that was to come" (*PM*63). Once economic
and political realities shifted in the 1930s, he changed his mind. "It
was all right, perhaps, for our generation to be lost," he considers,
"but had we any right to 'lose' another?" (*PM*250). Reconciliation
with the United States became a priority for Putnam and his family.
Harry Crosby's "symbolic" gesture may have haunted the Left Bank
in 1929, but Putnam wonders if the reaction to the execution of

Sacco and Vanzetti in 1927, "when French workers had invaded the terraces of Montparnasse and tossed the occupants into the street," did not portend a change in attitudes on the part both of expatriates and their French hosts (*PM*238–39). Certainly, in the period after the Wall Street crash, "the depression was making itself felt" (*PM*241), but among expatriate Americans "*la crise*" was first manifested in "spiritual" terms. The "shallowness" of American attitudes during the Coolidge administration gave way to "an unwonted seriousness" that marked a "coming of age" in the United States. With profound changes underway in their homeland, as well as the economic impact soon felt around the world, there were fewer reasons to be in Europe. "Although we did not realize it," Putnam observes, "the sustaining *raison d'etre* of our exile was being dragged from under us" (*PM*240). In the final analysis, Putnam admits that "it is difficult to form any precise idea" whether expatriation in the 1920s was a beneficial experience. Americans who went abroad "profited from that experience," on a personal level, "by becoming broader and more cosmopolitan in outlook" (*PM*218). They discovered "that America is part of . . . a larger world" (*PM*254). But when expatriates returned to those people left at home, in his opinion, "they brought with them little word of what was going on in France" (*PM*218). Upon arriving back in the United States himself, in 1933, Putnam encountered "a persisting gulf between those who went and those who stayed" (*PM*112). Disillusioned by the rise of fascism in Europe, he challenged himself to join with American radicals, efforts that gave "direction and employment" to his energies (*PM*245). He discovered "a strange and swirling America" that was "angry, bitter, disillusioned, cynically hardened." It was against this background, finally, that a generation that "had been *lost*" found itself or allowed itself, at least, to "be found by history" (*PM*244).

Elizabeth Bruss has argued that autobiographical texts may be written "to attain a publicly recognized identity" among their readers. In our examination of expatriate American autobiography, this motivation for life narrative is best illustrated, perhaps, by Samuel Putnam and Bravig Imbs. While Bruss reflects on the "responsibilities and complications" of living, thus, "in character,"[19] the position both Putnam and Imbs write for themselves in their texts reveals, precisely, a desire to define themselves entirely within an expatriate literary community in Paris. Emphasis on this physical location, much more than any genuine sense of camaraderie, is thus central to the effectiveness of both *Paris Was Our Mistress* and *Confessions of Another Young Man*. For Gerri Reaves, writing about the self demands an examination of "the emotional, cultural, and psychic landscape in which one conceives that self to exist," but any reliance on a "geographical paradigm for the self" threatens to invoke "collective" models of identity.[20] Expatriate American autobiography often willingly negotiates individual and collective notions of self, as we have seen, and neither Putnam nor Imbs seems concerned with losing himself in his surroundings, as these surroundings are firmly established as privileged ground for American modernism. In fact, while a text like *Exile's Return* examined expatriation by delineating people, both *Paris Was Our Mistress* and *Confessions of Another Young Man* examine expatriation by giving readers a greater sense of place. This is not to suggest that these texts lack either critical scrutiny or vividness of character; Putnam is quite systematic in his analysis, and Imbs provides readers with fascinating portraits of Gertrude Stein and George Antheil. But these two autobiographies still effectively reflect modernism's preoccupation with place. In fact, Leonard Lutwack argues that a "new interest in place" was a twentieth-century phenomenon, and "place as a formal element in literature" was but one important component. A reader may encounter this preoccupation with place in an author's "sense of loss of once-cherished" surroundings, a nostalgia that betrays fears of placelessness.[21] Putnam admits that "the Paris that we knew is, it may be, gone forever; there is no use trying to recapture it" (*PM*58). While some of the physical reminders of the city in the 1920s may remain, the place persists in the memory of those whom we read to examine how they saw themselves in that place, how they used shared space as a strategy to fix and revise their position in the emerging understanding of modernist art. Building on the work of geographer Edward Relph, J. Gerald Kennedy maintains that "a person's sense of place" is shaped by feelings of "insideness" or "outsideness" in a given location.[22] In this sense, writers like Putnam and Imbs use autobiography to transform a simple sense of physical connectedness to a wider assertion of imaginative belonging.

5

PATTERNS OF WOMEN'S STORIES

"Paris has often been imagined as a mysterious, seductive woman, both mistress and muse to generations of male poets," Andrea Weiss argues. "Women drawn to the allure of Paris were also responding to the female qualities of a city which allowed them to express themselves in less conventional, more substantive ways than simply as romanticized mistress or muse."[1] Notwithstanding the significant contribution of Gertrude Stein, however, the impression of modern American expatriation that emerged in autobiographies through the 1950s was dominated largely by stories told by men. This lack of development is significant. Not only do the stories women could tell about these years promise valuable records in themselves, but considering only men's voices limits substantially our view of the women they invoke frequently in their stories, as we never hear these women speak for themselves. When Jimmie Charters opines that, in Montparnasse, "one out of every ten women seems to be an exhibitionist," for example, no one thus implicated gets the opportunity to counter this claim.[2] The frank personal stories told by Peggy Guggenheim in *Out of this Century* (1946) and Caresse Crosby in *The Passionate Years* (1953) carry the reader well beyond artistic pursuits on the Left Bank. Lawrence Vail, Guggenheim's first husband, may have indeed been "the King of Bohemia," but the narrative she was "ripe" to share by her middle age, for example, concerned itself with lavish forays unimaginable to most Americans in Montparnasse: extensive travel over two continents to Algiers, Cairo, Jerusalem, Lausanne, London, Rome, and Venice.[3] So, it was not until the publication of Sylvia Beach's *Shakespeare and Company* (1956), in fact, that an expatriate woman brought forward remembrances from this period that received significant attention as an appraisal of literary life abroad.

Beach's contribution to literary Paris is unquestioned; Noël Riley Fitch, her biographer, credits her with having created with her bookshop "a literary center that magnetically attracted artists from all over the world."[4] Unfortunately, Beach's portrait of expatriation has limitations of scope that can be read as characteristic of its author's beneficent personality: while she had been in Paris since 1917, her text is most noteworthy for concentrating on the achievements of her contemporaries. Beach does grant in its opening pages that her father "was a Presbyterian minister who for seventeen years was pastor of the First Presbyterian Church in Princeton, New Jersey,"[5] and she concludes the book by revealing in a matter-of-fact manner that she spent "six months in an internment camp" before the liberation of Paris (*SC*216). In the interim, she writes about Adrienne Monnier, the French bookshop owner with "striking" eyes of "blue-gray" with whom she shared nearly twenty years of her life (*SC*13), but neither the basis of their relationship nor the details of its painful breakup is ever broached. On the other hand, she discusses in great detail the means by which she brought forward James Joyce's *Ulysses* (1922), dedicating more than ten years to that cause; yet his inconsiderate treatment of her is suffered in relative silence, at least in the autobiography as finally published. Fitch believes the decision to exclude any manuscript pages that may be "critical of anyone" is more a function of Beach's "social standards" than any external pressure from editors or publishers.[6] But, as a result, *Shakespeare and Company* reads as "self-effacing," in the opinion of Shari Benstock, to the point that the text becomes "disappointing" once the "indirect autobiographical technique" adopted by the author works "to deflect interest from herself."[7]

In the context of modern expatriate writing, however, one can argue that Sylvia Beach achieves a generational autobiography not unlike Malcolm Cowley's *Exile's Return*, though where Cowley concerned himself with the broad impulse to go abroad, Beach provides an illustration of expatriate life that reveals some of her personal conclusions, privately held. While he positioned his experience, in part, as representative of those of a self-consciously identified cohort, she merely recounts her interaction with members of the Lost Generation, though she attests that no group of people is "less deserving of this name" (SC206). Beach, who makes little of her contribution to the development of modern literature, does grant herself membership in "the Crowd" of Americans abroad based on the fact that her bookshop "was the first thing the pilgrims looked up" after arriving in Paris (SC23). But unlike Samuel Putnam and Bravig Imbs, she is not simply staking claim to ground sacred to expatriate Americans; as much as any American in Paris, perhaps, she has legitimate claim to that space. Regardless, her narrative strategy is less self-serving than those of her contemporaries who employed place as an organizing principle, and it is certainly less self-serving than that employed in *The Autobiography of Alice B. Toklas*. Like Gertrude Stein, Beach attempts to tell her story through an account of the lives of those around her. But while Stein used Toklas's life to frame her narrative, no one would suggest that Toklas was the true subject of that text. Sylvia Beach shares her autobiography in a most meaningful way with those individuals who surrounded her during her life, and by doing so, she further differentiates her story from the autobiographies of men that, according to Sidonie Smith, serve to diminish "personal and communal interdependency" by celebrating an "adversarial stance toward the world."[8]

That a woman may wish to tell her story in a different manner than men had heretofore told theirs may, in fact, be the seminal conclusion drawn from a reading of *Shakespeare and Company*. By now, critics of women's autobiography have long encouraged readers to consider most broadly what constitutes women's life stories. Traditionally, some of the other forms that women have employed to give voice to their experiences, forms like letters, diaries, and journals, have been excluded from a discussion of modern autobiography. If our understanding of the modes of life writing might be extended to forms other than the continuous retrospective narrative, however, a variety of voices emerge that enhance our knowledge of American expatriation. In this regard, there is no reason to think that women experience the world in a more fragmented way than do men, but they have had more demonstrable experience in making sense of their lives through forms that emphasize the fragmentary nature of that experience. In reading diaries as autobiography, for example, Judy Lensink sees their entries as forming a uniquely "female design—a supersubtle design, similar to a quilt's, made up of incremental stitches that define a pattern." As she further acknowledges, a "diary is obviously not a literal transcription of a day," and so it may be read as "one way in which women have made coherent their experiential lives."[9] One can argue that *Shakespeare and Company* thus shares similarities with the design of a diary. While there are no datelines, the strongest organizing principle is a fragmented chronology. There is no unifying narrative per se, but as critics like Nina Van Gessel have pointed out, the middle section of the book, devoted to the 1920s, "is propelled forward through a quick succession of sketches of writers and artists."[10] These sketches are arranged with little mind to thematic development, so outside of the broad story of the rise and decline of the bookshop, the text's form has less in common with conventional autobiography than it does with genres that concern themselves with the fragmented nature of consciousness, like the modern novels borrowed from Shakespeare and Company by Beach's faithful subscribers.

Although clearly not an autobiography in any conventional sense, the most extensive record of life abroad during these years may actually have been provided by Janet Flanner, whose fortnightly contribution of a letter to the *New Yorker* magazine endured for nearly a half century, beginning in 1925. Fleeing Greenwich Village with the writer and journalist Solita Solano, Flanner followed a pattern common to expatriate Americans, the two women hoping to find in Paris inspiration "to learn all about art and write our first novels," according to Solano's own remembrances.[11] Settling in the city in 1922, Flanner maintained a correspondence with her friend Jane Grant, whose husband was preparing to launch a new magazine in Manhattan. Eventually, Harold Ross committed to publishing Flanner's "Paris Letter" under the pseudonym Genêt, instructing the expatriate only to avoid writing about herself in a public venue. In fact, Grant later claimed that what the *New Yorker* really sought was "newsy letters . . . about anything except fashion."[12] In light of the persistent criticism of *Shakespeare and Company*, by which even Van Gessel concedes that the text willingly gives us "little insight into the author," one must acknowledge that Flanner seldom reveals anything about herself directly in the "Paris Letter." But if Beach emerges for her readers in the way "she meticulously orders, edits, and censors" the contents of her autobiography,[13] Janet Flanner lurks in her text behind tags like "your correspondent" and "this department." She resolved to write about what was important to her, in a style she herself described as "precisely accurate, highly personal, colorful, and ocularly descriptive."[14] Taken together, serially as they appeared in the *New Yorker* and excerpted in the collected volume *Paris Was Yesterday* (1972), her letters published from the mid-1920s to the beginning of the

Second World War again reveal much about the "I" through an investigation of the "we."

The manner in which Flanner took up this investigation, in fact, is read by some as a group effort. Biographer Brenda Wineapple describes Genêt as "a composite figure," arguing that from the help of friends in the research and typing of the columns from her base at the Hôtel Saint-Germain-des-Prés to the editing process in Manhattan, "Paris Letter" was nothing less than "a collaboration."[15] As Flanner herself allows, Harold Ross was a hands-on editor, someone she alternately describes as "strict"[16] and "a perfectionist" whose goal "was literally the publication of a technically flawless copy of *The New Yorker* every week."[17] In this regard, the efficacy of a collaborative model for women's autobiography offers both a means to reaffirm a sense of community undervalued in men's stories and a strategy to overcome the marginalization of women by men's control of the public discourse. For all his support of Flanner, it must be conceded, Ross first wished her to appear anonymously in the magazine, as was the necessity for contributors who were moonlighting from other writing jobs in Manhattan. By eventually publishing her as "Genêt," he imparted to her through an androgynous byline a pseudonym that challenged her identity as a woman. That Flanner drew upon the resources of her friends to reaffirm her agency in this context exposes, for Susan Friedman, "the differences in socialization in the construction of male and female gender identity" across a variety of discursive forms.[18]

In their recourse to "deflection" and "evasive self-definition," signatures of letter writing for Patricia Meyer Spacks, these contributions can be read as illustrations of a woman's effective use of "the epistolary form."[19] As letters, they seek to forge a personal connection with the reader; indeed, Flanner imagined she was writing them to Harold Ross alone.[20] It is clear to Shari Benstock that Flanner's words are intended for a specific audience: "literary, cultured, curious, sophisticated readers."[21] She writes as if her readers are familiar with Paris, but the affection with which she describes the city serves to endear it to Americans who were not. Her columns are, despite the fingerprints of high society, more relatable than the autobiographical works that commonly frame the achievement of high modernism. The irony employed by Flanner "offset" any suggestion of "arrogance," for Brenda Wineapple,[22] and a good deal of humor shines through. While comparing tourism in London and Paris, for example, she reports that it took "a guinea, including the tip" for a lunch for two in a decent establishment in London. "In

Paris," she adds, wryly, "there are hundreds of restaurants where you can drink and eat everything in sight, including the waiter, for that price."[23] In one report of a grand mystery play with "three stages, representing Heaven, Hell, and Calvary, erected on the sidewalks before Notre-Dame," Flanner runs through, with her usual dry wit, the problems encountered by the cast. "Owing to technical delays and the weather, the night of the dress rehearsal, Heaven wasn't finished," she announces, "the night set for the first performance, there was a hailstorm; the night of the actual première, the Devil had grippe and had to be replaced by an understudy." Ultimately, in her opinion, "none of it was or could be very holy."[24]

Critical readings of the epistolary mode cannot illuminate all of what Flanner achieves, though. A browse through the "Paris Letter" underlines how its accumulated impression seems "always in process," as Margo Culley understands a diary, in fact, and each of Flanner's contributions offers "in some sense a fragment" of a larger whole.[25] The original aim was for a regular weekly appearance, but even the fortnightly schedule eventually agreed upon was only adhered to erratically. Most of the columns still include a dateline, however, and thus they provide small, timely snapshots of what is happening in Paris, much like diary entries. Diaries thus achieve a "continuous present,"[26] not unlike that of critical discourse, and the power of Flanner's columns rests in a "critical edge, indeed double edge," that she herself acknowledges (*PY* xix). As with much of the ephemera from the interwar period, these contributions were not "self-conscious and self-serving" like most expatriate autobiographies, as Benstock describes them,[27] but unlike material not intended for publication, Flanner's columns were widely disseminated and thus helped shape public perceptions of life abroad. Culley sees as one of the diary's signature gestures its facility for revision, for the subject's "self-construction and reconstruction."[28] Through a tapestry spread out over frequent contributions, Flanner allows herself the opportunity to write and rewrite her impressions, fulfilling a desire for revision that many of her contemporaries struggled to bring to bear on their own autobiographical works. By thus contributing to the view of Paris between the World Wars, both Sylvia Beach and Janet Flanner have much in common. But unlike many of the expatriates who wrote of Paris after their return to the United States, Beach and Flanner stayed abroad past the middle of the twentieth century. In doing so, not only do they provide interesting perspectives, they contribute a great deal to their adopted countries, and both were acknowledged for such in their later lives.

In *My Thirty Years' War* (1929), a book Janet Flanner helped edit, Margaret Anderson comments upon the expatriate experience as one who wished, despite the time she spent in Europe, to have been spared it. The editor of the *Little Review* characterized herself, after all, as someone who simply visited Paris. Of her esteemed friends, she laments "the marks that one finds upon all expatriates who have remained away for too prolonged intervals perhaps from their native country." While she obviously feels sympathy for those individuals who longed to experience a world beyond the United States, she worries that "there is something alive at the American core and that cutting oneself off from it slackens the pulse."[29] This was clearly not the experience of Sylvia Beach. Her father first took the family to live in Paris when she was fourteen, and they quickly took to the city. "Paris was paradise to mother," Beach reveals. But as would later be the case with many expatriates during the 1920s, the family experienced a city that was not the Paris of the French native. Because of the nature of her father's work ministering to English speakers, the Beaches "knew very few French people" (*SC*4), but they fostered and maintained after their return to the United States "a veritable passion for France" (*SC*8). Once marital strife estranged her parents, it was with her mother that Sylvia Beach found herself once more in Europe, this time in Madrid. In *Shakespeare and Company*, she will allow simply, "I went to Spain in 1916, and spent some months there." She is a little more forthright in her decision to move to Paris, although she does not discuss even this event at length, telling her readers only that she "had had a peculiar interest in contemporary French writing." In Paris, she could nurture her study "at the source" (*SC*9). She does not explain fully her work with the Voluntaires Agricoles, where she filled in for "male farmers" who were at the front, or her position handing out "pajamas and bath towels" for the Red Cross (*SC*14). It was, in fact, the equivalent work available to an American woman who wanted to help the war effort, because no woman was permitted to drive an ambulance as did Ernest Hemingway and John Dos Passos. Her chance meeting with Adrienne Monnier precipitated a plan for a French bookshop in New York, but owing to the fact that what little money Beach had "would go much further" in France, as "rents were lower and so was the cost of living in those days," she decided instead to start an American bookshop in Paris (*SC*15). Thus, her reasons for staying abroad appear more pragmatic and personal than philosophical. "I was too far from my country to follow closely the struggles of the writers there to express themselves," she admits. But the surroundings she discovered in Paris helped keep her abroad, and the gathering assembly of talented individuals did more to attract Americans than did simply the promise of escaping conditions in the United States. "Of course, prohibition and suppressions were not entirely to blame for the flight of these wild birds from America," she claims. "The presence in Paris of Joyce and Pound and Picasso and Stravinsky and Everybody . . . had a great deal to do with it" (SC23–24).

Janet Flanner also discusses expatriate life with greater affection than did Margaret Anderson. Like Beach, the adolescent Flanner spent time abroad with her family, traveling throughout northern Europe for eighteen months, and the experience had a lasting effect upon her. Later in life, she credited this exposure with stirring a "pure aesthetic selfishness" that bred in her the wanderlust shared by all expatriates. Although she was forced to return to America when her father ran out of money, Flanner was unsatisfied with life in either the American Midwest or in Greenwich Village, where she subsequently sought refuge. "I wanted beauty, with a capital 'B.' I hadn't any in Indiana," she said years later. "I was consumed by my own appetite to consume—in a very limited way, of course—the beauties of Europe."[30] Flanner also had good reason to fear what she saw as the narrow prejudices of her native Indianapolis or even her adopted Chicago home, views that still resonated for her in New York. Having made the decision to leave her husband for Solita Solano, Flanner followed her, first to Greece and then to Paris, where they found greatest tolerance.

While Flanner would never reveal in the "Paris Letter" such personal motivations for living abroad, her descriptions of life in the city betray her enthusiasm for the freedom she believed she had found. Her discussion of the entertainer Josephine Baker, for example, hints at some of the liberties of a European life. While her description of Baker's "caramel-colored body" and "animal visage" are hardly enlightened by today's standards, Flanner's emphasis on the successes of a woman whose "voice" was a "magic flute" (PY72–73) underlines her assertion that "Paris has never drawn a color line" (PY3). While cultural tourists might be accused of coming abroad for nothing more than an opportunity to exploit the rate of currency exchange, Flanner believed that Americans abroad ultimately contributed to European cultural life. "Americans are still going through the city towards the northern ports in millions," she complains in her first letter, "carrying everything away that's portable, and the American Express is hard pressed to find crates enough to house the antiques that are on their way to make American homes beautiful."[31] But less than three months later, she reports, "It is necessary to note the sudden influence and interest caused in Parisian literary circles by the American literary middle West. The Chicago, Indiana, Ohio twang of verity is what the Parisian brain wants."[32] Her first columns teem with the exploits of a wider range of expatriates, including George Antheil, Djuna Barnes, Robert Coates, Julien Green, May Ray, and Glenway Wescott.

Sylvia Beach herself runs through a lengthy list of significant expatriate Americans of her acquaintance. Bill Bird, Hart Crane, John Dos Passos, Archibald MacLeish, and Man Ray are mentioned fleetingly, usually with some comment to confirm that they each made a favorable impression upon her. Sherwood Anderson was "a man of great charm" and "a mixture of poet and evangelist (without the preaching), with perhaps a touch of the actor" (*SC*30). Ezra Pound was "the acknowledged leader of the modern movement" (*SC*26) and "a great showman" (*SC*45). On the few occasions she is moved to offer criticism, her observations are couched among compliments. Robert McAlmon "neglected his craft, which was supposed to be writing," she observes, but the excessive socializing that distracted him from his work was brought about only because he "was so busy sharing his interesting ideas with his friends or listening attentively and with sympathy to their stories of frustration" (*SC*25). Harry Crosby, whose suicide brought such notoriety to Americans in Paris, may have been tragically "obsessed with death," but he remained always "generous" in his business dealings (*SC*134–35).

Shakespeare and Company is itself most generous in discussing the contributions of women, many of whom the reader is reminded help make up Sylvia Beach's crowd. While she suggests a genuine spirit of community really did bind together expatriates who "colonized the Left Bank of the Seine" (*SC*23), Beach associates herself most closely with American women, individuals whose contribution to modern letters had been forgotten by the 1950s. Tragically, Mary Butts had her promise "interrupted suddenly by her death," and Mina Loy was hindered by the fact that she had the opportunity to write verse only "whenever she had time" (*SC*113). Djuna Barnes was "so gifted," in Beach's assessment, "one of the most fascinating literary figures in the Paris of the twenties," but she laments that Barnes "doesn't seem to have been given her due in books on writers of the period" (*SC*112). Discreet always about her own lesbianism, she disapproves of the flamboyant spectacles of Natalie Barney, and she reveals that a customer who once came into the bookshop referred to the women of Barney's salon as "unfortunate creatures" (*SC*115). Beach herself is more restrained here, wondering only if Barney "ever took literary things very seriously" (*SC*114). Expatriate Hilda Doolittle is portrayed as "one of the most admired of the so-called imagists," but H.D. is also described in the text as the "lifelong friend" of Bryher, the British poet Winifred Ellerman (*SC*101). In doing so, Beach here employs the familiar cipher to discuss lesbian couples. While concealing the nature of her own relationship with Monnier, Beach is thus circumspect in discussing those of her friends and acquaintances. She handles material about Gertrude Stein and Alice Toklas carefully, remarking of their relationship simply that the two women were "perfectly congenial." Beach describes herself as "an early reader of *Tender Buttons* and *Three Lives*," but she also shows unusual frankness in describing Stein, by this time long dead, as "a child, something of an infant prodigy," who "took little interest, of course, in any but her own books" (*SC*27–28). In fact, Beach's support of James Joyce was more than any friendship with Stein could bear. "She was disappointed in me when I published *Ulysses*," Beach admits, "she even came with Alice to my bookshop to announce that they had transferred their membership to the American Library on the Right Bank" (*SC*32). Janet Flanner, herself, appears in *Shakespeare and Company* as a "brilliant" woman and "a great worker." In her capacity "as a roving writer," she "was always off, either to London or to Rome or to some other place," but as Beach avows, "she always found time to look after people." As one of Beach's "earliest American friends," Flanner was "in and out of the bookshop very often in the twenties" (*SC*110).

The "Paris Letter" accomplishes many of the same aims as *Shakespeare and Company* in underlining the achievement of Americans abroad. But where Beach is confirming positions and revising impressions in the 1950s, Flanner's writings are helping to make these reputations in the first place. It is Flanner, for example, who stresses to her audience in the United States the full significance to the expatriates of the success of Ernest Hemingway's *The Sun Also Rises*. Because "all these personages are . . . to be seen" at the locations the novel "so often placed them," she reports in the December 18, 1926 number of the *New Yorker*, Hemingway had animated the cafés anew (*PY*12). Sylvia Beach also receives frequent mention. She "is Shakespeare and Company," as Flanner personifies it, "the most famous American bookshop and young authors' fireside in

Europe" (*PY*128). Flanner also reports in the *New Yorker* on Beach's attempts to use a petition to stop Samuel Roth from pirating the work of James Joyce in the United States. "The list of signatures is amazing in its literary dignity and length," Flanner reports. "Already over two hundred of the most important intellectual names of Europe, England, and sometimes the United States have rallied to her aid" (*PY*17). Flanner was among the first Americans to write of the influence of *transition* magazine, reporting that while its first number hardly contains "a feast," it does provide "some good food for thought" for readers on both sides of the ocean (*PY*20).

As she demonstrates through the attention given Josephine Baker, Flanner uses the "Paris Letter" to discuss a wider range of figures than do conventional expatriate autobiographies. She reports on the May 1927 transatlantic flight of "the gallant Charles Lindbergh" that facilitated a dramatic reception in Paris, where "the Ministry of Foreign Affairs flew the Stars and Stripes, as did most of the tramcars" (*PY*22–24). When heavyweight boxing champion Gene Tunney visited France in 1928, Flanner reports a sighting at the Brasserie Lipp on the boulevard Saint-Germain. His appearance "broke up the shop," as "service was paralyzed" amid a flurry of activity. "The cashier, ordinarily a creature of discretion, ceased making her change," she reports. "The waiters rallied round Tunny's table shamelessly." The women on hand admired the pugilist with a breathless, "Comme il est beau!" and even the men had to acknowledge, "Quel homme magnifique!" (*PY*45–46).

Ultimately, it is not an American who preoccupies Sylvia Beach, as James Joyce becomes the focus of *Shakespeare and Company*. But among American writers, Ernest Hemingway holds Beach's regard most firmly. She views him as her "best customer" (*SC*77), thus titling the chapter devoted to a discussion of his life in Paris. She reveals deeply personal things about him, determined finally to say them "whether Hemingway shoots me or not" (*SC*78). He "can take any amount of criticism—from himself," and he stood in fact as "his own severest critic," but Beach acknowledges that "he is hypersensitive to the criticism of others" (*SC*83). Regardless, the impression that emerges here is remarkably admirable, in contrast to Stein's lingering portrait of an ungrateful apprentice. Hemingway's "knowledge of French was remarkable" (*SC*79), for example, and he was "serious and competent in whatever he did" (*SC*82). Beach writes, "He seemed to me to have gone a great deal farther and faster than any of the young writers I knew" (*SC*79). In fact, she believes that he was self-taught, essentially.

Though the question who has influenced such and such a writer has never bothered me, and the adult writer doesn't stay awake at night to wonder who has influenced him, I do think Hemingway readers should know who taught him to write: it was Ernest Hemingway. And, like all authentic writers, he knew that to make it "good," as he called it, you had to work.

Through his labors, he thus became "the acknowledged daddy of modern fiction" (*SC*81). But it is through her discussion of Hemingway's paternal nature in its truest sense that Beach attempts to coax out in her portrait another side of the writer who was defined by his ruggedness for readers in the United States and around the world. "Bumby was frequenting Shakespeare and Company before he could walk," she recalls of Hemingway's young boy, John Hadley. "I can see them, father and son, coming along hand in hand up the street." Once inside the shop, Hemingway set to "reading the latest periodicals" while balancing his child "carefully, though sometimes upside down." The boy would wait for Hemingway, "hoisted on a high stool . . . never showing any impatience," eager in his own childlike way to "go over all the questions of the day" at the neighboring bistro, just like any of the men of the quarter. "As for Bumby," she remembers fondly, "anything was all right as long as he was with his adored Papa" (*SC*82).

While Janet Flanner was herself great friends with Hemingway, it is Gertrude Stein who remains a constant for her through this period. As early as 1926, Flanner asserts, "No American writer is taken more seriously than Miss Stein by the Paris modernists" (*PY*9). Subsequently, she goes out of her way to publicize *The Autobiography of Alice B. Toklas*, described by Flanner as "a Paris-written book of extreme interest to both sides of the Atlantic." She does not discuss publicly the nature of Stein's relationship with Toklas, of course, but she does hint strongly as to the vexed question of the book's authorship by commenting that "any autobiography of the one must necessarily be a biography of, if not even by, the other." This "sly inscription," the "hoax" of the title page, is further magnified by Flanner's reassurance to the public that *The Autobiography of Alice B. Toklas*, unlike Stein's other work, would be accessible to readers. "However, on one point, the public will be glad to know, all the privileged agree," she says, "and that is that the book is written simply—not in the manner of *The Making of Americans*, but, rather, completely in Miss St—that is to say, Miss Toklas's first, or easiest, literary manner" (*PY*90). Flanner thus recognizes that Stein's renown was a matter of some contention, calling her "a popular problem child" and suggesting that this position was achieved "in her literary middle age,"[33] but by doing so Flanner always concentrates on Stein's standing as a writer.

Ironically, then, one of the more interesting invocations of Stein in the "Paris Letter" is as a collector of art. "Since Miss Gertrude Stein's collection of pictures practically ranks as one of Paris's private modern museums," she reports, "it is of interest to report that she and her canvasses have moved from her famous Montparnasse salon on the Rue de Fleurus to a remarkable seventeenth-century Latin Quarter flat formerly occupied by Queen Christina of Sweden and still containing her original wall *boiseries* and her reading cabinet." Claiming that "the moving men had to count up for Miss Stein what she had never bothered to inventory," Flanner gives an account of what Stein owns.

> Her collection today includes one hundred and thirty-one canvasses, including five Picassos which are still in the china closet. Ninety-nine of the pictures are hung. The salon alone contains four major masterpieces—Cézanne, Picasso's portrait of Miss Stein, Picasso's "Full Length Nude" (rose period) and his famous "Girl with Basket of Flowers." It also has two *natures mortes* by Braque and nineteen smaller Picassos, including four perfectly matched heads of the 1913 Cubist period, rare in their unity.

Years later, Janet Flanner admitted that she herself had actually been responsible for the inventory. "Actually I and not the moving men made the inventory of Miss Stein's pictures the day they were moved into the new apartment in the Rue Christine," she reveals. "I came to bring her a pot of white flowers (she always liked them that color) to decorate the new apartment, and she gave me a pencil and paper and said, 'Put the pot anywhere and make me an inventory of my art here,' which I did" (*PY*187–88).

In Sylvia Beach's text, the corresponding period is a sad time. "By the thirties, the Left Bank had changed," she observes. Indeed, many of her friends "had gone home," and she muses that "it had been pleasanter emerging from a war than going toward another one" (*SC*206). She noticed a shift in expatriate literature itself as Henry Miller and his "interesting" *Tropic of Cancer* replaced *The Sun Also Rises* as the book that captured the imagination of Americans abroad. As Beach's familiar cohort dwindles, the plight of Shakespeare and Company becomes more prominent in the narrative. "The bookshop was now famous," she writes. "It was always crowded with new and old customers, and was written up more and more in the newspapers and magazines." Sadly, as she discusses with some reluctance, the business "was beginning to be seriously hit by the depression" and "rapidly declined" (SC209). It managed to survive until the Nazis swarmed Paris, through the intervention of French supporters like André Gide who assembled a special committee for this purpose. "It was proposed that two hundred friends subscribe two hundred francs a year for two years," Beach reports. "The writers on the committee undertook to read in turn at the bookshop an unpublished work. These readings were to take place about once a month. Subscribers, as members of The Friends of Shakespeare and Company, would be entitled to attend the readings" (SC210). Motivated, in part, by the generosity of those around her, Beach was determined to deplete further her own resources for the sake of the bookshop. "Since my friends were doing so much for me, I thought I should sacrifice something myself," she confesses. "I decided to sell some of my most precious treasures." Her attempt to auction off Joyce manuscripts was notably unsuccessful. "Perhaps the catalogue failed to reach the Joyce collectors—or perhaps few were collecting Joyce in the thirties," she muses (SC211).

Janet Flanner reports on Americans in Paris through the 1930s, and one of her most downhearted entries publicizes that sale of manuscripts at Shakespeare and Company. She judges it "important if melancholy international news" (PY129), and she emphasizes the potential liquidation of "Joyceiana," those "collector's items" in Beach's possession "that no one else on earth has, not even Mr. Joyce" (PY128). Observing, years later, that Beach thus "gave more than she received," she confesses with her usual humility that "no Americans who later attended her sale and made purchases" had read of it in the New Yorker (PY129–30). Otherwise, Flanner's Paris by the mid-1930s seems largely devoid of Americans; she marks the end of an era with the repatriation of Arthur Moss in 1935. Moss claimed "to be the earliest edition of all expatriates," having arrived in Paris in late 1920 and made a name for himself as editor of "the first postwar Parisian transatlantic review," Gargoyle.

With respect to literary history, Flanner warns her readers against paying too much attention to such "dust on the shelves." Most of the Americans abroad who had animated Paris in the 1920s, she claims, "have long been best-sellers," and this commercial acceptance "was the condition that marked the demise of the epoch." Thus, she maintains, "the departure of those who founded it is posthumous."[34] In addition, economic hardship in the United States threatened the affluence of expatriates. "The Wall Street crash has had its effect here," she reports in late 1929. "In the Rue de la Paix the jewelers are reported to be losing fortunes in sudden cancellations of orders, and at the Ritz bar the pretty ladies are having to pay for their cocktails themselves." Sensing perhaps that this American plight did not bode well for Europe, even those French citizens who resented the extravagance of their guests chose not to revel in their troubles.

> Generally, the French people's sympathy in our disaster has been polite and astonishingly sincere, considering that for the past ten years they have seen us through one of the worst phases of our prosperity—which consisted of thousands of our tourists informing them that we were the richest country in the world, that they should pay their debts, that we had made the world safe for democracy, that we were the most generous people in the world, that they should pay their debts, and that we were the richest country in the world.

Flanner did allow herself to report some smugness, however. "Only in a few malicious French quarters had it been suggested that now certain small American investors can afford to paste Wall Street stocks on their suitcases or toss them to the crowd," she continues with some irony, "as they pasted and tossed five-franc notes here that marvelous summer when the franc fell to fifty" (PY61–62).

As late as July 1938, Janet Flanner makes reference to an "American colony" in Paris,[35] but this was not the vibrant Quarter of the 1920s. Writing in advance of the opening of Expo '37, she reaches out to what she imagines would be a wholly new wave of expatriates.

> About four hundred thousand Americans, the biggest crowd in ten years, have already arranged to come to Paris for the International Exposition of Arts and Technics, which is due to open on May 1st. Lots of these travelers haven't been here since the great days and nights of 1929; some have never been here at all. For both sorts, since it's human to forget the addresses you used to know and to lose the new ones given you, we have prepared the following conscientious list of Paris night clubs, bars, and restaurants. The addresses we have selected radiate geographically

from the gate of the Exhibition on the Place de l'Alma. If our list looks useful, keep it in your passport case; we'll never have the strength to eat, dance, and drink our way through the preparation for such a compendium again.[36]

Her comprehensive list of establishments is supplemented with a good deal of practical advice. "Take the waiter's advice of the house's wines and food specialties; he knows," she counsels. "Be sure you tip a full ten per cent; if you've been a lot of trouble to him because you do not speak French, give him a franc extra." Indeed, many of her suggestions are intended to make tourists less irritating to their hosts. "Don't talk too loud in public; remember that the American voice carries. Count your change carefully in night clubs," she chides. "And '*Doucement, s'il vous plaît*' is what you say to a taxi driver to make him go less fast—*peut-être*."[37] But this Paris for inexperienced American tourists demanded patience from even the seasoned expatriate. Flanner grumps in March 1935:

> Whatever travellers used to come to Europe for (they said it was culture) and whatever Europe used to have to offer (Europe said it was art), both travellers and Europeans, owing to the continued hard times, have now finally got down to brass tacks, and there's no culture of art nonsense about it. What travellers to the continent today want is to get the most fun for the least cash, and what the continentals have to offer has nothing to do with Mona Lisa's unsalable smile. Or so one gathers from *Paris-Midi*'s sensible and important recent series of articles entitled "Why Foreigners No Longer Come to France." Foreigners are mostly Americans, judging by the statistics quoted.

This vulgar exchange of pleasure for tourist dollars was related to menacing political developments through the 1930s. "The painful increase of nationalism all over Europe is only an increase of the necessity to have cash, to cease the wretched business of borrowing, tariffing, treatying. Tourists are bullion," she reports. "There's not a land in Europe today that wouldn't love tons of you this summer."[38]

Shari Benstock complains of expatriate autobiography that these works "focus on the expatriate community as an entity separate from and tangential to the French capital that encompassed it."[39] Sylvia Beach's emphasis on a "crowd" of Americans and a "colony" that grew up around her bookshop on the Left Bank helps propagate the idea that little was happening in Paris in the 1920s that did not directly involve visitors from the United States. However, she frequently invokes writers and artists she met through Adrienne Monnier, and while this hardly provides a comprehensive social history of Paris between the World Wars, it does present a broader picture of the city than that in many other expatriate autobiographies. "Half of my customers," she reminds us, "were, of course, French" (SC106). Léon-Paul Fargue, André Gide, Valery Larbaud, and Paul Valéry all visited Shakespeare and Company. But the best sense of the French is provided by her discussion of life in Monnier's own bookshop, La Maison des Amis des Livres. With "French authors . . . always dropping in" (SC13), this was not the Paris of an ordinary French citizen, though readers do get the sense of a place that "gave one the impression of peacefulness; you slowed down as soon as you entered it" (SC105).

Janet Flanner, on the other hand, had a genuine gift for drawing together different fragments of French existence. Benstock acknowledges that her letters "ceaselessly detailed a pattern of Paris life that went unobserved by the casual tourist and also remained, perhaps, unknown to the expatriate resident."[40] Writing in the autumn of 1936, for example, Flanner speaks of the hopes of well-heeled French skiers that they will have "snow by Christmas," for "ordinarily, they never get any except on heights where they can find snow but no hotels." This dry comment on the leisurely ambitions of one class of citizens gives way to a vivid description of the French countryside:

> In the forests around Paris, the common château bat—the little lop-eared *pipistelle*—hibernated exceptionally early. Barnyard swallows started for Egypt so soon after their second nesting that a flock of exhausted young ones was picked off the ground in southern France and kindly shipped across the Mediterranean by airplane. In Loire, eels have deserted the water to burrow into the banks; at Marennes, the oysters are unusually fat. All these are French nature's signs of a hard winter.

Immediately, she explains the relevance of these seasonal observations to an even greater number of French citizens. "Another sign, in a different sense, is coal," she continues. "It's going to be scarce, owing to bargemen's, deliverers', and miners' strikes."[41] This is not to suggest that she allowed herself to be drawn into every narrow political debate. "With the Rights here declaring that anyone who says Paris's Exhibition of Arts and Technics will open on May 1st is a Red, and with the Lefts announcing that anyone who says the Exposition won't be ready is a Fascist," she maintains, "we would like to state that we think that the Exposition will open on May 1st and that it won't be ready."[42] But her writing could not ignore wholly the unsettling international conditions of the time, and as Jane Grant observes, once Flanner began submitting political material and heard no objections from Harold Ross, she continued observations in her "Paris Letter" that were "sharp and authoritative" in assessing European politics.[43] "It will take more than the year 1939 for Europe to recover from 1938," she writes in her last New Year's column before the outbreak of war. "Not only the visible but the invisible map of the Old World has been altered. The frontiers of what men of good will believed in have been pushed around till nobody knows where they begin or end."[44] Flanner herself did not stay through the end of 1939; fleeing to the United States, she could not return to her adopted home for more than five years.

Having survived the German occupation of France, Sylvia Beach died in her Paris apartment in October 1962. In the years that remained to her after the publication of *Shakespeare and Company*, she seemed willing to finally temper, according to Noël Riley Fitch, the "modesty and reclusiveness" that defined both her life and her written record of that life. She made some concession to her celebrity to accept an honorary doctorate at the University of Buffalo.[45] But she maintained that she had published the definitive record of her life, and she had no reason—indeed, she would have no occasion—to revise her portrait of Paris. This was not the case with Janet Flanner. She resumed her "Paris Letter" in December 1944, and for much of the next three decades, she continued to provide a running social history of her adopted home. The advantage of Flanner's history, for Shari Benstock, is that "it is a record that is experienced, not remembered" long after her encounters. "Its perceptions are not dusted over with the span of years," she argues, "nor do they serve as belated repayment for disappointments, injustices, or youthful errors—as do many memoirs of the period."[46]

The opportunity for more self-conscious remembrance came to Flanner later in life. She steps outside Genêt to provide the *New Yorker* with a personal appreciation of *Shakespeare and Company* upon its publication, for example. In her affectionate notice of an "intimate, not scholarly" book "full of interesting information" and "lively illustrations," Sylvia Beach sounds much more lively than she appears in her own, self-effacing version of her life. Flanner proclaims the book written "with truth and in the vernacular."[47] Similarly, she reviews a posthumous edition of Alice B. Toklas's "rich, emotional" letters on a "heart-catching theme," *Staying on Alone* (1973).[48] As early as the 1920s, it had fallen to her to write death notices for eminent Parisians and foreigners who had taken up in the city. Fifty years later, she is performing this task in memory of friends, preparing a notable obituary for Margaret Anderson. "Her profile was delicious, her hair blonde and wavy, her laughter a soprano ripple, her gait undulating beneath her snug *tailleur*," Flanner writes. "The truth was that within her lay the mixture and mystery of her real consistence, in no way like her exterior. Her visible beauty enveloped a will of tempered steel, specifically at its most resistant when she was involved in argument, which was her favorite form of intellectual exercise, as I, who knew her for many years, can attest."[49]

The best illustration of Janet Flanner emerging from behind the mask of Genêt, however, comes with her own reassessment of her "Paris Letter." In the early 1960s, she was urged to publish a collection of these *New Yorker* pieces. As Brenda Wineapple reports, Flanner decided that William Shawn, her current editor, should discard her earliest letters, and only those written after World War II were judged valuable.[50] *Paris Journal: 1945–65* (1965) was a commercial and critical success, winning a National Book Award. A second volume covering 1965–1971 followed six years later, but at the same time Flanner agreed to allow Irving Drutman to edit a collection of her earliest material.[51] So it was that *Paris Was Yesterday* was published in 1972, a text that Flanner characterizes as "a kind of rag bag at best, with its violent mixture of time and topics."[52] Indeed, the excerpts from the "Paris Letters" published here, often only vignettes of individuals taken from the letters, are somewhat less engaging than the magazine contributions themselves, but her 7,500-word introduction to the volume provides a significant autobiographical gesture, itself. That piece was reprinted in the *New Yorker* and, according to Brenda Wineapple, "it was the most popular piece she had ever written."[53] Flanner observes, "Memories are the specific invisible remains in our lives of what belongs in the past tense" (*PY*vii). When she moves beyond Genêt this time, she leaves behind any pretense to journalistic objectivity, as illustrated by her recollection of eating at La Quatrième République, her favorite restaurant on the rue Jacob:

With my stomach stirred to hitherto unexperienced satisfactions, with my palate even now able to recall the sudden pleasure of drinking a tumbler of more than ordinary red or white French wine, I can recall the sensual satisfaction of first chewing the mixture in my mouth of a bite of meat and a crust of fresh French bread and then the following swallow of the wine itself, like the dominant liquid guide leading my nourishment down through my gullet into my insides. Eating in France was a new body experience. (*PY*xii)

She here imagines the Paris of her first experience as an idyll untouched by the influence of international business. She laments the "rash of colored cinema signs" that "suddenly burst out" along the Champs-Elysées at the end of the 1920s, "movie houses" being "always the first intruders" to harbinger the crassness of economic progress (*PY*xxiii). If her city is thus embellished, she is reverent in recalling people themselves, sensing that artists as part of an honored tradition deserve to be framed with respect. She still believes in the value of "living both home and abroad," understanding her expatriation as "living surrounded with the human familiarity of American friends and acquaintances, and the constant, shifting stimulation that came from the native French" (*PY*xvi). She identifies herself with those individuals she encountered after leaving Greenwich Village, "youngish American expatriates" that made up "a literary lot," each of whom "aspired to become a famous writer as soon as possible" (*PY*vii).

Much like Sylvia Beach, she uses her writing to discuss the Americans she encountered abroad: Kay Boyle, Hart Crane, e. e. cummings, John Dos Passos, and Glenway Wescott. Flanner is remarkably generous, saving serious criticism of her compatriots for Ezra Pound alone, his fascism still fresh in her mind. "I liked neither Pound's arbitrary historicity, nor his condensed violence," she complains most tellingly, "nor his floating Chinese quotations such as marked the poetry he wrote for the *Little Review*, nor all his weighty, ancient, mixed linguistics, like stony chips whacked off with *hauteur* from the old statuary of the scholarly mind." In contrast, she esteems Djuna Barnes as "the most important woman writer we had in Paris" (*PY*xvii). She revisits much of the material she had published in reviewing *Shakespeare and Company* two decades before to tell once more the story of the "extraordinary" Sylvia Beach, who provided the "hearth and home of the Left Bank American literary colony after 1920" (*PY*viii–ix). She is much more willing than was Beach to take to task James Joyce for his treatment of those who supported him. "Does anyone read *Ulysses* now, read it entire, word by word with the impetus we did fifty years ago?" she asks with the bitterness of one who had herself been deceived. "I wonder. And I disbelieve" (*PY*xii). As close as she gets to unbridled effusiveness is in her description of F. Scott Fitzgerald and his "beautiful" face, "like the visage of a poet," but she is also forced to fill in the details of his drinking, inevitably, though she remains grateful that he, alone among her writer friends, gave credit to her own "literary sensibilities" (*PY*xix). Most touching is her remembrance of Ernest Hemingway, whom she is able to discuss anew in light of his death in early 1961. She reveals that, like Hemingway, she endured the loss of her father by suicide, "a piece of personal duplicate history" that would never have made its way into the "Paris Letter," of course (*PY*viii). She sees the novelist's death by his own hand as "the ultimate melodrama of his spectacular existence," but she takes no issue with his action, which she views as "his mortal act of gaining liberty." She objects only to his family's initial attempt to conceal "the more profound truth" of his suicide by claiming that he had an "accident" with a firearm. In some ways, in Flanner's judgment, this desperate ruse was an extension of Hemingway's "state of ruin," his own "tottering faculties," and it revealed the same inability to grieve effectively that Flanner herself experienced a half century before. The legacy of his literary achievement is a testament to the work of all expatriates from the United States and a matter of more upbeat reflection for her. "As a special gift Ernest had a physical style of writing with his senses that was his own literary creation yet which soon influenced American male fiction-writing," she concludes (*PY*vii–viii).

In the 1974 afterword to the reprint edition of *The Cubical City* (1926), her only novel, Janet Flanner observes, "Writing fiction is not my gift. Writing is but not writing fiction."[54] She claims that from the time of her "fifth birthday," she knew she "wanted to be a writer." As evidenced from her own disappointment with that novel, her writing fell short of her ambition that she "was going to write books."[55] The esteem she herself granted longer narratives should not be discounted. The form on which she eventually settled was shorter, primarily, and not fictional in the sense that she would have recognized, though her magazine journalism evidenced many of the biases that inform the best novels of the twentieth century. Irving Drutman's edition of her earliest letters presents Flanner's works to readers in a form that mimics an autobiographical narrative, but by doing so he underlines the catholic range of her interests. A similar need to organize diverse material defines a work like Sylvia Beach's *Shakespeare and Company*, a text that itself examines the events of nearly forty years. The range of the material they cover thus imbues Beach and Flanner with their authority, and their writings provide a unique view of life abroad, affirming in particular the contribution of women authors to American modernism. In publishing *Women of the Left Bank* a generation ago, Shari Benstock sought to bring to even greater attention the "lives and works" of women who "have been considered marginal to the Modernist effort,"[56] and she counts among her subjects both Sylvia Beach and Janet Flanner. If some of the representative skepticism of the influence of expatriate women has ebbed since that time, readers still overlook examples of life writing that eschew the autobiographical "I," despite the best efforts of contemporary critics. So, beyond the narrowest definitions of genre, there still exist the autobiographical writings of expatriate women, long overshadowed by the stories of American men, that promise to complement our accumulated knowledge of life abroad. But by challenging the traditional structures of expatriate autobiography, Beach and Flanner shared a broader impulse, felt more widely by the beginning of the 1960s, to revise established conceptions of the Lost Generation.

6

REVISION AND TEXTUAL AUTHORITY

On April 8, 1933, Ernest Hemingway wrote to Janet Flanner, "By jeesus will write my own memoirs sometime when I can't write anything else. And they will be funny and accurate and not out to prove a bloody thing."[1] While this pledge should remind readers that some modern writers saw life narrative as a second-rate undertaking, it also betrays Hemingway's belief that Paris in the 1920s had not been accurately reflected in its earliest published accounts. His suggestion that he had no axe to grind, his professed desire to construct only "damned good memoirs" to illustrate how he was, in fact, "jealous of no one,"[2] belied frequent threats that reflect what Jacqueline Tavernier-Courbin characterizes as the author's "obsession with claiming that he had concrete evidence to damn his contemporaries."[3] He told *Esquire* editor Arnold Gingrich in 1934, for example, "I've written all the facts about Gertrude [Stein] so they'll be on tap if anything happens to me."[4] Ernest Hemingway would never publish such material during his lifetime, but by the end of the 1950s, he seemed finally prepared to do so. The text that appeared posthumously as *A Moveable Feast* (1964) was written between 1957 and 1960, at a time when a number of revisions of the Lost Generation were being undertaken. Ostensibly, Hemingway was inspired to write about his life in Paris after finding two old trunks of papers from that time, a "treasure trove" of background material described by biographer Carlos Baker.[5] The importance of these "blue-and-yellow-covered penciled notebooks," uncovered from the basement of the Ritz Hotel on the Place Vendôme, was asserted by Hemingway's widow, Mary, who claimed that these papers dominated his "afternoon reading" throughout early 1957.[6] Tavernier-Courbin has investigated fully the possible importance of the notebooks and finds the story "not overwhelmingly convincing," arguing that any found papers could have provided only miscellaneous "details," as Hemingway "made relatively small use" of old material in the composition of his subsequent book.[7]

A desire to set the record straight, more than nostalgia incited by providence, best explains the genesis of *A Moveable Feast*. Hemingway was well aware of the relevant autobiographies published in the decades after *The Autobiography of Alice B. Toklas*. He read Samuel Putnam's *Paris Was Our Mistress* upon its release in the late 1940s, for example, judging it "a strange mixture full of good intention, inaccurate journalism, and personal alibis for some pretty strange things."[8] As Sylvia Beach was at work on the manuscript for *Shakespeare and Company*, she consulted with Hemingway, according to Noël Riley Fitch, because "she was hesitant about publicly mentioning his early domestic life."[9] When he began to examine his own life in the 1920s, it was for Mary Welsh Hemingway simply because he wanted "to do something about Paris in the early days," to write his story "by *remate* . . . by reflection" through others. She was surprised that he played a less central role in the narrative of his own life, as his drafts were in her judgment "not much about" him, but she still maintained that the manuscript she eventually discovered after his suicide in 1961 was "finished except for the editing."[10] She concluded that "Ernest had expected his Paris memoirs to be his next published book," so she set out to bring it to the public by following two basic principles: nothing should appear that was "of quality inferior to the work published during Ernest's lifetime," and only "repetitions and redundancies" would be excised from manuscripts unburdened by supplementary text.[11] Tavernier-Courbin judges as "far more extensive" the work undertaken by the widow and by Scribner's editor Harry Brague, however, as much in *A Moveable Feast* "was changed, deleted, and added."[12] While the result was a text Hemingway would surely still have recognized, the copyediting and changes in the sequencing of material served to emphasize, repeatedly, only how an exceptional young man was challenged to transcend his surroundings. There are more than thirty places where the author's use of the pronoun "you" was replaced with "I" and "we," for example, an editorial decision that further "isolates Hemingway within his own experience and from the reader, who no longer participates in his life."[13] Gerry Brenner notes that readers thus never get to see in *A Moveable Feast* how Hemingway's manuscript "backs away from the harsh portrait he had sketched" of his contemporaries.[14] Indeed, as published, Ernest Hemingway's autobiography castigates expatriate Paris.

"There is not an associate of his, who conceivably might be his rival, or to whom he owed anything, that receives anything but denigration of character or profession," Andrew Lytle observes. "Not once does he show any human sympathy or charity towards his fellow man."[15] While many expatriates sought to define themselves by relational autobiography, implying throughout their works the importance of their involvement with others, the effect of *A Moveable Feast* is to develop Hemingway's reputation in contrast with the demonstrable shortcomings of those people around him. Susanna Egan is reminded when reading Hemingway's remembrances how "the self is constructed in relation to and in terms of other selves,"[16] but the others he draws here erode any sense of collective undertaking. His loathing of the English is pronounced. Wyndham Lewis "looked nasty" with the eyes "of an unsuccessful rapist,"[17] for example, and Ford Madox Ford was nothing more than "an ambulatory, well clothed, up-ended hogshead" roaming throughout Paris. "I had always avoided looking at Ford when I could and I always held my breath when I was near him in a crowded room," Hemingway avows (*MF*83).

Americans abroad do no better in his estimation. The consumptive Ernest Walsh, with his "marked-for-death look," revealed himself as a fraud for daring to even talk writing with Hemingway, and the editor of *This Quarter* thus suffers a defamatory comparison with "the whores in Kansas City" Hemingway knew as a young man (*MF*126–27). Katherine Mansfield was "near-beer," as her fiction amounted to nothing more than "carefully artificial tales of a young old-maid" (*MF*133). John Dos Passos, the parasitic "pilot fish" who attached himself to the wealthy socialites Gerald and Sara Murphy, was "a little deaf, sometimes blind" and brought only tragedy to "those who trust him" (*MF*207–8). The doomed Ralph Cheever Dunning is dismissed simply as "a poet who smoked opium and forgot to eat" (*MF*143). Hemingway derisively calls T. S. Eliot "the major," and he imagines the poet freed from his job as a banker, living in Natalie Barney's backyard, where admirers could "drop in to crown him with laurel" (*MF*112). Even Ezra Pound, who attained such perfection in the creation of his best work, who "was kinder and more Christian about people" than Hemingway ever is here, who emerged in fact as "a sort of saint," turned out to be little more than a provincial rube, chiding Hemingway for his literary curiosity while admitting himself to having "never read the Rooshians" (*MF*108, 134). Still, Hemingway reserves his cruelest treatment for the American with whom he was most closely associated during the Paris years, F. Scott Fitzgerald. Perhaps the most famous episode in *A Moveable Feast* sees Hemingway judge the size of his friend's genitals in a public restroom, in response to Zelda Fitzgerald's alleged complaint that, physically, her spouse "could never make any woman happy" (*MF*190). Hemingway believed her to be a constant distraction to her fragile and insecure husband. "He was always trying to work," Hemingway reports. "Each day he would try and fail" (*MF*182). But Fitzgerald's most serious problem was his drinking. "It was hard to accept him as a drunkard," Hemingway scoffs, "since he was affected by such small quantities of alcohol." Still, any drinking would, seemingly, transform him "into a fool" (*MF*166–67).

Ernest Hemingway's greatest preoccupation is with Gertrude Stein, of course, and her relentless drive for "publication and official acceptance" (*MF*17), an ambition that culminated with the treachery of *The Autobiography of Alice B. Toklas*. He can hardly "remember Gertrude Stein ever speaking well of any writer who had not written favorably about her work or done something to advance her career" (*MF*27). This pathological self-interest contrasted with the generosity shown Hemingway by Sylvia Beach. "No one that I ever knew was nicer to me," he says of the owner of Shakespeare and Company (*MF*35), though Gerry Brenner points out that the reorganization of the chapters in *A Moveable Feast* impoverishes even Beach's contribution to Hemingway's success and obscures her depiction as "the tolerant, nurturing and modest" mother figure.[18]

Hemingway's eventual success as a writer was a direct result of his ability to insulate himself from those people around him, in fact. "Birth of a New School," an excised chapter that was restored to the published text of *A Moveable Feast*, includes an extensive passage that explains how the author liked to work alone in the Closerie des Lilas. "The blue-backed notebooks, the two pencils in the pencil-sharpener (a pocket knife was too wasteful), the marble-topped tables, the smell of the early morning, sweeping out and mopping, and luck were all you needed," he attests. Immersed in an imaginative journey through the landscape of his fiction, the threat always came from some acquaintance who could disturb him with a simple, "Hi, Hem. What are you trying to do?" Such an interruption was "the worst thing that could happen" (*MF*91), and he set out to defend his solitude in his favorite café in as "cruel and heartless and conceited" a manner as necessary (*MF*94). "Now why is it that Hemingway wants to be the only one, the only artist and the only man?" Lytle asks of the desolate landscape the author leaves in his wake.[19] These passages represent Hemingway's memory of himself as a writer at the height of his powers, apprenticing to no one, relying on no one's inspiration or support. Although Paris itself was "the town best organized for a writer to write in that there is" (*MF*182), not even these surroundings could always be counted upon to nurture, and sometimes the city even mocked. "You got very hungry when you did not eat enough in Paris," he complains, "because all the bakery shops had such good things in the windows and people ate outside at tables on the sidewalk so that you saw and smelled the food" (*MF*69). More frequently, the elements themselves conspired against the writer, as "heavy cold rains would beat back" the spring, leaving a "cold, wintry light," threatening that the change of seasons "would never come" to lift his spirits. "This was the only truly sad time in Paris because it was unnatural," Hemingway laments (*MF*45). As he is represented in *A Moveable Feast*, the author is able, ultimately, to rise above his environment, to thrive in spite of Paris while other expatriates hoped desperately only to succeed because of it. "In those days you did not really need anything," Hemingway boasts (*MF*96), in one of the only places in which a munificent "you" persists in the text, a sad contrast to the state of anxiety into which the author had fallen by the end of his life.

For Jacqueline Tavernier-Courbin, the text draws Hemingway "as virtually perfect and almost everyone else as extremely flawed." *A Moveable Feast* is thus only "faithful to his personal vision of things,"[20] and he is careful to assert that, at some level at least, his work "be regarded as fiction." His further acknowledgment that "everyone has written about" some element of Paris in the 1920s leaves readers with the sense that this is a response, one to stand yet against those who "will doubtless write more" (*MF*ix). Indeed, Ernest Hemingway was not the only expatriate American readying a rejoinder to those contemporaries whose earlier works had framed life abroad. While *A Moveable Feast* was still a series of drafts culled from fragments of Hemingway's old notebooks, Harold Loeb published his own *The Way It Was* (1959), a collection of remembrances whose title reveals its author's desire to be definitive. Hemingway confided to Carlos Baker that he read Loeb's book, and while he would not grant that it influenced his own memories, he still found it "very touching and sad," reflecting how his old acquaintance "wished things to have been."[21]

The Way It Was seeks, in part, to retell the events that informed *The Sun Also Rises*. Loeb was clearly still hurt by his depiction in Hemingway's work as the ineffectual Robert Cohn, and he seemed eager to discuss Lost Generation fiction until the end of his life, concluding "that some interest must persist in those distant events" that informed its stories. In an article published in 1967, for example, Loeb sought to counter his "libelous" representation in Hemingway's novel by establishing its author's mean-spirited "propensity to assign disagreeable fictive characters and unpleasant behavior to the people he knew best."[22] But Loeb does not judge the merits of *The Sun Also Rises* in his autobiography, and his portrait of Hemingway is actually quite affectionate. "He had a shy, disarming smile and did not seem interested in the other guests; he wore sneakers . . . and a patched jacket," Loeb reports upon first meeting Hemingway at a party. "I thought never before had I encountered an American so unaffected by living in Paris."[23] Loeb's real purpose is to examine his own motives for living abroad, of course, transcending the "pleasures" that colored his earliest impressions of the city "as a place in which to live."[24] Precisely because they "were 'lost' for a time, separated from our traditional moorings and attached to nothing whatsoever," he finds among his contemporaries enough similarities to draw together expatriate experience, a continuity that differentiates his cohort from other groups of Americans. "We were not so different from those who had preceded us," he maintains. "Perhaps our hopes were a little higher, our disappointments deeper: but at least ours was a generation that had set out to discover, a generation that had chosen to dare."[25]

On the other hand, Matthew Josephson's *Life among the Surrealists* (1962) tries to answer more directly these "other published accounts" of Americans abroad, taking as a starting point the need to question the homogeneity of cohort implied in a text like Loeb's. Besides the autobiographies of those expatriates who shared his experience, Josephson was aware of current "searchers and scholars" whose reading of American expatriation "abounds in errors of fact and interpretation." He hoped to "retell what actually happened, before error becomes so thickly rooted that men after us will not know how to distinguish fact from fancy."[26] His analysis thus begins with an acknowledgment of the proliferation of expatriate autobiographies. "As the decade of the 1920's recedes into the past, some of us who were then in our own twenties have been greatly tempted to look back with the perspective of a third of a century and recapitulate our adventures, our friendships, our follies and our little triumphs, such as they were," Josephson reflects. "It would seem I have failed to resist this temptation." He grants that this time "seems to form a distinct epoch in history," and his examination of that time also underlines a great deal of similarity among those Americans who lived in France. "The lives of a good many of us were stamped with a common pattern of experience," he acknowledges. "For some years many of us considered Paris our Second Country, and I confess that whenever I had occasion to leave it and return to my First Country, my native land, the fear would come to me that I would never be so happy again."[27] But Josephson doubts that anyone could be an "authorized spokesman" for Americans abroad, and his "group portrait" ultimately emphasizes difference, refuting the "misleading nomenclature" of the Lost Generation. While Josephson comes to question this "very idea of a generation," however, accepting it reluctantly as "only a convenient mental construct,"[28] novelist Kay Boyle was preparing to embark upon a project that would reassert the coherence of a recognizable cohort of expatriate Americans, connecting their journey to the struggles of contemporary youth, and by doing so would declare the continued relevance of the innovations that defined their art. *Being Geniuses Together* is a text that exceeds the achievement of Harold Loeb in arguing a sense of community among these expatriates and, by doing so, seeks to counter the approach of individuals like Hemingway and Josephson who hoped above all else to refute accounts of a cohesive generation abroad.

By the mid-1960s, Boyle was in possession of a three-book contract from Doubleday publishers in New York. The cornerstone of this deal was to have been a history of Germany, a manuscript on which she began work as early as 1958. Boyle encountered difficulties completing the project, and after lobbying successfully to undertake a history of German women instead, she was forced eventually to abandon the project altogether. To help her meet her professional obligations, Boyle hoped that her new publisher would accept a new plan to reissue *Three Short Novels* (1958), a work that had appeared under the Beacon imprint. That publisher still had four thousand copies of the book in its warehouse, however, and so Doubleday editor Ken McCormick was unable to agree to Boyle's proposal.[29] McCormick suggested instead that she undertake work revising Robert McAlmon's 1938 autobiography, *Being Geniuses Together*.[30] Indeed, in the years following his death in 1956, Boyle had been seeking an American publisher for her friend's book, but when Doubleday brought forward a new edition of the work in 1968, it contained alternate chapters written by Kay Boyle herself. McAlmon's original text was approximately 110,000 words in length; Boyle's edition is 160,000 words, only 70,000 of which were written by Robert McAlmon. "This present book is his," Boyle writes of McAlmon's achievement in her 1984 afterword (*BG*333), and while one might argue that this is the case, no one can question the fact that she altered his book from its original form in a far more dramatic fashion than Mary Welsh Hemingway had altered *A Moveable Feast*.

There are, in fact, two immediate questions raised by an examination of Boyle's strategy for revising *Being Geniuses Together*. First, what is the significance of the 90,000 words she added to the work? Second, what is revealed through an analysis of McAlmon's edited contribution—including a consideration of the 40,000 words of McAlmon's work omitted from the 1968 edition, seven full chapters excised and significant passages from at least a half-dozen others? McAlmon himself had suffered editorial interference during his lifetime. Born in Kansas, the son of an exacting Presbyterian clergyman, he had difficulty finding a publisher for his autobiography in the 1930s because, as Sanford Smoller explains, no one seemed "in the mood to read about the escapades of writers and artists in the ebullient and innocent twenties." Eventually, Secker and Warburg in London agreed to bring forward the text, but only after excising those passages they judged likely to attract "libel and obscenity suits."[31] Soon after his death, the writer's sister Victoria tried to have *Being Geniuses Together* reissued, but she found in his earlier drafts little she judged worthy of inclusion. Once Boyle undertook the work, she found many places in which the earlier "typescript differs from the published version," and she claims to have "frequently substituted McAlmon's undeleted text rather than the edited sections which appeared in the original edition" (*BG*xi). She restored material to *Being Geniuses Together*, but most of the changes, as outlined above, replaced McAlmon's original material with her own.

The effect of Boyle's editorial strategy in all instances is that the sense of community is tightened between American writers discussed in the narrative. While some of her changes removed references to forgotten poets and novelists like Carlyle MacIntyre and Ken Sato, most of her emendations excluded references to things that happened outside Paris, things that happened beyond the temporal frame she enforces. Clearly, her writing of the Lost Generation and the privileging of the time and space it occupied is a strategy mainly undertaken by expatriates of lesser achievement than she. Boyle leaves no doubt that she feels insecure about her place among her contemporaries, though, for the simple reason that she followed a somewhat unusual path to Paris. But it is also likely that Boyle recognized in recent works of expatriates like Ernest Hemingway and Matthew Josephson an ill-timed disparaging of the expatriate impulse. While Gertrude Stein hoped to see herself as separate from her contemporaries, and even a writer as accomplished as Malcolm Cowley had misgivings about drawing a generation, neither of them seriously questioned the experience of living abroad. If, to this point, only marginal figures enthusiastically embraced the idea of a cohort in their desire to belong, Boyle saw the defense of the concept of a generation itself as inherent to the justification of expatriation in the 1920s. Modernism came under careful scrutiny during the 1960s, and Boyle's revision of the Lost Generation sought to reaffirm both the achievement of her cohort and the relevance of the cultural undertaking in which they participated.

Like many expatriate Americans between the World Wars, Kay Boyle was by no means an established writer when she left for France in June 1923. By sheer industry, she had positioned herself among a small group of artists in Greenwich Village that was handling in the United States the affairs of the expatriate magazine *Broom*, but for her own literary output she could claim nothing more than a few lines in *Poetry* and a couple of unsigned reviews in the *Dial*. Boyle's first husband, Richard Brault, was a French engineer, and the couple spent their first months abroad living with his family in Brittany. She claims that they planned to stay in Europe "three or, at the most, four months" (*BG*39), and she recognizes that this particular situation "would seem to disqualify me as a member of the lost generation" (*BG*11). In her daily life, she "surrendered totally" to French customs, so that even in her appearance she "scarcely recognized" herself as a young woman from St. Paul, Minnesota (*BG*147). Brault's search for work took them to the shores of the English Channel and, eventually, Stoke-on-Trent, and so it would be some time before Boyle actually established herself in Montparnasse.

As for McAlmon, his memories of the time are defined by responses to place, responses that for Boyle are largely deferred.

So, while McAlmon describes his earliest interactions with Ezra Pound, Wyndham Lewis, and James Joyce, for example, geography above all else is privileged in his account throughout *Being Geniuses Together*, and for him Paris itself quickly becomes a character with whom he forges an uneasy relationship.

> Now, after a month of Paris, I felt I must get away. I had no love, merely an infatuation for the place. Upon arriving there after an absence, I was always in a fever of excitement, and couldn't do quickly enough the bars of Montparnasse and the cabarets of Montmartre, and the Champs Elysées district. Like Fanny Hill, however, my fever for curiosities abated as the blood stream flowed more coolly and the arteries hardened. Crossing the Seine into the Place de la Concorde on a misty spring morning, or seeing Notre Dame des Champs from river level at dawn, when well on with drink, still brought a foaming ecstasy into me, a stroke of lightning to the heart or mind about the wonder of it. But I knew all too well that Paris was a bitch, and that one shouldn't become infatuated with bitches, particularly when they have wit, imagination, experience, and tradition behind their ruthlessness. (*BG*113–14)

Against this spirited description of the city, Boyle's contribution appears much less concerned with place, initially, underlining the importance of the emotional rather than the physical connection that binds together the writers of her growing acquaintance. Indeed, Donna Hollenberg observes that Boyle's earliest fiction, books that also feed upon her first experiences abroad, reversed the traditional connection of the United States "with convention and entrapment" so that it is Europe that stifles a young woman's "freedom and independence."[32] In *Plagued by the Nightingale* (1931), the story of a young American who chafes under the demands of her new French relatives, Boyle trades on images of confinement and the symbolism of a caged bird to examine her own feelings of captivity. With her own artistic ambitions discouraged by her uncultured in-laws, she first "entered into a sly and secretive life" of letter writing with her mother and with the poet Lola Ridge, discussing at length the works of William Carlos Williams and Marianne Moore (*BG*67). She admits that, by the time she moved to a dingy apartment in Le Havre so that her husband could take a position with the local electric company, "every day I wrote so many letters that often I did not have the price of postage to send them off" (BG139). Through sheer perseverance, she forged a friendship with Emanuel Carnevali, and it was the Italian poet who gave her address to Ernest Walsh, just then in the process of launching *This Quarter*. When Boyle grew ill with pneumonia, she moved to the south of France to recuperate with Walsh in early 1926 and began with him there an affair that ended only because of his death from tuberculosis in October of that year.

In that brief period of time, Boyle assumed responsibility for the magazine's correspondence, expanding her network of contacts considerably. By her own admission, letters grew ever more important to her emerging artistry, as well. "Letters became the means of relating with familiar, living people the mystery of the dreams and realizations of the night, a way of marking my return to a native coast after the long voyage of drifting in seemingly interminable loneliness," she explains. "It was necessary to write these letters at once, soon after awaking, and not relegate the writing of them to the evening, or to one day set aside in the week, while I got on with the daily concerns of life. They must be written quickly; I must reach out quickly to these spokesmen who were my bond and contact with humanity before the dark, lonely tide of dreams had ebbed entirely away" (BG214–15). Boyle's direct contact with her cohort was thus deferred through much of the 1920s. She admits that while staying in Paris in 1923, for example, she lurked outside Shakespeare and Company without "the courage to approach the door" and introduce herself to Sylvia Beach and whomever else might be inside (BG84). In this sense, it was her emerging sense of a community, more than the communal contact of shared endeavor, that was most important to Kay Boyle. Even her first meetings with Robert McAlmon were unremarkable, and she admitted that by the time he came to visit her in Monte Carlo in April 1927, "he and I exchanged not more than a dozen sentences" (BG210).

If Kay Boyle's Lost Generation was not based on actual proximity and camaraderie, it did rely on the recognition of common intellectual and artistic concerns expressed within a temporal frame clearly demarcated. Indeed, Boyle's revisions emphasize her chronological reorganization of the narrative. McAlmon's original title *Being Geniuses Together: An Autobiography* was replaced in the 1968 edition with *Being Geniuses Together, 1920–1930*. The omission of McAlmon's last five chapters, besides suggesting some haste in completing a manuscript that was itself more than a year overdue, was consistent with Boyle's decision to end the tale with the events of 1930. This focus upon the specific definition of a period or an era was also reflected in her decision to reorganize events from four of McAlmon's original chapters in an attempt to preserve her tidy, chronological sequence. Boyle replaced McAlmon's descriptive chapter headings with dates, substituting for example "The Nightinghoul's Crying" with "Robert McAlmon, 1923" and "Nights of Venice" with "Robert McAlmon, 1924." McAlmon allows at one point that "this tale is certainly not chronological" (*BG*198), but Boyle's revisions have made it so, suggesting an orderly history of a precisely defined generation of writers abroad, ending with unprecedented abruptness after the Wall Street crash and the consolidation of American newspapers in Paris that supported many of these figures. In fact, neither McAlmon nor Boyle returned to America in 1930, but Boyle reports that by this time "the good days of the Quarter were finished," at least as she remembers McAlmon characterizing it, and she had thus "come too late" to participate in all the revels of expatriate American writers on the Left Bank (*BG*286). Because Boyle only established herself in Paris after the spring of 1928, she uses her contribution to *Being Geniuses Together* to confirm her place in a generation she imagines and uses her emphasis on chronological organization to highlight its late bloom, thereby giving this community a sense of continuity granted it by no other autobiography.

There was, of course, an actual company of American writers living in Paris throughout the 1920s, though we have seen most expatriates describe it as different collections of writers, shifting and changing through the decade. So, while McAlmon uses *Being Geniuses Together* to record his impressions of people, he refuses to draw the self-conscious connections essential for defining a single community of writers. In rejecting the cliques that defined artists in London, for example, McAlmon muses, "There were groups in New York, too, but why be alive if you can't like the battle of measuring their contempt or indifference or interest against that of others?" (*BG*4). He questions the virtue of Ezra Pound's identification of a recognizable group of "us" in Paris (*BG*116) and participates in nothing more systematic than "to compile a list of the foreign artists" present in the city in the 1920s (*BG*163). "I never felt myself an expatriate or anything but an American, although not through excess of patriotism," he maintains. "I had left America because of events and had never been, and am not now, romantic about Europe" (*BG*256). He has a devil-may-care attitude about his travels, in fact. "If the world's going to hell, I'm going there with it, and not in the back ranks either," he writes (*BG*203). In a section cut from the 1968 edition, McAlmon laments how people "in New York" saw *The Sun Also Rises* as a true "depiction of life . . . in Paris" because it ignores the "working, producing, alert, and competent" expatriates who contradict wild images of Americans abroad.[33] But just because he hates the idea that Americans at home had the impression that expatriates led "non-working and dissolute lives" (*BG*163) does not mean that he respects everyone around him. In fact, reflecting what Boyle describes as his "ruthless honesty" (*BG*24), McAlmon offers disparaging comments about just about every writer he met, American or otherwise. Harry Crosby was "too full of hero-worship" (*BG*308), and, in the earlier edition, McAlmon claims, "His writing I found impossible to believe valid."[34] T. S. Eliot wrote "mouldy poetry" (*BG*6), while Ford Madox Ford was "a mythomaniac . . . who likes to believe that all of the young come to sit at his feet" (*BG*116). James Joyce is described as "a Dublin-Irish provincial" (*BG*25); W. B. Yeats was "too Irish twilighty and sweetly mystic" (*BG*227). Sinclair Lewis was not "even a good second-rater" (*BG*33). While Gertrude Stein possessed "a child's vanity and love of praise," he writes of Amy Lowell only that she "did weigh a good deal more than Gertrude" (*BG*204). For McAlmon, no cohort of laudable colleagues emerges in his account among which he seeks to place himself. As does Hemingway in *A Moveable Feast*, Robert McAlmon reserves some of his harshest criticisms for those closest to him. Hemingway himself got interested in the bullfighting by which he came to define masculinity only through "Gertrude Stein's praise of it" and out of a need to define a process of "self-hardening" by which he might live (*BG*161). William Carlos Williams, from whom he would grow estranged over the poet's assertion that McAlmon had been "browbeaten and emasculated" by the women in his life,[35] is here "inclined to go literary and nostalgic" (*BG*165). Kay Boyle herself, influenced "by the swooning moonlight" of contemporary prose, "goes too, too fine for the ordinary mortal" according to her friend, and the resulting work was "pretentious, and therefore vulgar or cheap" (*BG*253).

Boyle, on the other hand, identifies all these writers as "self-exiled revolutionaries" (*BG*336), allowing their experiences to define a nurturing environment that sustained expatriate Americans. McAlmon fashioned himself a loner, prowling from engagement to engagement without forging meaningful connections, though Boyle is careful not to include his admission that some expatriates, including Ezra Pound, thought him "the American most about town and most aware of low and night life."[36] In the meantime, Boyle seeks to justify even the fractures between expatriate writers among all nationalities in Paris. While it is Boyle and not McAlmon who makes an issue of the famous estrangement between Gertrude Stein and James Joyce, it was for Boyle no petty, personal disagreement. Rather, these two literary behemoths held "opposite concepts of a new syntax and a new vocabulary," meaningful differences that emerge in the search for a common literary goal (*BG*242). Similarly, Boyle attempts to explain away here the differences in literary strategy that saw McAlmon exclude himself from Eugene Jolas's *transition* magazine, in much the same manner in which she attempted to minimize their differences so as to broker a friendly truce between the two men in 1928. While McAlmon writes that the magazine "was a constant example of how not to write" (*BG*252), and even Boyle admits that the views of its editor on the importance of the unconscious in writing were "in total opposition to McAlmon's universe and conjecturings" (*BG*268), she lent both men her unquestioned loyalty. Because preserving a sense of unity was of no importance to Robert McAlmon, readers may be tempted to read his title as ironic; indeed, the concept of "genius" resists collaborative effort. But as Kay Boyle seeks above all else to posit the existence of some underlying unity, even her most bitter enemies are treated with tact or diplomatically ignored. She writes of "rocking and cradling" Ethel Moorhead "as if she were my little child" as they mourned Ernest Walsh (*BG*191), even though Moorhead's jealousy over Boyle's relationship with Walsh often led Moorhead into paroxysms of rage. While Boyle had a long and bitter feud with Laura Riding, begun in disagreement over the poetry of Hart Crane, there is mention in this text only of an abandoned luncheon for which Boyle claims to be "ashamed ... for a long time afterwards" (*BG*265).

By drawing with such care an expatriate community, Kay Boyle reveals how she herself sought so desperately for a place to belong. As early as 1924, for example, she toyed with the idea of joining Raymond Duncan's colony of artists in Neuilly. Founded by the brother of the dancer Isadora Duncan, the group preached simplicity in living, but Boyle was perhaps more interested in practical matters: Sharon, the daughter she had with Ernest Walsh, presented by 1928 what Joan Mellon describes as "a responsibility with which she had no means of coping."[37] In *Being Geniuses Together*, Boyle claims that she regarded life with the group as an opportunity to ease her "social conscience" (*BG*292), but she experienced a total breakdown instead, going "off the deep end" to suffer "a symbolic suicide." The manifestation of this collapse was a period of frenzied sexual promiscuity. "I consorted with this one and that one, love having nothing to do with it," she confesses (*BG*317). Boyle aborted the resulting pregnancy, and she discusses the procedure with chilling frankness in her autobiography. "All I knew was that it could not, must not be born," she says, "and I denied it its life with the cold calculation of an executioner" (*BG*320). From the depths of this experience, she felt a reawakening of spirit, beginning with a frank self-assessment: "These things I had done were all the flowering of the tenderest care and cultivation, the results of a privileged upbringing, of a youth in which the spirit had been gently nurtured," she attests. "I had never for a moment doubted that the integrity of that spirit would be extended without effort, without the necessity of conscious thought, to integrity of conduct. I could not have been more mistaken" (*BG*320–21). Her physical condition continued to deteriorate, however, and she eventually contracted cerebral meningitis. As the story is retold in the novel *My Next Bride* (1934), it was at this time that she finally saw Raymond Duncan's colony as a fraud, and she concludes in the autobiography that "the things I had come to work for there simply didn't exist" (*BG*323). With the help of Harry and Caresse Crosby, Robert McAlmon, and Lawrence Vail, she escaped the colony with her daughter. Her portrait of her rescuers and their friends, as artificially cohesive as it might be, depicts a family far more loyal to her than what she left behind in Neuilly.

The redeeming feature of the 1968 edition of *Being Geniuses Together* may be that Boyle is unsuccessful, however, in sustaining this centripetal effect throughout. Like modernism itself, the array of characters at the heart of the book defies easy classification; tensions spill out and reveal the inner contradictions of the group. Near the end of the text, the differences that estrange her from McAlmon erupt in a moment of farcical violence, as he rejects her attempt to anthologize the writings of their contemporaries:

> But it was a sad evening, an evening of goodbyes being said for the summer, and suddenly McAlmon got down from the bar stool he was sitting on, and walked to the end of the counter and leaned across it and jerked the handsomely printed announcement of Archie's and my yearbook of poetry from the wall. He looked me straight in the eye with his glacial blue stare as he tore

the announcement in two, and then into four, and flung it on the floor. "That's what I think of your crazy, senseless undertakings! That's what I think of your taste in poetry!" he said. At our feet lay the scattered uproarious words: "the best . . . ever published . . . most sought-after . . . renowned . . . LIVING POETRY . . ." screamed the poor hysterical words with their throats cut now, writhing their last on the bar room floor. I had been drinking from a tall glass stein of beer, and before Richard could stop me, or before I myself knew what I was about to do, I threw the stein after McAlmon, who had started back to his seat again. (BG316–17)

In her reading of *Being Geniuses Together*, Christine Hait sees Boyle's textual strategy as inspired by lines of McAlmon's poetry repeated in the text: "Oh, let me gather myself together / Where are the pieces / quivering and staring and muttering / that are all to be a part of me?" By seeking "to collect . . . multiple elements," in Hait's words,[38] Boyle wishes to compose a seamless and stable written history of herself, of McAlmon, and of her cohort. But any reading of such an essential component of American modernism truthful to the antagonistic spirit of modern art can only hope for an uneasy equilibrium between and within groups. In one gleaming flash of anger quoted above, Boyle reveals the spirit of a modernist movement marked by its own diversity and open to interrogation.

Boyle sees *Being Geniuses Together* as a dialogue with her dead friend, and Hait chooses to define its form as "dual autobiography."[39] Indeed, Boyle addresses McAlmon directly at places in the text. When writing of her determination to repay a loan of $250 given her by Harold Loeb's estranged wife, Marjorie, she admits, "All right, this was romanticizing, McAlmon. You would have known right off that the debt was never to be repaid" (BG40). While McAlmon and Boyle seldom contradict each other, and their voices never overlap, she chooses to reveal incidents from her life that illuminate salient aspects of his story, even avoiding material that "is only obliquely concerned with McAlmon" (BG294). She acknowledges that there are few direct comparisons to be made between their experiences, and "few parallels can be drawn between McAlmon's life and mine" (BG44). Still, Boyle arranges material to emphasize similarities, extending once more the sense of unity she wishes to maintain. Following the chapter in which McAlmon reveals that his overbearing mother-in-law, "starved for emotional outlet," would stand over his marriage bed "to see her darlings in bed together" (*BG*58), for example, Boyle reports that her own meddling father-in-law "would come on silent slippers into our room and close our windows against the treacherous night air of Brittany" (*BG*66).

Certainly, Boyle had a fraught relationship with life narrative. She leaves out details here when she believes readers can learn many of these things from her early fiction, especially when what happened to her "is only obliquely concerned with McAlmon" (*BG*294). She admits to having been contracted to ghostwrite the memoirs of Gladys Palmer, the Dayang Muda of Sarawak, a British aristocrat whose title came from marrying the brother of a British rajah in Borneo. *Relations and Complications* (1929) thus put forward "a life that had actually never been" its subject's, so that Boyle "reconstructed for her what had perhaps never taken place" (*BG*257–58). Boyle maintains at this point that autobiography "should be primarily a defense of those who have been unjustly dealt with in one's own time" (*BG*333), and she believes that through her actions McAlmon's literary reputation will be reinvigorated. "It is my hope that the present revision will do more than provide a deeply sympathetic portrait of a writer and publisher who deserves to be remembered for his unique qualities," she claims, "but that it will help to accord to Robert McAlmon his rightful and outstanding place in the history of the literary revolution of the early nineteen-twenties" (*BG*xi). Her earliest ambition was to give "daily allegiance to the words that others were able to set down, or to the musical notes that others were able to put on paper, or the brush strokes with which others would transform a canvas into history" (*BG*103). She repeats here Ernest Walsh's claim that she is best seen as "homage-giver to the great" (*BG*214), and she believes McAlmon is worthy of this treatment. *Being Geniuses Together* is intended, in part, to connect him with a modernist enterprise from which his own writing sought to effect distance. While McAlmon told Boyle that he hoped the "God-damned, fucking, quivering pieces" of his life she wished to collect should be left to "fall apart" (*BG*328), Boyle makes McAlmon a central figure of the Lost Generation. She cuts passages like McAlmon's confession that Djuna Barnes once exclaimed to him, angrily, "You know you hate my guts."[40] Instead, Boyle reports only that Katherine Mansfield thought McAlmon's writing "extraordinarily good"; she cites Ezra Pound's claim that the strength of McAlmon's work provided him with a reason "for starting" his literary magazine the *Exile*; she raises Ernest Walsh's assertion that McAlmon's writing excelled because it was effective in "contemplating all human-ity"; she quotes Katherine Anne Porter's admiration of McAlmon's "nice sour humour and sharpness of eye and the ability to size up people and situations" (*BG*104–5). In all these cases, Boyle places McAlmon among a group of writers she conjures up herself, and, in a gesture typical of the self-consciousness of modernism, she uses the testimonials of group members themselves to accomplish the feat.

The nature of autobiography is that it seeks, in part, to create a surface narrative to represent the essence of a life. The critical component of Boyle's textual practice recreates this narrative for McAlmon, revoicing his story on her terms. Perhaps the most in-teresting editing Boyle undertakes is in her treatment of McAlm-on's sexuality and his marriage to British poet Winifred Ellerman. A union of convenience between the homosexual McAlmon and the lover of American writer Hilda Doolittle, the true nature of their relationship is only hinted at by McAlmon. Biographer Joan Mellon goes to great lengths in speculating about the difficulties Boyle had in accepting her friend's sexuality. While she almost cer-tainly had hopes for a relationship with him herself while he lived, her trepidation in the 1960s was fueled, Mellon maintains, by her fears "that any admission of McAlmon's essential homosexuality would damage the reputation she was working so diligently to res-urrect."[41] Although Boyle stops well short of reporting slurs Ernest Hemingway apparently shot at McAlmon over his "old tricks"[42] with young men, for example, she acknowledges that McAlmon's sexuality was a topic of some interest to his contemporaries. With little precedent in the narrative and no further explanation, Boyle quotes Morley Callaghan's assertion that McAlmon "was willing to be interested in women" (*BG*184n), and she reports a corroborative conversation she had with writer Evelyn Scott.

> The first day she told me she had seen McAlmon the night
> before, and that she had known him in New York before his
> marriage, but that he was always alien and cold. Remote, like a
> homosexual, she said. No, I said; that I don't believe. She said she
> didn't believe it either, but she could find no explanation of why
> no fire was ever struck between them. . . . She wanted McAlmon
> to respond, she said; she wanted him to be seduced in the mind
> at least. She was asking surrender of him. (*BG*153)

Certainly, McAlmon was cagey about his preferences, never

pronouncing his sexuality publicly. He regales readers with stories of carousing "amid the clink of glasses, jazz music played badly by a French orchestra, the chatter and laughter of whores" where he dances with "Jeanette, a big draught horse of a girl," who "pranced about like a mare in heat and restrained no remark or impulse which came to her." But this relationship was mostly innocent, as Jeanette, "six foot and buxom," often "seemed not to realize I was there," he reports (*BG*28). Similarly, he proudly makes it known that Sylvia Gough, a South African woman often found at Ada "Bricktop" Smith's nightclub, proclaimed him "the only man who doesn't try to come to bed with me every time we get drunk together" (*BG*36). In this way, his writing follows conventions established by other expatriate Americans; after all, the excesses of life abroad were still often represented in popular accounts of "deviant" activity. Malcolm Cowley believed that their critics undertook "a general offensive . . . based on the theory that all modern writers, painters and musicians were homosexual."[43] Perhaps because of this, McAlmon is careful to make frequent, if chaste, references to women encountered during his nights on the town, passages faithfully preserved here by Kay Boyle.

When faced with the evidence of McAlmon's unconventional marriage and his close friendships with various men in Paris, however, Boyle has a dilemma. To include this material is to give evidence to those who would propagate what she describes as "filth about McAlmon";[44] to exclude this material is to acknowledge that there is a secret to keep. Sometimes, Boyle simply defers to McAlmon's own voice, quoting in one of her chapters, for example, his letter to William Carlos Williams in which he admits that his "marriage is legal only, unromantic, and strictly an agreement." He tells Williams, "You can use your imagination and perhaps know what I mean" (*BG*45). But her apparent willingness to ignore the possible implications of some other episodes allows Boyle to restore even some contentious passages that had been omitted from the first edition of McAlmon's autobiography. According to Michael Gnarowski, Boyle chanced to re-establish contact with Canadian writer John Glassco during the period in which she was revising the book.[45] Privately, Glassco claimed to have had an affair with McAlmon,[46] but no reference to him appeared in 1938. Confident, perhaps, in the knowledge she had carried on a relationship with Glassco, herself, Boyle reinserts here a number of references to him and Graeme Taylor, whom she describes as "McAlmon's two Canadian disciples" (*BG*294). McAlmon's restored account of the playful encounters between the three men, read now, contains a great deal of sexual ambiguity and even some mischievous irony:

> In Nice were two Canadian boys from Montreal whom I had known in Paris when they spent a year in the Quarter. They had discovered an Italian tea room *pension*, and the compact little apartment above it the proprietor let the three of us have, charging for it and the meals very low *pension* rates. The rooms faced the sea, and the beach was not a minute's walk away. We settled in, Buffy Glas[s]co and Graeme Taylor and I, and each of us writing. . . . The doorway between their room and mine was left open, and I could hear the clatter of typewriters, which helped me to work and to concentrate. (BG272–73)

While this passage is hardly as flamboyant as Glassco's assertion that McAlmon spent much of his time frolicking "in his B.V.D.'s" and wearing a hairnet while he wrote,[47] the absence of references to this trip to Nice reminds readers of the inevitable gap between events in McAlmon's life and their representation in *Being Geniuses Together*. "I read a great many travel books, biographies, autobiographies, and books of scientific adventure," McAlmon affirms. "It was not startling, it was pathetic rather, to note how differently from their conversation most authors presented themselves in writing" (BG198).

In his *Telling Lies in Modern American Autobiography*, Timothy Dow Adams points out that life narrative must always be understood as the play between "memory and imagination," an embellished story that is only ever "rooted in what really happened."[48] McAlmon's willingness to evade questions of his sexual orientation provides only the most blatant example of creating a fictive structure around which he, like those writers already considered, builds a version of his life. Even *Nightinghouls of Paris* (2007), described by editor Sanford Smoller as McAlmon's "thinly fictionalized" account of the time, is "perfectly direct about sexual couplings and uncouplings" of his friends while remaining "reticent about" his own affairs.[49] Strictly speaking, Boyle's retrospective is no more truthful, of course; she is mythologizing: "But how do I know that I am telling the truth now about what I believed and wanted then?" she frets (BG103). While McAlmon in the 1930s was being coy about events that had occurred over a period of fifteen years, Boyle is writing thirty years later under the weight of modernist immortality. She hopes to be true to an imagined "mural . . .

of such continuity that people would look on it for a long time to come as literary history" (*BG*175). *Being Geniuses Together* thus functions as her provisional rewriting of modernism, her attempt as a spokesperson for the Lost Generation to reaffirm the relevance of their work and draw connections between "our revolt and that of the young of 1968" (*BG*14). She believes "that young people in every generation, in every century, find themselves imprisoned" by social expectation "without honour and against their wills" (*BG*44). So, against the background of new literary insurrections that questioned the achievement of modernism, Boyle asserts that "the tumult of my spirit" shares "in the same history of protest that is being acted out by the tormented young today" (*BG*106). An instructor at San Francisco State University during the turbulent 1960s, Kay Boyle attempted to live her later years in keeping with those words, in fact, whether it was advocating on behalf of civil rights or marching against the Vietnam War.

An examination of *Being Geniuses Together* underlines the ways in which writing a community, charting the complex connections that may be used to discuss American expatriation between the World Wars, continued to be a gesture relevant to modernism itself. Read this way, Boyle's revision of McAlmon's autobiography fleshes out social context while seeking with a singularity of purpose to identify and connect figures that might constitute a group. Thus, a text like *Being Geniuses Together* attempts to obscure differences that, while obviously working against the creation of a homogenous movement Boyle desires, still remain central to the resistance at the heart of the modern project. While she was certainly guilty of attempting to minimize difference, it is her bold experimentation with the autobiographical form, ironically, that ties this narrative most closely to the spirit of the time about which she writes. By alternating McAlmon's text with her own, by subverting the voice of an apparently unwilling collaborator a decade after his death, Boyle questions the very nature of life narrative and shows the same boldness in an examination of literary form that gave life to the artistic experimentation rooted along Paris's Left Bank during the 1920s. By the time Boyle produced this text, however, much of this spirit was long extinguished. It was during the 1960s, as David Harvey has argued, that "counter-cultural . . . movements" defined themselves firmly as "anti-modernist." Modernism had been by this time aligned, definitively, with the establishment, and so what remained of modernism found itself assailed by the sorts of cultural protests in which Kay Boyle had involved herself. While Boyle attempted to connect the political action of the sixties with the artistic insurrection of the twenties, the "individualized self-realization" of the latter ran counter to the sort of rhetorical pulling together at the center of her text.[50] So if Boyle was less than successful in making relevant to her students the undertakings of the Lost Generation, the relentless fragmentation of her cohort, presaged in the work of Josephson and Hemingway, would soon come to define more recent rereadings of modernism, rereadings in which expatriate American autobiography would continue to play a role.

7

THE AFTERLIFE OF EXPATRIATE AMERICAN AUTOBIOGRAPHY

"The American twenties in Paris . . . was the decade when the idea of the American in Paris got fixed in the American imagination," Adam Gopnik maintains. "But, as with vineyards, it is stress that makes for flavor, and there is something disappointingly flabby and crowded about the endless number of memoirs of that time that bombard the reader, feeding, as they do, on each other. The Lost Generation, as it was called, was perhaps not lost enough."[1] Indeed, George Wickes pronounced the idea of "rootless expatriates of the lost generation" an "overworked subject" as early as 1969,[2] but subsequent decades still have seen no discernable falling off of interest in Americans abroad between the World Wars. Hugh Ford's influential *Left Bank Revisited* (1972) and *Published in Paris* (1975) appeared soon after Wickes's declaration, and *The Lost Generation Journal*, a scholarly periodical devoted to the subject of expatriation, was published throughout most of the 1970s. This period of academic inquiry culminated with the appearance of a volume in Gale Research's Dictionary of Literary Biography series edited by Karen Rood, *American Writers in Paris, 1920–1939* (1980). The 1980s and 1990s brought related monographs from, among others, Shari Benstock, Humphrey Carpenter, Marc Dolan, Noël Riley Fitch, Arlen Hansen, Donald Pizer, and J. Gerald Kennedy. *News of Paris* (2006), Ronald Weber's study of American journalists in France, reflects its author's belief that there persists today a need "to add to the familiar portrait of the expatriate period."[3] Curiously, perhaps, the first years of the twenty-first century have been especially fruitful for new inquiry, beginning with "Americans in Paris, Paris in Americans," an international conference sponsored by the city's Mona Bismarck Foundation in 2001. Reflecting Sophie Lévy's belief that "art from the interwar period" still "seems to fascinate and preoccupy art historians," the Musée d'Art Américaine Giverny sponsored in 2003 "A Transatlantic Avant-Garde: American Artists in Paris, 1918–1939," an exhibition of expatriate American visual pieces.[4] "In Paris, the American artists encountered the international avant-garde, and seeing their own art in relationship to a new context," Elizabeth Glassman argues in the preface to its catalogue, "they were able to affirm or reaffirm their artistic identity that was simultaneously modern and American." Thus, she maintains "that the American artists who traveled to and from France in the interwar period created works of art that contribute simultaneously to the history of the Parisian avant-garde and to the history of American art."[5] Reflecting the belief that expatriation itself played a fundamental role in the development of modernism, interest in the experience of Americans abroad has also not abated. New biographies of expatriates from Hart Crane to Peggy Guggenheim, Caresse Crosby to Ezra Pound have appeared since 2000. More surprisingly, perhaps, autobiographies have appeared posthumously from the mid-1980s onwards, contributing new voices to ongoing debates about the nature of modernism itself.

In his reading of the movement, political scientist Marshall Berman sees great continuity over the past two centuries of cultural production. While "the modern world has changed radically," Berman positions "the modernist" as a constant figure, "trying to survive and create in the maelstrom's midst." The artist of this period thus lives a "life of dialogue," a "keeping alive the bonds" with cultural production of the past, by which "modernist culture" endures and proliferates. The substance of a modernism understood this broadly is precisely those "scraps and tatters" that persist,[6] and critics who read any current relevance for the movement similarly emphasize diversity. This diversity, in turn, belies fears of an excluding colossus that accompanies what Fredric Jameson describes as modernism's "shift from an oppositional to a hegemonic position."[7] Peter Nicholls has most famously used the term "modernisms" to assert the kind of diversity Berman recognizes, to underline "a highly complex set of cultural developments" that define the art of the first half of the twentieth century.[8] While many expatriate American autobiographies emphasized a sense of unified community that runs counter to this reimagining of modernism, those published posthumously since the mid-1980s, interestingly, have largely sought instead to reflect greater diversity in defining the Lost Generation.

In his introduction to *The Norton Book of American Autobiography* (1999), Jay Parini reflects on the "open-ended" form of life narrative by reaffirming that, naturally, writers of autobiography "cannot be dead," though many seek "to achieve a kind of finality" in their works, nonetheless.[9] Ernest Hemingway may have been near death as he worked on *A Moveable Feast*, but his widow's subsequent handling of his manuscript illustrated the promise of an afterlife for expatriate American autobiography. Clearly, Hemingway's text was not the final word on Paris in the 1920s, and the work of editors has continued to make available to the reading public autobiographies like Gorham Munson's *The Awakening Twenties* (1985), Wambly Bald's *On the Left Bank* (1987), Waverley Root's *The Paris Edition* (1987), Eugene Jolas's *Man From Babel* (1998), and Maria Jolas's *Woman of Action* (2004). The appearance of these volumes attests to the faith readers continue to place in the truth of the narrated firsthand experiences of Americans abroad. This "authority of experience," as Sidonie Smith and Julia Watson have defined it, remains persuasive despite the broader skepticism of the veracity of autobiographical fact.[10] The "Publisher's Note" to Munson's *The Awakening Twenties*, for example, proclaims the manuscript its author left at the time of his death in 1969 "a near-flawless study of a fascinating period in literary history, written from the unique perspective of a participant-observer whose craft, indeed whose very life, was language, the written word." By "serving as proxy for the author," Munson's widow Elizabeth Delza edited the text "without sacrificing its heart or losing the powerful presence of its author." While the examination of the editorial practices of Mary Welsh Hemingway and Kay Boyle brings into question any claim that *The Awakening Twenties* represents definitively Gorham Munson's "voice," an account that is the embodiment of "his spirit" still provides an important supplementary account of the Lost Generation.[11]

Munson launched the little magazine *Secession* while abroad, hoping that his "*tendenz* review" would help "concentrate the new impulses" of writers like Malcolm Cowley, Hart Crane, Matthew Josephson, Marianne Moore, and Yvor Winters (*AT* 162). But what might readers make of Wambly Bald, a columnist and proofreader at the Paris *Tribune*? Benjamin Franklin V, who edited *On the Left Bank*, claims that the newspaper clippings collected here depict the "less well known . . . artistic Paris" of the early 1930s, "with such verve, such style, such vividness," though in contrast to the columns of Janet Flanner, for example, these writings may be of less interest as autobiography, as Bald himself appears "unimportant to the reader of his column, except as its author, as the voice that relates the events."[12] Waverley Root, another *Tribune* staffer, began his autobiography "in self-defense" according to editor Samuel Abt, as he worried that others might continue to use his stories as "source material." Root acknowledges, "About the interest in the Paris of the 1920s and 1930s—it seems to come in waves. I am conscious of this because everybody who wants to write anything about that period seems to come to me, as one of the last survivors, for information."[13] Andreas Kramer and Ranier Rumold, however, undertook an edition of *Man from Babel* because they believed that "literary posterity has hardly registered Eugene Jolas's remarkable accomplishments." Indeed, these editors hoped to effect "a re-evaluation of the moral dimension of modernism," finding in Jolas's experiences "popular and provincial energies" that contradict the elitism of the movement.[14] But by publishing an edition of his wife's *Woman of Action*, Mary Ann Caws hoped to show Maria Jolas as a "heroic figure" in her own right, her story "effaced" though it may have been "behind that of her colorful husband and their famous friends."[15] In each of these cases, editors and publishers have judged that the stories these expatriates tell about themselves and the people they encounter in Europe may challenge our conceptions of life abroad in the 1920s and 1930s. Beyond complementing, and sometimes contradicting, other stories of expatriation, however, these accounts often refute the aloofness that, for many people, remains a hallmark of modernism. As Sean Latham reaffirms, "modernism has thrived on a smug sense of cultured superiority," but the posthumous stories of these expatriate Americans seek instead to reconnect their experience to "the tastes and expectations of the general reading public"[16] and thus define the enduring value of modernism by emphasizing the continuing relevance of modernist experience instead of the autonomy of its art.

The nearly two hundred weekly installments of Wambly Bald's "La Vie de Bohème" provided one of the "most closely followed features" in the Paris *Tribune*. From October 1929 to July 1933, his view of expatriation was, as Ronald Weber describes it, a "scatter-shot collection of Left Bank reporting, gossip, barbs, and publicity blurbs . . . finely attuned to the paper's audience, wastrel or otherwise." A trained journalist, Bald had shipped out of New Orleans as a seaman, stopping in France only after discovering for himself the joys of life as an American in Paris.[17] It was, perhaps, because he brought to the *Tribune* this varied background that his contributions captured "a picture, a mood, a sense of personality and time and place," according to the editor of *On the Left Bank*. "Bald knew and wrote about the personalities who congregated in or visited Montparnasse," Benjamin Franklin attests. And the particular value of these columns for revisions of expatriate life is that they highlight "the less exalted, the regulars of Montparnasse, the people who created and promoted the new, which did not always become the lasting" (*LB*xiii). "La Vie de Bohème" announces, for example, a "recent vacation at the American Hospital" for the novelist Michael Arlen, who described his illness simply as "a trifling nuisance" and "an interruption in my work" (*LB*9). Bald marks the arrival on the Left Bank of Bob Brown's so-called reading machine, by which writers seemed ready to embrace a new mechanization in their art. "The idea of the 'readies' is to publish books in microscopic type on a tape measure controlled by an electric motor," he explains. "A magnifying glass enlarges the words as they roll through the machine. The purpose is to save time and space, and Bob thinks that a library can thus be carried in a small suitcase" (*LB*67). Bald foreshadows the tragic death of Ralph Cheever Dunning, Ezra Pound's doomed protégé who starved to death in his "precarious" apartment on the Notre Dame des Champs. "He is seldom seen at the Dôme; he prefers to hug his coal-burner, read the Upanishads, and dream," Bald reports (*LB*12). The reader here meets nonsense poet Abraham Lincoln Gillespie, whose decade-long struggle for fame culminated with a speech at the Chateau Madrid in Cannes. "Everyone applauded but no one knew what he was talking about," Bald records, "because words are juicy things and Link is capable of squirting the juice with more abandon than most of his contemporaries" (*LB*24). When Gillespie returns to the United States in 1932, "La Vie de Bohème" laments his departure by quoting his line "ghoubrel / i shing my ostracization / come back!" while describing how the poet "astonished strangers by squirting seltzer at them if they didn't like his poetry" (*LB*99). Julien Green, once acclaimed as a novelist, appears only as a "popular Montparnassian" (*LB*4). Before his novels colored Paris of the 1930s, Henry Miller is described as "a legitimate child of Montparnasse, the salt of the Quarter." As Bald describes him, "He is never definite. Miller has been out of a job for some time and he hasn't a cent. But he's lucky. He has friends. They always take care of him" (*LB*77–78). The selection of columns thus anthologized in *On* *the Left Bank* provides offbeat views of both the famous and the forgotten, but the intimate knowledge of their lives read on the pages of the *Tribune* seems like the views of a perceptive outsider.

Throughout *The Paris Edition*, however, Waverley Root positions himself consciously as an outsider, asserting an objectivity similar to Janet Flanner's in her "Paris Letter." He sees expatriate Americans in Paris as forming "an enclave" from which he was able to maintain some distance (*PE*161). Its heart "was centered on the café terrace, and the personal relationships that were built up there were the products of long hours of café sitting." And as a working newspaperman, he claims, "I didn't have time for this" (*PE*13). While Root sought to avoid the kinds of literary friendships from which many stories of the Lost Generation were fashioned, he still concedes that "an interlocking society" emerged along the Left Bank. "If everybody didn't know everybody else," he observes, "everybody at least knew about everybody else" (*PE*15). Though he shares his views of Paris on this basis, any rereading of these opinions serves only to confirm the judgments he made in the 1920s and 1930s. As he did then, Root looks here to diminish figures central to understandings of expatriation that had begun to take hold even as he edited copy on the *Tribune*. As "every other young American with any interest in cultural matters" (*PE*115), Root had heard of Harold Stearns years before he arrived in Paris in 1927, but he finds the principal expatriate intellectual "a master of the art of silence" whose "spark" of intelligence was "no longer operating" (*PE*117). He was no more in awe of the reputation grown up around the author of *The Sun Also Rises*. "The first question asked, inevitably, of anyone who lived in Paris during the 1920s and 1930s," according to Root, "is 'Did you know Ernest Hemingway?'... The invariable answer, whether it is true or not, is 'Yes.' Nobody wants to admit that he was on the spot and did not know Hemingway" (*PE*12).

As it appears in *The Paris Edition*, the Lost Generation is as much a confluence of *Tribune* staffers as it was of major literary figures. Indeed, Root returns on a number of occasions to his longstanding criticism of Gertrude Stein and the program of *transition* magazine, even though critical opinion had long ago turned against him. He had been a vocal opponent of Stein's linguistic experiments, and his position did not soften after the commercial success of *The Autobiography of Alice B. Toklas*. "It would have been my opinion that if Gertrude Stein was leading young writers anywhere," he maintains, "it was up a blind alley" (*PE*42). Still, Root argues here, in fact, that such views were not "particularly unfair" to her. "Gertrude Stein did indeed have a gift for putting together sentences so concise and so spare that they fall from the page with the thump of the inevitable," he maintains. "She possessed a recognizably true style, by which I mean one that is distinguished not merely by a pattern of writing, which is ornamental, but by a pattern of thinking, which is structure." The "beat" she worked so hard to create generally "serves no good purpose," and the related austerity seemed only to have instructed Ernest Hemingway (*PE*39). Similarly, Root criticized what he viewed as a cynical veneration of opacity in *transition*, serializing James Joyce's *Finnegans Wake* as "Work in Progress." At the time, he contributed terse letters of dissent to the magazine; in his autobiography, he calls the underlying principles of its editors "doctrinaire ideologies, artificial theories, and empty manifestos" (*PE*136).

Despite the ruthless tone with which Waverley Root conducts this reassessment of American expatriation, the desire to answer existing accounts of the Lost Generation is best represented by Gorham Munson's *The Awakening Twenties*. Writing near the end of his life, Munson would have read more than thirty years' worth of secondhand accounts of the twelve months he spent in Europe during the early 1920s. It is impossible, according to Munson, to "get the whole story" of life abroad "from *The Way It Was* by Harold Loeb, *Life among the Surrealists* by Matthew Josephson, and *Exile's Return* by Malcolm Cowley" (*AT*171). While he hoped his text would provide "a sufficiently coherent account of the creative sources of the decade" (*AT*xv), Munson's primary concern is with the record of the collapse of his expatriate journal *Secession*. Munson was almost immediately homesick after he left New York in July 1921, and he was back in the United States before the publication of the third number of the magazine in August 1922. *Secession* could be published for twenty dollars a number in Europe, but to bring the operation home to print its five hundred copies would have cost him many times more. By collaborating with Matthew Josephson, Munson hoped to be able to continue printing abroad, but editorial clashes exacerbated by the distance led to the eventual "hijacking" of *Secession*, as he characterizes it, by Josephson, Malcolm Cowley, and John Wheelwright (*AT*171). Having eventually regained control of the magazine, Munson completed its run with its eighth number in April 1924.

These events, as was the case with the majority of expatriate undertakings, were marked for him by "arrogant juvenility." Munson opines, "Perhaps that is why I cannot, in the manner of several chroniclers of the early jazz age, review my immersion in it with romantic regret over time's passing. The period was something to be outgrown" (*AT*169). According to Malcolm Cowley, returned expatriates at the end of 1923 tried to merge their talents at "a catholic meeting" in New York, but the assembled group failed to "preserve the decorum customary in an Italian speakeasy."[18] The flashpoint seemed to have been a critical letter sent by Munson from Woodstock, "unusually well written for him," according to Harold Loeb.[19] It is only in the 1951 edition of *Exile's Return* that Cowley revealed the unfortunate postscript to the gathering: Josephson marched upstate so he and Munson could settle matters "with their fists." Cowley was not present, but he reported secondhand accounts of "a dull spectacle, a war fought horizontally more than vertically."[20] Matthew Josephson wrote in *Life among the Surrealists* that a "very fat" Munson had "fists . . . like pillows." Josephson's account of the pitiable altercation ennobled neither the combatants nor the issues that estranged them. "The slow-moving Munson, after a few exchanges, clinched with me and we fell to the wet ground, rolling about a while and becoming well covered with mud," he reports. "I struggled to break from him. We were both out of breath as we got to our feet and could scarcely swing at each other." Apparently unfazed by the "flabby blows" he received, Josephson believed himself to have been "sitting on Munson's chest" by the conclusion of the mêlée.[21]

Munson objects to his characterization in Cowley and Loeb's autobiographies, but he is particularly galled by Josephson's view of him as "a priceless comic figure of the literary scene in that period."[22] Munson writes, "I shall not clutter this narrative with corrections of earlier errors," but he still hopes to provide in *The Awakening Twenties* all that is "essential and relevant" in differentiating between the sundry personalities that characterized American life abroad during the decade (*AT*171). While there is little chance that readers could ever mitigate the differences that divided expatriates, Munson hopes through his account of the "scuffle," best described as "a scene in the theatre of the absurd," to disparage the legacy of the expatriate experience itself (*AT*185). "Most of the American expatriates were," after all, "minor writers—very minor," according to Munson (*AT*158). Josephson identified himself as an American Dadaist, and as Munson understands it, their fight represented Josephson's "significant gesture," the transplanting of avant-garde antagonism to American soil. Munson's description of the imbroglio thus seeks to refute the potency of Josephson's dissent:

The encounter was more nearly a scuffle than a fight. Its high point—or better, the low point since it occurred on the ground—was reached when the Dadaist lay supine under the rump of the Secessionist, his body writhing beneath the weight of a convalescent who had been on a building-up diet for six weeks, his arms pinioned by the knees of his critic, the dampness of the ground chilling his temper. "Let me up" was the manifesto of the upsetting moment in the history of American Dadaism when instead of Dada attaining to its apex, the movement's chief was thrown struggling beneath the podex of the opposition. (*AT*185)

The significance of expatriation thus dissolved into farce among the muddy surroundings of Woodstock, long before the Lost Generation had even asserted itself in *The Sun Also Rises*.

If expatriation was, for Munson, an adolescent rite of passage beyond which young Americans had to move, he is still interested in revisiting the familiar question of the motivations that took those Americans abroad in the first place. He cites the familiar influence of Harold Stearns, whose command "to get the hell out of his brazen country" helped Munson and his wife decide in July 1921 to use their "savings from a year of school teaching" to go to Europe to take advantage of "the advantageous exchange-rates for the dollar." But Stearns was "already bankrupt in ideas" before he reached Paris (*AT*158–59), and so Munson looks to the work of progressive essayist Randolph Bourne for a more reputable influence behind the expatriate impulse. As a contemporary of T. S. Eliot and Ezra Pound who undertook but a brief tour of Europe on a visiting fellowship from Columbia University, Bourne could not be seen as an American in Paris, of course, though Munson traces his influence in the desire of young writers "to battle . . . the standard of the genteel generation" (*AT*31). Suffering perpetually frail health, Bourne died in the Spanish influenza outbreak of 1918, but Munson sees him as "youth's partisan in the generational conflict" that defined Greenwich Village's intellectual life after the First World War (*AT*23). He sought "to perform surgery on the colonial attitudes of America" by promoting a "cosmopolitanism" (*AT*28) expatriates soon embraced by taking up "the adventure of life" (*AT*32). The precedent they set in the early 1920s gave rise to greater diversity in American art later in the decade.

Some people like Waverley Root made the decision to go abroad impulsively. "About eight o'clock one evening in April 1927 it occurred to me that I was out of job, that I had little money, and that I had long wanted to go to France," he reflects glibly. "At noon the next day I was aboard the S. S. *President Harding* steaming down the Hudson, outwardbound. I had no definite plans" (*PE*3). Having arrived in Paris, Root experienced "an interlocking society" of expatriates that fed developing myths of a cohesive life abroad. "It was difficult to disentangle those you knew at firsthand because you had talked to them, knowingly, face to face, from those you knew at secondhand, because somebody else had talked to you about them," he claims (*PE*14–15). Still, the advantages of expatriation in "the capital of nonconformism" were genuine. "Paris was a city in which the expression of all ideas was permissible, at least in the part of its society that I entered," he explains. "There was no dominant body of public opinion so sure of its own standards that it dared tell everybody else what to think. This nearly complete tolerance and freedom often led to extravagance, but extravagance was more interesting than well-worn ruts." While Root did not leave the United States with a sense of disillusionment, he still discovered surroundings that caused him to question all he had learned at home. "Everything of intellectual importance was happening in Paris and I was privileged to be occupying a ringside seat at its immense cultural circus," he continues. "Paris was open to all ideas, to all opinions, to every mode of thinking. That is why we were all happy there" (*PE*124–25).

Some other paths to the Left Bank were more circuitous. Maria Jolas first traveled abroad before the outbreak of the First World War. A young woman from the southern United States who had already turned twenty, she was expected by that time to "have been married and starting to raise a family" (*WA*49). Instead, she went to Berlin at the end of 1913 in hopes of studying voice. "I was carrying no passport, no identity papers of any kind, in fact, except a steamship ticket made out in my name," she marvels at the informality of foreign travel, experienced even in the shadow of war (*WA*55). While her musical training went slowly, she enjoyed her first experiences in Europe, discovering for herself a fascination with language that would come to define the modernist experience. "Principally, however, the sound of the new language was both exciting and frustrating," she admits. She sought opportunities to hear German particularly "well spoken" and followed her interest to attend services at the neighborhood church. "The sermons particularly, which were long and earnest, I simply let drench me, until gradually certain words," as she describes the experience, "began to have meaning for me" (*WA*57–58). She returned to her family home in Louisville, Kentucky, in June 1914, and what began as a summer vacation extended five years because of the war. Europe, torn by the conflict, was changed in the popular American imagination. Suddenly, it was known simply as "over there," a continent "of blood and mud" rather than the site of cultural enlightenment. "It was a culturally bleak moment in the United States," she asserts. "My political confusion was great" (*WA*64).

Soon after her return, Jolas moved to New York to continue her education and took there a job with Charles Scribner and Sons. This first contact with the publishing industry foreshadowed later work among expatriate Americans. In September 1919, she followed abroad her voice teacher Giulia Valda, beginning a "new life in Paris" at twenty-six, "finally an adult" (*WA*65). If expatriation was thus an act of self-realization for Maria Jolas, traveling to Europe was a journey of self-discovery for the man she would marry. Born to immigrant parents in New Jersey, Eugene Jolas was actually raised in Alsace-Lorraine, "an American in exile, in the hybrid world of the Franco-German frontier" (*MB*5). He eventually experienced his country in the years before the First World War in the same manner as did first-generation Americans. "The thought came to me with explosive force that I was returning to my native land, a land whose language I did not know, a land whose customs were alien to me, but whose wonders I was eager to explore," he exclaims. "However much of a greenhorn I might seem, paradoxically, I was coming home" (*MB*18). Eventually, he was drafted into the military, and while he never saw combat, the shared experience helped effect his "Americanization" (*MB*32). Thus, his decision to travel abroad in the early 1920s was also an expatriation, though the impulse was stirred in him through contact with his family. "Letters from Europe were becoming more frequent and their contents seemed more real to me," Eugene Jolas explains. "They spoke of the latest metamorphosis of the frontier, the new conflicts, the liberation from German militarism. Passing by a steamship agency one day, I stopped to look at pictures of boats and harbors. I was lured by an unnamed desire" (*MB*51). Other hopeful American writers felt "the emotional pull of the European world," but none shared his experience of "always pendulating between the two continents" (*MB*2). He saw his time in Paris as an opportunity "to serve as interpreter of European civilization to my native America and of American culture to Europe" (*MB*65). While he acknowledged that "many of the writers, painters and musicians who had fled from prohibition and Babbittism felt they were engaged in a conscious revolt against their native land," he bristled at the resulting "exaggerated admiration for all things European." In fact, oft-repeated "cultured clichés about Continental superiority over America" gave rise to "angry outbursts" from Eugene Jolas, whose "American nostalgia" went unabated (*MB*117).

Because of the somewhat unusual circumstances surrounding their expatriation, perhaps, the autobiographical records left by the Jolases contribute a great deal of additional color to readers' understanding of American experiences abroad. Maria Jolas first boarded with a Madame Langlois in the seventeenth arrondissement, her house "a barely furnished, make-do gamble" to make money from paying guests. "However, I was so happy to be in Paris, to be taking in once more a new city and a new language," she writes, "that its bareness and the need to buy an oil-burning stove and fetch the oil myself, in order to keep warm and have warm water to wash in, did not seem a hardship" (*WA*66). The younger of the two Langlois daughters whose acquaintance she made "was dowdy and lived in her mother's uncomfortable boarding-house," while "the other was elegant and lived elsewhere," in what is described as a "mutually acceptable and usually impermanent arrangement that existed between French men with money and women with none." While Jolas was expected to accept this "social institution," the basic concern she showed for the well-being of the Langlois's servant, the "slavey" Berthe, was seen as a far more serious "indiscretion" for a woman of her social standing (*WA*67–68). Similarly inexplicable behavior for the well-cultured was an evening of voyeurism at a French brothel arranged by Madeleine Boyd, wife of American critic Ernest Boyd, apparently "sophisticated entertainment" interpreted by Jolas as a "tasteless practical joke" (*WA*70–71). Single until her early thirties, she eventually inherited a portion of her father's estate, and this afforded her the "complete independence" to keep for the rest of her life a degree of the autonomy that so far had kept her from marrying any of the young men of her acquaintance. "And I am inclined to think that this mutual lack of attraction," she suggests further, "in addition to what is quaintly described as 'late flowering,' was also due to my desire for independent action and thought, which may well have frightened off most of the young men of my generation." But Eugene Jolas, on the other hand, was someone "whose mind and heart" she "immediately respected and loved." She judged that "he had the strengths" that she "lacked," but she, too, similarly "complemented" him. "I would fit my life to Gene's," she concludes simply (*WA*76–77).

The changing circumstances of her personal life came, then,

to match her wonder at her surroundings. Life abroad opened her mind to new arts. "Thus far my aesthetic surroundings had been confined to music and literature. Now I was acquiring an entirely new vocabulary, words whose English equivalents I had not yet used, and which opened up for me new avenues of sensibility, accessible this time, through the eye," she enthuses. "That in itself was exciting: learning to read what a painter or a sculptor had expressed, to recognize the artist's personality as one would a handwriting or a tone of voice." But she attributed this growth to the influence of her adopted city. "And I became convinced that in a city like Paris—does there exist another such city?—where the visual arts have flourished for so many centuries," she continues, "even the most insensitive eye would eventually see forms and colours with increased awareness. It is not for nothing that Paris has been called the painter's city" (*WA*73). Before the end of the 1920s, however, the Jolases left the city to rent an old hunting lodge in Colombey-les-deux-Eglises, a dwelling later bought by Charles de Gaulle. "The house stood in a clearing facing the village," Maria Jolas remembers, capturing the spirit of the pastoral retreat. "Behind the house was a wide open space of lawn with a few fruit trees, and up above, along the highroad wall, an avenue of lilac bushes. Close to the other end of the house, to break the wind from across a wide, sparsely populated valley, there was another cluster of tall old trees" (*WA*88). Surrounded here by local farmers who "lived in a machineless age," working "their fields and vineyards with the same stubborn love of the loam which their ancestors had shown," Eugene Jolas recalls, expatriate Americans edited a magazine that nurtured international writers of a burgeoning modern literature. Everyone from Gottfried Benn to James Joyce, André Breton to Gertrude Stein, Hart Crane to Tristan Tzara appeared on the pages of *transition*. On the weekends, the Jolases' country house filled with an equally impressive collection of Americans in Europe, including coeditor Elliot Paul, escaping Paris so as "to forget for a while the dynamo-whirl of the capital" (*MB*95).

It was ironic, therefore, that the decision the Jolases made to leave the city was a reaction to the "alarming amount of social activity" necessary to bring out the magazine. Its Paris base was "a modest hotel on the Place des Invalides," as Jolas describes it. "Our 'offices,' as Paul used to call our cluttered-up ex-bedroom (complete with all French plumbing features)," he continues, "were eventually to become the mecca of the numerous manuscript-laden 'exiled' writers from every state in the Union" (*MB*87–88). But it was James

Joyce, whose *Finnegans Wake* appeared in *transition*, who was their "bellwether." His "colossal elegy to the night-mind" embodied the experimentation with language Jolas hoped would bring "a polysynthetic quality" to English (*MB*89, 96). Lest anyone think Joyce was systematic in this undertaking, Jolas assures his readers that the author "would improvise whenever something particularly interesting occurred to him during the reading" of his proofs, "and occasionally even allow a *coquille*—a typographical error—to stand, if it seemed to satisfy his encyclopedic mind, or appeal to his sense of grotesque hazard." Jolas's provincial French printer was frustrated by Joyce's endless emendations, seemingly nonsensical changes that could double the length of the proofs, sometimes telephoned from Paris. "Often, however, his last-minute additions really taxed the patience of the excitable Monsieur Noël. 'Joyce, alors!' he would shout," as Jolas describes the reaction, "while the editors kept discreetly silent. Joyce chuckled when I told him that his name was being used as an objurgation." There was thus nothing uncanny about the creation of *Finnegans Wake*, and Joyce's worried response to the early reception of his work similarly contradicts assumptions about modernism's remoteness. "He was very anxious to have people like the work," Jolas reports, "and seemed astonished that the first reactions were for the most part negative in tone. He would look carefully over the list of our subscribers in France, England, Ireland and the United States, and sometimes suggest names for circulation." Indeed, it was "at Joyce's suggestion" that *transition* began a series of "interpretative" works explaining Joyce's new technique, published as *Our Exagmination Round His Factification for Incamination of a Work in Progress* (1929) by Sylvia Beach's Shakespeare and Company (*MB*99–100).

This level of detail also defines Waverley Root's *The Paris Edition*. He gives, for example, an unusually thorough account of his transatlantic voyage aboard the *President Harding*. "I often stayed on deck until late at night. As it grew dark, the black water seemed to rise about the flanks of the ship until I felt that I could dip my fingers into it if I put my arm over the side," he describes. "It was on this first Atlantic crossing that I saw an iceberg gleaming majestically white in the distance; a whale spouting a few rods from the ship; flying fish skimming just above the waves; and several times porpoises leaping along beside us, happy for our company" (*PE*5). He found travel by sea a particularly apt means of escape from his life in the United States. "The great charm of ocean travel in those days was its complete detachment from the world and its worries," Root explains. "From the moment you lost sight of land, you belonged to a self-sufficient universe within which nothing could go wrong." This isolated environment rendered him from his old life to a life of new possibilities:

> You experienced, suddenly, a great lightening of heart, a feeling of complete liberty, unthinkable on land, where you could move in the direction of trouble and were frequently forced, by one form of pressure or another, to do so. At sea you were being moved inexorably toward your destination with no possibility of exchanging it by the exercise of volition. It proved pleasant to give volition a rest. No matter what disaster might occur behind you, on land, you could do nothing about it; you were therefore relieved of all responsibility. (*PE6*)

The carefree attitude engendered on the ship flowered in Paris itself. "I was blinded by the brilliance of a city that presented itself like a rapid succession of explosions of light too bright to illuminate the objects on which it fell, demanding exclusive attention to itself, like fireworks," he enthuses. "I wandered through Paris in a dream, incapable of paying attention to people—I was soaking up the city like a sponge and with just about a sponge's capacity of comprehension" (*PE12–13*).

But these remembrances do not always run so poetic. No expatriate American autobiography of the period speaks with such frankness about sex, certainly. Hérol Egan, the sports editor of the Paris *Tribune*, a native of the state of Texas, describes here to Root his assignations as "the daily grind," walking "over to the nearby Luxembourg Gardens, selecting one of the women sunning themselves there and leading her back to his newly abandoned bed." Few of the women there were "professionals"; they "were there for sex also," simply "players of the same sport" as Root's colleague (*PE146*). "There were plenty of warmhearted amateurs about," Root boasts, "and it was our opinion that it was as unnecessary to pay for love as to pay for breathing." But this is not to suggest that expatriate Americans never brokered time with prostitutes. Readers are first introduced to the Chabanais, for example, "then the most celebrated bordello in Paris." As it was "too expensive" for all but the aristocracy, expatriate Americans called at other "*maisons closes*" (*PE126*). It was in such an establishment Root first saw "a room that not only had all its walls covered with mirrors but even had one on the ceiling." In places of "respectability and refinement," clients chose from among "boarders" by viewing photographs;

only in houses "well down the ladder" were men "ushered straight into a large public room filled with girls" (PE127). The modest Root claims, "It was rare for any of us to go upstairs. I succumbed only once myself, when a girl with whom I was talking proved to be irresistibly seductive." Visits to these establishments were most popular with American tourists. Root and his colleagues often frequented two establishments, "one in the rue Blondel and the other in the rue Ste. Apolline," where "most of the girls . . . wore nothing but shoes." While these clubs were fine for expatriate drinking and "ogling," activities not always undertaken in that order, some of the recent arrivals who demanded a tour of these entertainments preferred something more upscale (PE128). Fortunately for them, the Sphinx opened on the rue Edgar-Quinet in the mid-1930s, "a model of modernity, spotless and blazing with light, teeming with healthy girls." Here, visitors could be introduced to "the wickedness of Paris in a tolerable degree," Root judges. "I even took my wife along on some excursions to the Sphinx" (PE130–31).

When the subject matter makes such careful frankness less important, Root still describes his surroundings in a most exacting detail. He discusses eating at Gillotte's, an unassuming establishment that distinguished itself at a time "when one ate well at all levels, even the humblest." If diners were seeking "truffles and foie gras," there was little to satisfy at Gillotte's; however, it did feature "hearty French home cooking, *la cuisine bourgeoise*," valued even by taxi drivers who were "comparatively free to roam in search of fodder" throughout Paris (PE107). "Gillotte's was open twenty-three hours out of twenty-four, closing from four to five in the morning," he explains, "and probably would never have closed at all if the license fee for round-the-clock cafés had not been something like double that for places that took at least an hour off" (PE111). He is similarly meticulous in his discussion of lodging. At the Hôtel de Lisbonne, "a picturesque if squalid place . . . at the corner of the rue Monsieur-le-Prince and the rue de Vaugirard" (PE97), entrance was granted through a central courtyard where guests were forced "to keep to its center" while they passed because "lodgers had a habit of disposing of waste, of whatever kind, by tossing it out the window." There were no private baths, "but every room had a washbowl with running water." No other expatriate American autobiography concerns itself with the perils of using a "Turkish toilet," with its hole in the floor "and two islands on either side of it designed to provide standing room for the feet." In fact, Root complains, the "inrush of water" was always so severe that it was impossible for him to get "off the islands onto the mainland before the tide reached the ankle-tops." But if Root suffered these indignities, he also found at the Hôtel de Lisbonne the unusual "luxury" of central heating, in addition to the high ceilings and large bookcases that gave his room "a feeling of spaciousness." In the final analysis, however, the monthly rent of ten dollars may have been the hotel's most appealing feature: his average salary in the late 1920s was but thirty dollars a fortnight (*PE*98–99).

Eventually, Root settled on a studio apartment that cost sixteen dollars a month, up six flights of stairs in a building on the rue de l'Ancienne Comédie. But while he admits that "the cold calculating eyes of real estate men would have been seen as making it less valuable" than his old digs, he was more happy there than in any other residence because of its redeeming charm.

> Picturesqueness! The place was steeped in it. It was not an ordinary apartment, but an artist's studio, with one wall almost all glass, an authentic artist's skylight even though it faced west, not north. From it I looked over the rooftops of Paris with, in the foreground, the perfectly proportioned old stone tower of St. Germain des Prés and, in the background, the Eiffel Tower. The view from the bedroom window was even better. It commanded one of the oldest parts of Paris, whose roofs in 1927 still looked like those of a village, covered with red tiles and bristling with chimneys, each enclosing a tight bundle of pale red tubes, one for each fireplace. The houses were clustered around narrow winding medieval streets. The backdrop was the cathedral of Notre Dame. (*PE*101)

Indeed, these moments of wistfulness always balance Root's cynicism. He remembers the open markets where fresh food was brought to Paris by "horse-drawn farm carts," for example, but he contrasts this image with the "phalanxes of trucks" that blocked city streets by the 1950s (*PE*104). Still, he is mindful of the deviousness of nostalgia. Before he ever set foot in the city, he was enchanted by the stories of Paris told him by Courtney Bruerton, his French professor at Tufts University, of standing "at the window of his hotel in the rue des Beaux-Arts" and watching "the art students returning from the Bal des Quat'z-Arts in the early morning, carrying their naked models on their shoulders." But this turns out not to be all it was supposed to be. "When I inspected the same scene some years later," Root discovers, "I decided that if Professor Bruerton had really viewed this spectacle from his hotel window, he must have used a telescope" (*PE*3).

As these remembrances make the expatriate experience more accessible to contemporary readers, as they make the world to which modernists responded more comfortably familiar, they thus question the aloofness of which modernism is commonly accused. But the most effective challenge to the elitism of the movement is the connection traced between modernism and mass culture through art's roots in the popular press. As John Carey argues so effectively, newspapers were anathema to the elitist tendencies of the movement by threatening "an alternative culture" that disseminated information to its readers without "the traditional cultural élite" shaping its message.[23] If Bravig Imbs's *Confessions of Another Young Man* established a paradigm by which marginal writers of the modern period might attempt to connect themselves to a modernist nobility, later autobiographies go so far as to reverse this pattern by connecting expatriate Americans to popular culture. Certainly, Hugh Ford points out that the Paris *Tribune* originally brought to its readers "the activities of the cultural adventurists from America . . . who were turning the old Latin Quarter of Montparnasse into an artistic and social *pied-à-terre*." But, over time, the paper "annexed (or was annexed by) the Left Bank, or Latin Quarter, or Montparnasse," as "*Tribune* managing editors sometimes hired and fired" expatriates "with monotonous regularity" while enduring "their eccentric behavior—up to a point."[24] These most recent stories of the Lost Generation examined here emphasize similarly how American expatriation became entwined with a decidedly populist form, and how newspaper work thus fed the impulses that helped shape modernism itself.

"The Paris *Tribune* had its origin in the *Chicago Tribune*'s Army Edition," as Ronald Weber explains it, "launched in Paris with patriotic pride on July 4, 1917, and directed to the American Expeditionary Forces that had joined the European War."[25] But publisher Robert McCormick decided not to disband the paper after the armistice. "Without missing a day," Waverley Root marvels, "the army edition" of the paper gave way to its "European edition" (*PE*51). To rival the Paris *Herald*, in hopes of furthering his business and political ambitions, the eccentric McCormick ran what was known as "the poorest-paying paper" in the city (*PE*22). Though it was never wildly profitable at any point before its eventual demise in 1934, Weber still finds it "a familiar feature of expatriate life" with its "restless collection of drifters, literary hopefuls, and able professionals."[26] Root calls the paper "a cultural phenomenon" (*PE*52), and by the time the operation was sold to the *New York Herald*, its circulation had grown to twenty-five thousand copies, surpassing its rivals (*PE*201).

In Paris without a job, Root first sought work at the well-heeled *Herald*, but like most expatriates he found a warmer welcome for him at the *Tribune*. After all, this was the outfit that sheltered a dissolute Harold Stearns and gave a translating job to Bravig Imbs, though the latter knew no French. Working initially with the day staff, Root drew impressions of the paper's offices on the rue Lamartine that stressed the informality of the operation. Walking through the door for his first shift, he ducked "just in time to escape an unidentified flying object hurtling down" the staircase. What he encountered was "a laborsaving device" rigged from a "wicker wastebasket" and a long rope, for the benefit of the staff of a French newspaper with offices above those of the *Tribune*. "To save themselves the effort of walking down six flights of stairs to pick up mail, newspapers, or other deliveries and then toiling up again," he explains, "*Paris-Midi* had improvised a dumbwaiter from a wastebasket on a long rope, which was tossed into the void of stairway and hauled up again from time to time with the catch" (*PE*22). Similarly haphazard was the manner in which the *Tribune* day staff gathered news stories, "on a large spike placed in the center of the copydesk for the inspection of the night staff." It is these men who "decide whether to use the story and what prominence to give it, or even to have it rewritten by more competent journalists," and very quickly Root joined them in creating the "daily miracle," as expatriate Whit Burnett coined it. From chaos, seemingly, a paper emerged each morning "bursting with news of the city, the country, the continent, America, and the world" (*PE*26–27).

Wambly Bald played a number of roles in helping to create this miracle, working primarily with Henry Miller and Alfred Perlès as proofreaders on the *Tribune*. While he was not interested in joining the editorial staff, Bald was persuaded for four years to contribute a weekly column. Described as "the Walter Winchell of the Lost Generation" (*PE*58), Bald betrays in his "La Vie de Bohème" the self-consciousness that defined American expatriation by the end of the 1920s. "One hundred years from now," he writes, "professors will be lecturing on Montparnasse: its development and decay" (*LB*117). While acknowledging that Gertrude Stein coined "the lost generation" for "the aimless tribe" that found its way from the United States to Europe (*LB*15), he laments the narrow thinking in defining "the term 'real' Quarter or 'real' Montparnasse" to describe the expatriate experience (*LB*28). The Left Bank was "the focal point for the accredited and discredited alike" (*LB*6), and so Bald uses the *Tribune* to examine the appeal to expatriates of this privileged ground. Eighteen months after the Wall Street crash, he reports that most people assume "that Montparnasse has died." Concerned that perhaps "the grand old colony has become a rendezvous for loungers and fakirs," Bald asks, "Has Bohemia folded? Is the Dôme just a café? Has the 'lost generation' found itself?" (*LB*68). He believed that "Montparnasse has had so many eras that it will not be easy to decide which one this is." But he laments that "Most of our contemporaries have called it the last one and run away to other districts" (*LB*71). Maintaining that "new ideas are the coin of the Quarter" (*LB*89), he first concludes that "Montparnasse has been dying for many years, but its death rattle will survive this generation" (*LB*84). Still, it would be Bald's ultimate fate to chart the decline of the Left Bank in the early 1930s. He marks what he sees as its passing in his last column on July 25, 1933.

> I've had a good time. I've seen them all: Derain and Braque and Chirico and Lillian Fisk and Foujita and Joe the barman. I've seen James Stephen and Huxley and Norman Douglas and Colette and Marie Laurencin and Brancusi and Paul Fort and—but this could go on and on; I no longer wish to do on and on. I've seen the Coupole expand over the Quarter like a mushroom or like a weight-lifter's chest, the Select go Oscar Wilde and the Rotonde go Nordic. I've seen the Dôme, that place of cheap bliss, that ugly wart on the face of the earth, turn into an American bar. I've seen all that—but it's all over now. I'm not deserting a sinking ship; it's been sunk for ages. You get something out of Montparnasse, and then it gets something out of you—just like bad liquor. (*LB*141)

He thus mourns for "the parade of silhouettes": George Antheil to Flossie Martin, Ernest Hemingway to Harold Stearns. In the end, Wambly Bald found the expatriate impulse spent. "The world is leveled off," he concludes. "Montparnasse is Main Street, and the 'plastic' modernists have won their battle against cliché. Even automobiles and furniture are going Picasso. The staunch army may disband" (*LB*142).

It was a job opportunity at the *Tribune* that first brought Eugene Jolas to Paris in the early 1920s. Having been given responsibility for the paper's "literary page," Jolas used his "Rambles through Literary Paris" to underline the international composition of modern art. "My aim was to apply American reporting methods to the creative and aesthetic issues of the day," he explains. "I considered myself primarily a reportorial observer and recorder of the ideological currents in post-war Paris" (*MB*71). He used the pages of the *Tribune* to juxtapose the exploits of George Antheil with Tristan Tzara, Ernest Hemingway with Léon-Paul Fargue, Man Ray with James Joyce. The experiments with language so important to *transition* had actually begun in the New York tabloids. "We transmuted facts into myths, twisted them into grotesque sensations, made them emerge in distorted contours, surrounded them with the magic of the modern epic," Jolas writes of his time on the *New York Daily News*. "We were the verbal mirrors of the city's explosive tumult, we responded to the morbid hunger of a mass unconscious" (*MB*43). He found at the Paris paper a similar opportunity to "jazz up" stories, "growing lurid and sensational over the leads" (*MB*66), and the writers he met in the city provided fuel for his own creative ambitions. "It was during these years, too, that I set forth on a long pilgrimage through language," he reflects, "a journey of exploration through the titanic forest of words, many thousands of words, a columbiad through the empires of three languages, in search of new language which I envisioned as the synthesis of a future tongue" (*MB*65).

The world featured on the pages of the Paris *Tribune* was thus an inspiration for the launch of *transition*, a magazine that sought to foster expatriates' "daring experimentation with words, colors, and sounds" (*MB*87). Like his work on the paper, this new endeavor was to be seen as "not only a workshop, but a kind of higher journalism, a simultaneous attempt to report to the English-speaking world the main intellectual movements of the continent" (*MB*93). He was driven, throughout, by the residual frustrations of his newspaper work. "I should like to ask any sensitive police reporter, any political or city hall reporter, any correspondent, any feature writer what he really thinks of the iterant, trite words he is compelled to use, day in, day out. Does he not finally come to feel repugnance at having to continue to use the same overworked, hollowed-out phraseology?" he wonders. All people who work with words thus sought "a more precise, richer and more fluid speech," but in the hands of artists, these experiments with language addressed "the paucity of vocabulary and the poverty of the lyrical phrase" that kept writers "from expressing the deeper emotions which his unconscious might have evoked" (*MB*108–9). While Jolas's experiments, like those of many modernists, were criticized for their abstruseness, it is clear that his basic motivations were rooted in a search for purer expression. He believed that if the artist ultimately refused "to lower his intellectual values in order to reach the masses," it was only to avoid yet another "echo of the powers that be." His "Revolution of the Word," a program first printed in *transition* in 1929 (*MB*110–11), sought "to push back the frontiers of the mind and its means of expression" so that art could change the world in ways meaningful to all (*MB*119).

Kirk Curnutt emphasizes again in his study of expatriation that the infamy of Americans abroad in the 1920s was bolstered through "the help of the mass media" that enkindled rivalry between the "dangerous counterculture" of "modernist rebels" and those who stayed home.[27] While some modern artists certainly profited from this exposure, many expatriate autobiographies sought actively to redress the injustices of these portrayals. The writings of Wambly Bald, Eugene Jolas, and Waverley Root serve to remind readers, however, that the popular press played a more direct role in the development of the Lost Generation, sustaining many of the expatriate Americans in Paris through these years and reflecting on its pages many of the issues that shaped the concerns of modern writers. These later autobiographies, as well as those of Maria Jolas and Gorham Munson, supplement established accounts of life abroad and question perceived truths about expatriate life. Indeed, the introduction to Chris Baldick's *The Modern Movement* (2004) stresses how "writers who had grown up" within a developing modernism understood it as "a broad church that embraced a variety of forms, techniques, styles, and attitudes, all of which were in some way innovative and in some way representative of new twentieth-century modes of awareness."[28] And, in fact, as critics have attempted to recapture a more catholic sense of the movement, it is appropriate to underline where diversity has been stressed in autobiographies more recently published. From the 1920s, readers have been interested in the lives of those expatriate Americans who make up what is often called the Lost Generation, and so the autobiographies of its participants, both minor and major, have effectively shaped and reshaped perceptions of life abroad. Although Paris already had, by the early twentieth century, a long history of hosting writers from other countries, the American writers who spent time there between the World Wars embraced the city with an enthusiasm that only reaffirmed its mystique while bolstering their individual reputations. Similarly, it must be said, autobiography had an established critical pedigree before the modern period, but subsequent decades have illustrated how Americans abroad embraced the form—and by so doing enriched its tradition while creating texts that vividly portray expatriates in their Parisian surroundings.

NOTES

Introduction

1. Ernest Hemingway, *A Moveable Feast* (New York: Charles Scribner's Sons, 1964; New York: Touchstone Books, 1996), 29.

2. Noël Riley Fitch, *Sylvia Beach and the Lost Generation: A History of Literary Paris in the Twenties and Thirties* (New York: W. W. Norton and Company, 1983), 442.

3. Philip Young, "The Lost Generation: War, Home, and Exile," in Lawrence H. Broer and John D. Walther, eds., *Dancing Fools and Weary Blues: The Great Escape of the Twenties* (Bowling Green, Ohio: Bowling Green State University Press, 1990), 82.

4. Lawrence H. Broer and John D. Walther, introduction to Broer and Walther, *Dancing Fools and Weary Blues*, 1.

5. Marc Dolan, *Modern Lives: A Cultural Re-Reading of "The Lost Generation"* (West Lafayette, Ind.: Purdue University Press, 1996), 5.

6. Dolan, *Modern Lives*, 26–27.

7. F. Scott Fitzgerald, *The Crack-Up*, ed. Edmund Wilson (New York: New Directions, 1945), 13.

8. Dolan, *Modern Lives*, 21.

9. Dolan, *Modern Lives*, 26.

10. Dolan, *Modern Lives*, 44.

11. Bruce Robbins, "Modernism in History, Modernism in Power," in Robert Kiely, ed., *Modernism Reconsidered* (Cambridge: Harvard University Press, 1983), 233.

12. Malcolm Bradbury, "The Nonhomemade World: European and American Modernism," *American Quarterly* 39, no. 1 (Spring 1987): 27.

13. Malcolm Bradbury and James McFarlane, "The Name and Nature of Modernism," in Malcolm Bradbury and James McFarlane, eds., *Modernism: A Guide to European Literature, 1890–1930* (New York: Penguin Books, 1991), 22.

14. Dolan, *Modern Lives*, 16.

15. Tom Wood, "Origin of the Term Lost Generation," *Lost Generation Journal* 1, no. 1 (May 1973): 5.

16. Hugh Kenner, "The Making of the Modernist Canon," *Chicago Review* 34, no. 2 (Spring 1984): 60.

17. Lawrence Rainey, *Institutions of Modernism: Literary Elites and the Public Culture* (New Haven: Yale University Press, 1998), 6.

18. Edmund Wilson, *Axel's Castle: A Study in the Imaginative Literature of 1870–1930* (New York: Charles Scribner's Sons, 1931), 1.

19. Laura Riding and Robert Graves, *A Survey of Modernist Poetry* (London: Heinemann, 1927), 9.

20. Riding and Graves, *A Survey of Modernist Poetry*, 11–12.

21. Peter Childs, *Modernism* (New York: Routledge, 2000), 13.

22. Morrill Cody, afterword to John Thomas, *Dry Martini: A Gentleman Turns to Love* (New York: George H. Doran; Carbondale: Southern Illinois University Press, 1974), 252.

23. Ernest Hemingway, *The Sun Also Rises* (New York: Charles Scribner's Sons, 1926; New York: Simon and Schuster, 1995), 25.

24. Ernest Hemingway, *The Sun Also Rises*, 120.

25. Janet Flanner, *Paris Was Yesterday: 1925–1939*, ed. Irving Drutman (New York: Viking Press, 1972; San Diego: Harcourt Brace Jovanovich, 1998), 12.

26. Richmond Barrett, "Babes in the Bois," *Harper's* 156, no. 936 (May 1928): 724.

27. Barrett, "Babes in the Bois," 730–31.

28. Louis Bromfield, "Expatriate—Vintage 1927," in Grant Overton, ed., *Mirrors of the Year: A National Review of the Outstanding Figures, Trends and Events of 1926–7* (New York: Frederick A. Stokes Company, 1927), 233–34.

29. Frederick Lewis Allen, *Only Yesterday: An Informal History of the Nineteen-Twenties* (New York: Harper and Brothers, 1931), 203.

30. Nathan Asch, *Love in Chartres* (New York: Alfred and Charles Boni, 1927), 48, 51. Further references to "*LC*" in this chapter are made parenthetically in the text.

31. Quoted in Geoffrey Wolff, *Black Sun: The Brief Transit and Violent Eclipse of Harry Crosby* (New York: Random House, 1976), 293.

32. Philip Horton, *Hart Crane: The Life of an American Poet* (New York: Viking Press, 1937), 103.

33. Bromfield, "Expatriate—Vintage 1927," 238–39.

34. John Downton Hazlett, *My Generation: Collective Autobiography and Identity Politics* (Madison: University of Wisconsin Press, 1998), 14.

35. Sidonie Smith and Julia Watson, *Reading Autobiography: A Guide for Interpreting Life Narratives* (Minneapolis: University of Minnesota Press, 2001), 10.

36. Anita Susan Grossman, "Art Versus Truth in Autobiography," *Clio: A Journal of Literature, History, and the Philosophy of History* 14, no. 3 (Spring 1985): 298.

37. Candace Lang, "Autobiography in the Aftermath of Romanticism," *Diacritics* 12, no. 4 (Winter 1982): 11.

38. Roy Pascal, *Design and Truth in Autobiography* (London: Routledge and Paul, 1960), 2, 9.

39. Philippe Lejeune, *On Autobiography* (Minneapolis: University of Minnesota Press, 1989), 5.

40. Smith and Watson, *Reading Autobiography*, 13.

41. Paul de Man, "Autobiography as Defacement," *Modern Language Notes* 94, no. 5 (December 1979): 921–22.

42. Donna Perreault, "What Makes Autobiography Interrogative?" *Biography: An Interdisciplinary Quarterly* 13, no. 2 (Spring 1990): 133.

43. de Man, "Autobiography as Defacement," 919.

44. Ezra Pound, "Date Line," in *Literary Essays of Ezra Pound*, ed. T. S. Eliot (New York: New Directions, 1968), 74–75.

45. T. S. Eliot, "The Function of Criticism," in *Selected Prose of T. S. Eliot*, ed. Frank Kermode (Boston: Faber and Faber, 1975), 73.

46. John Pilling, *Autobiography and Imagination: Studies in Self-Scrutiny* (Boston: Routledge and Kegan Paul, 1981), 5.

47. Ezra Pound, *The Selected Letters of Ezra Pound, 1907–1941*, ed. D. D. Paige (New York: New Directions, 1950), 212.

48. Olav Severijnen, "The Renaissance of a Genre: Autobiography and Modernism," *New Comparison: A Journal of Comparative and General Literary Studies* 9 (Spring 1990): 42.

49. Albert E. Stone, "Modern American Autobiography: Texts and Transactions," in Paul John Eakin, ed., *American Autobiography: Retrospect and Prospect* (Madison: University of Wisconsin Press, 1991), 95.

50. Stone, "Modern American Autobiography," 98.

51. John Carey, *The Intellectuals and the Masses: Pride and Prejudice among the Literary Intelligensia, 1880–1939* (Boston: Faber and Faber), vii, 21.

52. Ezra Pound, "The New Sculpture," in *Ezra Pound's Poetry and Prose: Contributions to Periodicals in Ten Volumes*, ed. Lea Baechler, A. Walton Litz, and James Logenbach (New York: Garland Press, 1991), 1:222.

53. Pound, "The New Sculpture," 1:221.

54. William Wordsworth, "Essay, Supplementary to the Preface 1815,"

in *The Prose Works of William Wordsworth*, ed. W. J. B. Owen and Jane Worthington Smyser (Oxford: Clarendon Press, 1974), 3:80.

55. Pound, "On Criticism in General," in *Ezra Pound's Poetry and Prose*, 4:266.

56. Ezra Pound, "The Serious Artist," in *Literary Essays of Ezra Pound*, 41.

57. Ezra Pound, "How to Read," in *Literary Essays of Ezra Pound*, 21.

58. T. S. Eliot, "The Function of Criticism," in *Selected Prose of T. S. Eliot*, 69, 73–74.

59. William Carlos Williams, *The Autobiography of William Carlos Williams* (New York: Random House, 1951; New York: New Directions, 1967), xi.

60. Albert E. Stone, *Autobiographical Occasions and Original Acts* (Philadelphia: University of Pennsylvania Press, 1982), 2.

61. Gertrude Stein, "The Story of a Book," in Gertrude Stein, *How Writing is Written: Volume II of the Previously Uncollected Writings of Gertrude Stein*, ed. Robert Bartlett Haas (Los Angeles: Black Sparrow Press, 1974), 62.

1. *Beyond the Sermonic Tradition*

1. Thomas Cooley, *Educated Lives: The Rise of Modern Autobiography in America* (Columbus: Ohio State University Press, 1976), 4–5.

2. Philip Abbott, *States of Perfect Freedom: Autobiography and American Political Thought* (Amherst: University of Massachusetts Press, 1987), 18.

3. Peter Dorsey, *Sacred Estrangement: The Rhetoric of Conversion in Modern American Autobiography* (University Park: Pennsylvania State University Press, 1993), 9.

4. Philip Dodd, "Criticism and the Autobiographical Tradition," in Philip Dodd, ed., *Modern Selves: Essays on Modern British and American Autobiography* (London: Frank Cass, 1986), 5.

5. Geoffrey Harpham, "Conversion and the Language of Autobiography," in James Olney, ed., *Studies in Autobiography* (New York: Oxford University Press, 1988), 44.

6. Alfred Kreymborg, *Troubadour: An Autobiography* (New York: Boni and Liveright, 1925), 414. Further references to "*T*" in this chapter are made parenthetically in the text.

7. Smith and Watson, *Reading Autobiography*, 16.

8. Robert F. Sayre, *The Examined Self: Benjamin Franklin, Henry Adams, Henry James* (Princeton: Princeton University Press, 1964), 198.

9. James Muldoon, introduction to James Muldoon, ed., *Varieties of Religious Conversion in the Middle Ages* (Gainesville: University Press of Florida, 1997), 1, 8.

10. Abbott, *States of Perfect Freedom*, 18.

11. John Dos Passos, *The Best Times: An Informal Memoir* (New York: New American Library, 1966), 23, 25.

12. Arlen J. Hansen, *Gentlemen Volunteers: The Story of the American Ambulance Drivers of the Great War, August 1914–September 1918* (New York: Arcade Publishing, 1996), xiv–xv.

13. Donald Pizer, *American Expatriate Writing and the Paris Moment: Modernism and Place* (Baton Rouge: Louisiana State University Press, 1996), 1.

14. Williams, *The Autobiography of William Carlos Williams*, 174.

15. Williams, *The Autobiography of William Carlos Williams*, 146.

16. Williams, *The Autobiography of William Carlos Williams*, 178.

17. Alfred Kreymborg, *The Little World: 1914 and After* (New York: Coward-McGann, 1932), 65.

18. Alfred Kreymborg, *Our Singing Strength: An Outline of American Poetry, 1620–1930* (New York: Coward-McGann, 1929), 539.

19. Allen Tate, *Sixty American Poets, 1896–1944* (Washington, D.C.: Library of Congress, 1945), 64.

20. Kreymborg, *Our Singing Strength*, 334.

21. Williams, *The Autobiography of William Carlos Williams*, 148.

22. Kreymborg, *Our Singing Strength*, 337.

23. Van Wyck Brooks, Alfred Kreymborg, Lewis Mumford, and Paul Rosenfeld, preface to Van Wyck Brooks, Alfred Kreymborg, Lewis Mumford, and Paul Rosenfeld, eds., *The American Caravan* (New York: Macaulay Company, 1927), x.

24. "Why Do Americans Live in Europe?" *transition* 14 (Fall 1928): 100, 111, 117.

25. Gertrude Stein, review of *Troubadour: An Autobiography*, by Alfred Kreymborg, *Ex Libris* 2, no. 9 (June 1925): 278.

2. Self-Aggrandizement and Expatriate Reputation

1. Kreymborg, *Troubadour*, 370.

2. Ulla E. Dydo, "*Stanzas in Meditation*: The Other Autobiography," *Chicago Review* 35, no. 2 (Winter 1985): 4.

3. Gertrude Stein, *The Autobiography of Alice B. Toklas* (New York: Harcourt, Brace, and Company, 1933; New York: Vintage Books, 1990), 251. Further references to "*AA*" in this chapter are made parenthetically in the text.

4. Catherine N. Parke, "'Simple through Complication': Gertrude Stein Thinking," *American Literature: A Journal of Literary History, Criticism, and Bibliography* 60, no. 4 (December 1988): 554, 556.

5. Rainey, *Institutions of Modernism*, 3.

6. Constance Pierce, "Gertrude Stein and Her Thoroughly Modern Protégé," *Modern Fiction Studies* 42, no. 3 (Fall 1996): 607.

7. Quoted in Catherine Turner, *Marketing Modernism between the Two World Wars* (Amherst: University of Massachusetts Press, 2003), 120.

8. Shirley Neuman, *Gertrude Stein: Autobiography and the Problem of Narration* (Victoria, B.C.: English Literary Studies, 1979), 13.

9. Joseph Fichtelberg, *The Complex Image: Faith and Method in American Autobiography* (Philadelphia: University of Pennsylvania Press, 1989), 209.

10. Alice B. Toklas, *What Is Remembered* (New York: Holt, Rinehart, Winston, 1960), 160.

11. James R. Mellow, *Charmed Circle: Gertrude Stein and Company* (New York: Praeger Publishers, 1974; New York: Owl Books, 2003), 149.

12. Mellow, *Charmed Circle*, 9.

13. *Testimony against Gertrude Stein* (The Hague: Servire Press, 1935), 2, 11.

14. Timothy Dow Adams, *Telling Lies in Modern American Autobiography* (Chapel Hill: University of North Carolina Press, 1990), 18.

15. *Testimony against Gertrude Stein*, 2.

16. Edward Burns, ed., *The Letters of Gertrude Stein and Carl Van Vechten, 1913–1946*, vol. 1 (New York: Columbia University Press, 1986), 404.

17. Shirley Neuman, "The Observer Observed: Distancing the Self in Autobiography," *Prose Studies* 4, no. 3 (1981): 320.

18. Laurel Bollinger, "'One as Not Mistaken but Interrupted': Gertrude Stein's Exploration of Identity in the 1930s," *Centennial Review* 43, no. 2 (Spring 1999): 228.

19. Susan M. Schultz, "Gertrude Stein's Self-Advertisement," *Raritan* 12, no. 2 (Fall 1992): 71.

20. Carolyn A. Barros, "Getting Modern: *The Autobiography of Alice B. Toklas*," *Biography* 22, no. 2 (Spring 1999): 184.

21. Mellow, *Charmed Circle*, 127.

22. Gertrude Stein, *Everybody's Autobiography* (New York: Random House, 1937; Cambridge, Mass.: Exact Change, 1993), 101. Further references to "*EA*" in this chapter are made parenthetically in the text.

23. Turner, *Marketing Modernism*, 116–17.

24. Quoted in Mellow, *Charmed Circle*, 353.

25. Lawrence Raab, "Remarks as Literature," *Michigan Quarterly Review* 17 (1978): 480–81.

26. Pizer, *American Expatriate Writing*, 28.

27. Suzanne Rodriguez, *Wild Heart: Natalie Clifford Barney and the Decadence of Literary Paris* (New York: HarperCollins Publishers, 2002; New York: Ecco Press, 2003), 263.

28. Catherine R. Stimpson, "Gertrude Stein and the Lesbian Lie," in Margo Culley, ed., *American Women's Autobiography: Fea(s)ts of Memory* (Madison: University of Wisconsin Press, 1992), 152.

29. Leigh Gilmore, "A Signature of Lesbian Autobiography: 'Gertrice/Altrude,'" *Prose Studies* 14, no. 2 (September 1991): 63–64.

30. Neuman, *Gertrude Stein*, 34.

31. Quoted in Mellow, *Charmed Circle*, 348.

32. Mellow, *Charmed Circle*, 354.

33. Turner, *Marketing Modernism*, 120.

34. W. G. Rogers, *When This You See Remember Me: Gertrude Stein in Person* (New York: Rinehart, 1948), 8–9.

35. Virgil Thomson, *Virgil Thomson* (New York: A. A. Knopf, 1966), 156, 183.

36. Bravig Imbs, *Confessions of Another Young Man* (New York: Henkle-Yewdale House, 1936), 171.

37. Thomson, *Virgil Thomson*, 50.

38. Ernest Hemingway, *A Moveable Feast*, 29, 31.

39. Cynthia Secor, "Gertrude Stein: The Complex Force of Her Femininity," in Kenneth W. Wheeler and Virginia Lee Lussier, eds., *Women, the Arts, and the 1920s in Paris and New York* (New Brunswick, N.J.: Transaction Books, 1982), 30.

40. Gertrude Stein, *The Geographical History of America* (New York: Random House, 1936), 214.

41. Quoted in Marianne DeKoven, *A Different Language: Gertrude Stein's Experimental Writing* (Madison: University of Wisconsin Press, 1983), 36.

42. Sandra M. Gilbert and Susan Gubar, *No Man's Land: The Place of the Woman Writer in the Twentieth Century* (New Haven: Yale University Press, 1988), 1:189.

43. Paul Bowles, *Without Stopping* (Hopewell, N.J.: Ecco Press, 1972), 119.

44. Ernest Hemingway, *A Moveable Feast*, 15, 17.

45. Marianne DeKoven, "Gertrude Stein and the Modernist Canon," in Shirley Neuman and Ira B. Nadel, eds., *Gertrude Stein and the Making of Literature* (Houndsmill, Hampshire: Macmillan, 1988), 12.

46. Ernest Hemingway, *A Moveable Feast*, 20.

47. Adams, *Telling Lies*, 24.

48. Imbs, *Confessions of Another Young Man*, 240.

49. Imbs, *Confessions of Another Young Man*, 298, 300.

50. Cynthia Secor, "Gertrude Stein," in Wheeler and Lussier, eds., *Women, the Arts, and the 1920s*, 27.

51. Phoebe Stein Davis, "Subjectivity and the Aesthetics of National Identity in Gertrude Stein's *The Autobiography of Alice B. Toklas*," *Twentieth-Century Literature* 45, no. 1 (Spring 1999): 18, 28.

3. *Searching for a Representative Expatriate*

1. Malcolm Cowley, *Exile's Return: A Narrative of Ideas* (New York: W. W. Norton, 1934), 12. Further references to "*EN*" in this chapter are made parenthetically in the text.

2. Malcolm Cowley, *Exile's Return: A Literary Odyssey of the 1920s*, ed.

Donald W. Faulkner (New York: Viking Press, 1951; New York: Penguin Books, 1994), 10. Further references to "*EO*" in this chapter are made parenthetically in the text.

3. John Downton Hazlett, "Conversion, Revisionism, and Revision in Malcolm Cowley's *Exile's Return*," *South Atlantic Quarterly* 82, no. 2 (Spring 1983): 181.

4. Hazlett, *My Generation*, 14.

5. Hazlett, *My Generation*, 32.

6. Hazlett, *My Generation*, 14.

7. Hazlett, *My Generation*, 15–16.

8. Hazlett, "Conversion, Revisionism, and Revision," 182.

9. Donald Faulkner, introduction to Cowley, *Exile's Return: A Literary Odyssey of the 1920s*, xvi.

10. Dolan, *Modern Lives*, 89.

11. Caresse Crosby, *The Passionate Years* (New York: Dial Press, 1953), 292.

12. Edward Germain, introduction to Harry Crosby, *Shadows of the Sun: The Diaries of Harry Crosby*, ed. Edward Germain (Santa Barbara, Calif.: Black Sparrow Press, 1977), 16.

13. Harold Stearns, "A Prodigal American Returns," *Scribner's Magazine* 91, no. 5 (May 1932): 293.

14. Hugh Ford, foreword to Harold Stearns, *Confessions of a Harvard Man: The Street I Know Revisited*, ed. Hugh Ford (Santa Barbara, Calif.: Paget Press, 1984), xiii.

15. Malcolm Cowley, "Young Mr. Elkins," *Broom* 4, no. 1 (December 1922): 52–53.

16. Harold Stearns, *The Street I Know* (New York: Lee Furman, 1935), 92. Further references to "*SK*" in this chapter are made parenthetically in the text.

17. Gerald W. McFarlane, *Inside Greenwich Village: A New York City Neighbourhood, 1898–1918* (Amherst: University of Massachusetts Press, 2001), 2, 191, 225.

18. Ross Wetzsteon, *Republic of Dreams, Greenwich Village: The American Bohemia, 1910–1960* (New York: Simon and Schuster, 2002), 89.

19. Paul Jay, ed., *The Selected Correspondence of Kenneth Burke and Malcolm Cowley: 1915–1981* (Berkeley: University of California Press, 1990), 135.

20. Harold Stearns, "America and the Young Intellectual," *Bookman* 53, no. 1 (March 1921): 48.

21. Harold Stearns, *America and the Young Intellectual* (New York: George H. Doran, 1921), 159, 167.

22. Harold Stearns, introduction to Harold Stearns, ed., *Civilization in the United States: An Inquiry by Thirty Americans* (New York: Harcourt, Brace, and Company, 1922), iii.

23. Harold Stearns, "The Intellectual Life" in Stearns, *Civilization in the United States*, 150.

24. William L. Shirer, *20th Century Journey: The Start, 1904–1930* (New York: Simon and Schuster, 1976), 218–19.

25. Robert McAlmon, *Being Geniuses Together: An Autobiography* (London: Secker and Warburg, 1938), 113–14.

26. Robert McAlmon and Kay Boyle, *Being Geniuses Together, 1920–1930* (Garden City, N.J.: Doubleday, 1968; Baltimore: Johns Hopkins University Press, 1997), 292.

27. Harold Stearns, "The Intellectual Life," in Harold Stearns, ed., *America Now: An Inquiry into Civilization in the United States by Thirty-Six Americans* (New York: Charles Scribner's Sons, 1938), 377.

28. Harold Stearns, introduction to Stearns, *America Now*, vii.

29. Donald Faulkner, introduction to Cowley, *Exile's Return: A Literary Odyssey of the 1920s*, ix.

30. Hazlett, "Conversion, Revisionism, and Revision," 179.

31. Hazlett, "Conversion, Revisionism, and Revision," 179, 188.

32. Donald Faulkner, introduction to Cowley, *Exile's Return: A Literary Odyssey of the 1920s*, xxiv.

4. *Place as a Strategy of Attachment*

1. J. Gerald Kennedy, *Imagining Paris: Exile, Writing, and American Identity* (New Haven: Yale University Press, 1994), 29.

2. Jerrold Seigel, *Bohemian Paris: Culture, Politics, and the Boundaries of Bourgeois Life, 1830–1930* (Baltimore: Johns Hopkins University Press, 1986), 367–68.

3. Kennedy, *Imagining Paris*, 29.

4. Eric Cahm, "Revolt, Conservatism and Reaction in Paris, 1905–1925," in Bradbury and McFarlane, eds., *Modernism*, 162.

5. Arlen J. Hansen, *Expatriate Paris: A Cultural and Literary Guide to Paris of the 1920s* (New York: Arcade Publishing, 1990), xxi.

6. Malcolm Bradbury, "The Cities of Modernism," in Bradbury and McFarlane, eds., *Modernism*, 97.

7. Noël Riley Fitch, *Walks in Hemingway's Paris: A Guide to Paris for the Literary Traveler* (New York: St. Martin's Press, 1989), 11.

8. Samuel Putnam, *Paris Was Our Mistress: Memoirs of a Lost and Found Generation* (New York: Viking Press, 1947), 7. Further references to "*PM*" in this chapter are made parenthetically in the text.

9. Kennedy, *Imagining Paris*, 24.

10. Pizer, *American Expatriate Writing*, xiv.

11. Pizer, *American Expatriate Writing*, 47–48.

12. Imbs, *Confessions of Another Young Man*, 276. Further references to "*CM*" in this chapter are made parenthetically in the text.

13. David Gross, *Lost Time: On Remembering and Forgetting in Late Modern Culture* (Amherst: University of Massachusetts Press, 2000), 102.

14. Pizer, *American Expatriate Writing*, 142–43.

15. Fitch, *Walks in Hemingway's Paris*, 144.

16. Jimmie Charters, *This Must Be the Place: Memoirs of Montparnasse*, as told to Morrill Cody (London: Herbert Joseph, 1934; New York: Collier Books, 1989), 11. Further references to "*TP*" in this chapter are made parenthetically in the text.

17. Seigel, *Bohemian Paris*, 3.

18. George Antheil, *Bad Boy of Music* (Garden City, N.Y.: Doubleday, Doran, and Company, 1945), 109.

19. Elizabeth W. Bruss, *Autobiographical Acts: The Changing Structure of a Literary Genre* (Baltimore: Johns Hopkins University Press, 1976), 12.

20. Gerri Reaves, *Mapping the Private Geography: Autobiography, Identity, and America* (Jefferson, N.C.: McFarland and Company, 2001), 2.

21. Leonard Lutwack, *Role of Place in Literature* (Syracuse: Syracuse University Press, 1984), 2, 184.

22. Kennedy, *Imagining Paris*, 6.

5. Patterns of Women's Stories

1. Andrea Weiss, *Paris Was a Woman: Portraits from the Left Bank* (San Francisco: Harper Collins, 1995), 25.

2. Charters, *This Must Be the Place*, 20.

3. Peggy Guggenheim, *Out of This Century: The Informal Memoirs of Peggy Guggenheim* (New York: Dial Press, 1946), 1, 33.

4. Fitch, *Sylvia Beach and the Lost Generation*, 12.

5. Sylvia Beach, *Shakespeare and Company* (New York: Harcourt, Brace, 1956; Lincoln: University of Nebraska Press, 1991), 3. Further references to "*SC*" in this chapter are made parenthetically in the text.

6. Fitch, *Sylvia Beach and the Lost Generation*, 412.

7. Shari Benstock, *Women of the Left Bank: Paris, 1900–1940* (Austin: University of Texas Press, 1986), 221.

8. Sidonie Smith, *A Poetics of Women's Autobiography: Marginality and the Fictions of Self-Representation* (Bloomington: Indiana University Press, 1987), 39.

9. Judy Nolte Lensink, "Expanding the Boundaries of Criticism: The Diary as Female Autobiography," *Women's Studies* 14, no. 1 (1987): 41–42.

10. Nina Van Gessel, "Re-Casting the Midwives of Modernism: Autobiographies of American Expatriate Women Publishers and Editors" (Ph.D. diss., McMaster University, 1996), 71.

11. John C. Broderick, "Paris between the Wars: An Unpublished Memoir by Solita Solano," *Quarterly Journal of the Library of Congress* 34 (1977): 308.

12. Jane Grant, *Ross, The New Yorker and Me* (New York: Reynal and Company, 1968), 223.

13. Van Gessel, "Re-Casting the Midwives of Modernism," 69.

14. Flanner, *Paris Was Yesterday*, xx. Further references to "*PY*" in this chapter are made parenthetically in the text.

15. Brenda Wineapple, *Genêt: A Biography of Janet Flanner* (Lincoln: University of Nebraska Press, 1989), 103.

16. Janet Flanner, afterword to Flanner, *The Cubical City* (New York: G. P. Putman's Sons, 1926; Carbondale: Southern Illinois University Press, 1974), 429.

17. Janet Flanner, "The Unique Ross," introduction to Grant, *Ross, The New Yorker and Me*, 11.

18. Susan Stanford Friedman, "Women's Autobiographical Selves: Theory and Practice" in Sidonie Smith and Julia Watson, eds., *Women, Autobiography, Theory: A Reader* (Madison: University of Wisconsin Press, 1998), 72.

19. Patricia Meyer Spacks, "Female Rhetorics" in Smith and Watson, eds., *Women, Autobiography, Theory*, 232.

20. Grant, *Ross, The New Yorker and Me*, 224.

21. Benstock, *Women of the Left Bank*, 102.

22. Wineapple, *Genêt*, 99.

23. Janet Flanner, "Paris Letter," *New Yorker* 11, no. 5 (March 16, 1935): 80.

24. Janet Flanner, "Paris Letter," *New Yorker* 11, no. 21 (July 6, 1935): 50.

25. Margo Culley, introduction to *A Day at a Time: Diary Literature of American Women, from 1764 to 1985*, in Smith and Watson, eds., *Women, Autobiography, Theory*, 220.

26. Culley, introduction, 220.

27. Benstock, *Women of the Left Bank*, 5.

28. Culley, introduction, 219.

29. Margaret Anderson, *My Thirty Years' War* (New York: Covici-Friede, 1930; New York: Horizon Press, 1969), 233–34.

30. John Bainbridge, *Another Way of Living: A Gallery of Americans Who Choose to Live in Europe* (New York: Holt, Rinehart, and Winston, 1968), 16.

31. Janet Flanner, "Paris Letter," *New Yorker* 1, no. 34 (October 10, 1925): 26.

32. Janet Flanner, "Paris Letter," *New Yorker* 1, no. 46 (January 2, 1926): 35.

33. Janet Flanner, "Paris Letter," *New Yorker* 13, no. 50 (January 29, 1938): 45.

34. Janet Flanner, "Paris Letter," *New Yorker* 11, no. 37 (October 26, 1935): 48.

35. Janet Flanner, "Paris Letter," *New Yorker* 14, no. 22 (July 16, 1938): 58.

36. Janet Flanner, "Paris Letter," *New Yorker* 13, no. 6 (March 27, 1937): 56.

37. Flanner, "Paris Letter," *New Yorker* 13, no. 6, 58.

38. Flanner, "Paris Letter," *New Yorker* 11, no. 5, 78, 80.

39. Benstock, *Women of the Left Bank*, 100.

40. Benstock, *Women of the Left Bank*, 100.

41. Janet Flanner, "Paris Letter," *New Yorker* 12, no. 40 (November 21, 1936): 74.

42. Janet Flanner, "Paris Letter," *New Yorker* 13, no. 9 (April 17, 1937): 56.

43. Grant, *Ross, The New Yorker and Me*, 224.

44. Janet Flanner, "Paris Letter," *New Yorker* 14, no. 46 (December 31, 1938): 50.

45. Fitch, *Sylvia Beach and the Lost Generation*, 413.

46. Benstock, *Women of the Left Bank*, 100.

47. Janet Flanner, *Janet Flanner's World: Uncollected Writings, 1932–1975*, ed. Irving Drutman (New York: Harcourt Brace Jovanovich, 1979), 310–11.

48. Flanner, *Janet Flanner's World*, 334.

49. Flanner, *Janet Flanner's World*, 320.

50. Wineapple, *Genêt*, 271.

51. Wineapple, *Genêt*, 287.

52. Quoted in Janet Flanner, *Darlinghissima: Letters to a Friend*, ed. Natalia Danesi Murray (New York: Random House, 1985), 463.

53. Wineapple, *Genêt*, 290.

54. Flanner, afterword to *The Cubical City*, 430.

55. Flanner, afterword to *The Cubical City*, 427.

56. Benstock, *Women of the Left Bank*, x.

6. Revision and Textual Authority

1. Ernest Hemingway, *Selected Letters, 1917–1961*, ed. Carlos Baker (New York: Charles Scribner's Sons, 1981), 388.

2. Ernest Hemingway, *Selected Letters*, 396.

3. Jacqueline Tavernier-Courbin, *Ernest Hemingway's "A Moveable Feast": The Making of Myth* (Boston: Northeastern University Press, 1991), 8.

4. Ernest Hemingway, *Selected Letters*, 411.

5. Carlos Baker, *Ernest Hemingway: A Life Story* (New York: Charles Scribner's Sons, 1969), 536.

6. Mary Welsh Hemingway, "The Making of the Book: A Chronicle and a Memoir," *New York Times Book Review* (May 10, 1964): 26–27.

7. Tavernier-Courbin, *Ernest Hemingway's "A Moveable Feast*," 18.

8. Ernest Hemingway, *Selected Letters*, 619.

9. Fitch, *Sylvia Beach and the Lost Generation*, 412.

10. Mary Welsh Hemingway, "The Making of the Book," 27.

11. Mary Welsh Hemingway, *How It Was* (New York: Knopf, 1976), 520.

12. Tavernier-Courbin, *Ernest Hemingway's "A Moveable Feast,"* 171.

13. Tavernier-Courbin, *Ernest Hemingway's "A Moveable Feast,"* 175.

14. Gerry Brenner, "Are We Going to Hemingway's Feast?" *American Literature: A Journal of Literary History, Criticism, and Bibliography* 54, no. 4 (December 1982): 542.

15. Andrew Lytle, "*A Moveable Feast:* The Going To and Fro," *Sewanee Review* 73 (1965): 340.

16. Susanna Egan, "Lies, Damned Lies, and Autobiography: Hemingway's Treatment of Fitzgerald in *A Moveable Feast,*" *a/b: Auto/Biography Studies* 9, no. 1 (Spring 1994): 81

17. Ernest Hemingway, *A Moveable Feast,* 109. Further references to "*MF*" in this chapter are made parenthetically in the text.

18. Brenner, "Are We Going to Hemingway's Feast?" 532.

19. Lytle, "*A Moveable Feast:* The Going To and Fro," 341.

20. Tavernier-Courbin, *Ernest Hemingway's "A Moveable Feast,"* 97, 99.

21. Quoted in Baker, *Ernest Hemingway,* 552.

22. Harold Loeb, "Hemingway's Bitterness," *Connecticut Review* 1 (1967): 7.

23. Harold Loeb, *The Way It Was* (New York: Criterion Books, 1959), 190.

24. Loeb, *The Way It Was,* 65.

25. Loeb, *The Way It Was,* 300.

26. Matthew Josephson, *Life among the Surrealists* (New York: Holt, Rinehart and Winston, 1962), 4–6.

27. Josephson, *Life among the Surrealists,* 3–4.

28. Josephson, *Life among the Surrealists,* 4, 6.

29. Joan Mellon, *Kay Boyle: Author of Herself* (New York: Farrar, Straus, and Giroux, 1994), 444.

30. McAlmon and Boyle, *Being Geniuses Together,* 333. Further references to "*BG*" in this chapter are made parenthetically in the text.

31. Sanford J. Smoller, *Adrift among Geniuses: Robert McAlmon, Writer and Publisher of the Twenties* (University Park: Pennsylvania State University Press, 1975), 263, 275.

32. Donna Hollenberg, "Abortion, Identity Formation, and the Expatriate Woman Writer: H.D. and Kay Boyle in the Twenties," *Twentieth Century Literature* 34, no. 3 (Fall 1988): 509.

33. McAlmon, *Being Geniuses Together,* 230.

34. McAlmon, *Being Geniuses Together,* 299.

35. Smoller, *Adrift among Geniuses,* 307.

36. McAlmon, *Being Geniuses Together,* 94.

37. Mellon, *Kay Boyle,* 121.

38. Christine H. Hait, "Life-Giving: Kay Boyle's Innovations in Autobiography in *Being Geniuses Together,*" in Marilyn Elkins, ed., *Critical Essays on Kay Boyle* (New York: G. K. Hall, 1997), 304.

39. Hait, "Life-Giving," 299.

40. McAlmon, *Being Geniuses Together*, 22.

41. Mellon, *Kay Boyle*, 460.

42. John Glassco, *Memoirs of Montparnasse* (New York: Oxford University Press, 1995), 43.

43. Cowley, *Exile's Return: A Literary Odyssey of the 1920s*, 190.

44. Mellon, *Kay Boyle*, 460.

45. Glassco, *Memoirs of Montparnasse*, 220n.

46. Glassco, *Memoirs of Montparnasse*, 228n.

47. Glassco, *Memoirs of Montparnasse*, 97.

48. Adams, *Telling Lies*, 3.

49. Sanford J. Smoller, introduction to Robert McAlmon, *The Nightinghouls of Paris*, ed. Sanford J. Smoller (Urbana: University of Illinois Press, 2007), xxviii, xxxii–xxxiii.

50. David Harvey, *The Condition of Postmodernity* (Malden, Mass.: Blackwell Publishers, 1990), 38.

7. *The Afterlife of Expatriate American Autobiogaphy*

1. Adam Gopnik, introduction to Adam Gopnik, ed., *Americans in Paris: A Literary Anthology* (New York: The Library of America, 2004), xxi.

2. George Wickes, *Americans in Paris, 1903–1939* (New York: Doubleday, 1969), 4.

3. Ronald Weber, *News of Paris: American Journalists in the City of Light between the Wars* (Chicago: Ivan R. Dee, 2006), 16.

4. Sophie Lévy, introduction to Sophie Lévy, ed., *A Transatlantic Avant-Garde: American Artists in Paris, 1918–1939* (Berkeley: University of California Press, 2003), 15.

5. Elizabeth Glassman, preface to Lévy, *A Transatlantic Avant-Garde*, 13.

6. Marshall Berman, *All That Is Solid Melts into Air: The Experience of Modernity* (New York: Penguin Books, 1988), 346.

7. Fredric Jameson, "The Politics of Theory: Ideological Positions in the Postmodernism Debate," in *The Ideologies of Theory: Essays, 1971–1986* (Minneapolis: University of Minnesota Press, 1988), 2:104.

8. Peter Nicholls, *Modernisms: A Literary Guide* (New York: Macmillan, 1995), vii.

9. Jay Parini, introduction to Jay Parini, ed., *The Norton Book of American Autobiography* (New York: W. W. Norton and Company, 1999), 16.

10. Smith and Watson, *Reading Autobiography*, 27.

11. "Publisher's Note" to Gorham Munson, *The Awakening Twenties: A Memoir-History of a Literary Period* (Baton Rouge: Louisiana State University Press, 1985), xiii–xiv. Further references to "*AT*" in this chapter are made parenthetically in the text.

12. Benjamin Franklin V, introduction to Wambly Bald, *On the Left Bank, 1929–1933*, ed. Benjamin Franklin V (Athens: Ohio University

Press, 1987), xi, xxii–xxiii. Further references to "*LB*" in this chapter are made parenthetically in the text.

13. Samuel Abt, introduction to Waverley Root, *The Paris Edition*, ed. Samuel Abt (San Francisco: North Point Press, 1987), vii, xii. Further references to "*PE*" in this chapter are made parenthetically in the text.

14. Andreas Kramer and Ranier Rumold, introduction to Eugene Jolas, *Man from Babel*, ed. Andreas Kramer and Ranier Rumold (New Haven: Yale University Press, 1998), xi, xxx. Further references to "*MB*" in this chapter are made parenthetically in the text.

15. Mary Ann Caws, introduction to Maria Jolas, *Woman of Action: A Memoir and Other Writings*, ed. Mary Ann Caws (Columbia: University of South Carolina Press, 2004), x–xi. Further references to "*WA*" in this chapter are made parenthetically in the text.

16. Sean Latham, *Am I a Snob? Modernism and the Novel* (Ithaca: Cornell University Press, 2003), 2.

17. Weber, *News of Paris*, 91.

18. Cowley, *Exile's Return: A Narrative of Ideas*, 193.

19. Loeb, *The Way It Was*, 196.

20. Cowley, *Exile's Return: A Literary Odyssey of the 1920s*, 183–84.

21. Josephson, *Life among the Surrealists*, 266–67.

22. Josephson, *Life among the Surrealists*, 238.

23. Carey, *The Intellectuals and the Masses*, 6–7.

24. Hugh Ford, introduction to Hugh Ford, ed., *The Left Bank Revisited: Selections from the Paris Tribune, 1917–1934* (University Park: Pennsylvania State University Press, 1972), 1.

25. Weber, *News of Paris*, 78.

26. Weber, *News of Paris*, 81–82.

27. Kirk Curnutt, *Ernest Hemingway and the Expatriate Modernist Movement* (Farmington Hills, Mich.: Gale Group, 2000), 73.

28. Chris Baldick, *The Modern Movement, The Oxford English Literary History*, vol. 10, 1910–1940 (Oxford: Oxford University Press, 2004), 5.

BIBLIOGRAPHY

Abbott, Philip. *States of Perfect Freedom: Autobiography and American Political Thought.* Amherst: University of Massachusetts Press, 1987.

Adams, Timothy Dow. *Telling Lies in Modern American Autobiography.* Chapel Hill: University of North Carolina Press, 1990.

Allen, Frederick Lewis. *Only Yesterday: An Informal History of the Nineteen-Twenties.* New York: Harper and Brothers, 1931.

Anderson, Margaret. *My Thirty Years' War.* New York: Covici-Friede, 1930; New York: Horizon Press, 1969.

Antheil, George. *Bad Boy of Music.* Garden City, N.Y.: Doubleday, Doran, and Company, 1945.

Asch, Nathan. *Love in Chartres.* New York: Alfred and Charles Boni, 1927.

Bainbridge, John. *Another Way of Living: A Gallery of Americans Who Choose to Live in Europe.* New York: Holt, Rinehart, and Winston, 1968.

Baker, Carlos. *Ernest Hemingway: A Life Story.* New York: Charles Scribner's Sons, 1969.

Bald, Wambly. *On the Left Bank, 1929–1933.* Edited by Benjamin Franklin V. Athens: Ohio University Press, 1987.

Baldick, Chris. *The Modern Movement. The Oxford English Literary History Vol. 10, 1910–1940.* Oxford: Oxford University Press, 2004.

Barrett, Richmond. "Babes in the Bois." *Harper's* 156, no. 936 (May 1928): 724–36.

Barros, Carolyn A. "Getting Modern: *The Autobiography of Alice B. Toklas.*" *Biography* 22, no. 2 (Spring 1999): 177–208.

Beach, Sylvia. *Shakespeare and Company.* New York: Harcourt, Brace, 1956; Lincoln: University of Nebraska Press, 1991.

Benstock, Shari. *Women of the Left Bank: Paris, 1900–1940.* Austin: University of Texas Press, 1986.

Berman, Marshall. *All That Is Solid Melts into Air: The Experience of Modernity.* New York: Penguin Books, 1988.

Bollinger, Laurel. "'One as Not Mistaken but Interrupted': Gertrude Stein's Exploration of Identity in the 1930s." *Centennial Review* 43, no. 2 (Spring 1999): 227–58.

Bowles, Paul. *Without Stopping.* Hopewell, N.J.: Ecco Press, 1972.

Bradbury, Malcolm. "The Nonhomemade World: European and American Modernism." *American Quarterly* 39, no. 1 (Spring 1987): 27–36.

Bradbury, Malcolm, and James McFarlane, eds. *Modernism: A Guide to European Literature, 1890–1930.* New York: Penguin Books, 1991.

Brenner, Gerry. "Are We Going to Hemingway's Feast?" *American Literature: A Journal of Literary History, Criticism, and Bibliography* 54, no. 4 (December 1982): 528–44.

Broderick, John C. "Paris between the Wars: An Unpublished Memoir by Solita Solano." *Quarterly Journal of the Library of Congress* 34 (1977): 306–14.

Broer, Lawrence H., and John D. Walther, eds. *Dancing Fools and Weary Blues: The Great Escape of the Twenties.* Bowling Green, Ohio: Bowling Green State University Press, 1990.

Brooks, Van Wyck, Alfred Kreymborg, Lewis Mumford, and Paul Rosenfeld, eds. *The American Caravan.* New York: Macaulay Company, 1927.

Bruss, Elizabeth W. *Autobiographical Acts: The Changing Structure of a Literary Genre.* Baltimore: Johns Hopkins University Press, 1976.

Burns, Edward, ed. *The Letters of Gertrude Stein and Carl Van Vechten, 1913–1946.* 2 vols. New York: Columbia University Press, 1986.

Carey, John. *The Intellectuals and the Masses: Pride and Prejudice among the Literary Intelligensia, 1880–1939.* Boston: Faber and Faber, 1992.

Charters, Jimmie. *This Must Be the Place: Memoirs of Montparnasse.* As told to Morrill Cody. London: Herbert Joseph, 1934; New York: Collier Books, 1989.

Childs, Peter. *Modernism.* New York: Routledge, 2000.

Cooley, Thomas. *Educated Lives: The Rise of Modern Autobiography in America.* Columbus: Ohio State University Press, 1976.

Cowley, Malcolm. *Exile's Return: A Literary Odyssey of the 1920s.* Edited by Donald W. Faulkner. New York: Viking Press, 1951; New York: Penguin Books, 1994.

———. *Exile's Return: A Narrative of Ideas.* New York: W. W. Norton, 1934.

———. "Young Mr. Elkins." *Broom* 4, no. 1 (December 1922): 52–56.

Crosby, Caresse. *The Passionate Years.* New York: Dial Press, 1953.

Crosby, Harry. *Shadows of the Sun: The Diaries of Harry Crosby.* Edited by Edward Germain. Santa Barbara, Calif.: Black Sparrow Press, 1977.

Culley, Margo, ed. *American Women's Autobiography: Fea(s)ts of Memory.* Madison: University of Wisconsin Press, 1992.

Curnutt, Kirk. *Ernest Hemingway and the Expatriate Modernist Movement*. Farmington Hills, Mich.: Gale Group, 2000.

Davis, Phoebe Stein. "Subjectivity and the Aesthetics of National Identity in Gertrude Stein's *The Autobiography of Alice B. Toklas*." *Twentieth-Century Literature* 45, no. 1 (Spring 1999): 18–45.

DeKoven, Marianne. *A Different Language: Gertrude Stein's Experimental Writing*. Madison: University of Wisconsin Press, 1983.

de Man, Paul. "Autobiography as Defacement." *Modern Language Notes* 94, no. 5 (December 1979): 919–30.

Dodd, Philip, ed. *Modern Selves: Essays on Modern British and American Autobiography*. London: Frank Cass, 1986.

Dolan, Marc. *Modern Lives: A Cultural Re-Reading of "The Lost Generation."* West Lafayette, Ind.: Purdue University Press, 1996.

Dorsey, Peter A. *Sacred Estrangement: The Rhetoric of Conversion in Modern American Autobiography*. University Park: Pennsylvania State University Press, 1993.

Dos Passos, John. *The Best Times: An Informal Memoir*. New York: New American Library, 1966.

Dydo, Ulla E. "*Stanzas in Meditation*: The Other Autobiography." *Chicago Review* 35, no. 2 (Winter 1985): 4–20.

Eakin, Paul John, ed. *American Autobiography: Retrospect and Prospect*. Madison: University of Wisconsin Press, 1991.

Egan, Susanna. "Lies, Damned Lies, and Autobiography: Hemingway's Treatment of Fitzgerald in *A Moveable Feast*." *a/b: Auto/Biography Studies* 9, no. 1 (Spring 1994): 64–82.

Eliot, T. S. *Selected Prose of T. S. Eliot*. Edited by Frank Kermode. Boston: Faber and Faber, 1975.

Elkins, Marilyn, ed. *Critical Essays on Kay Boyle*. New York: G. K. Hall, 1997.

Fichtelberg, Joseph. *The Complex Image: Faith and Method in American Autobiography*. Philadelphia: University of Pennsylvania Press, 1989.

Fitch, Noël Riley. *Sylvia Beach and the Lost Generation: A History of Literary Paris in the Twenties and Thirties*. New York: W. W. Norton and Company, 1983.

————. *Walks in Hemingway's Paris: A Guide to Paris for the Literary Traveler*. New York: St. Martin's Press, 1989.

Fitzgerald, F. Scott. *The Crack-Up*. Edited by Edmund Wilson. New York: New Directions, 1945.

Flanner, Janet. *The Cubical City*. New York: G. P. Putman's Sons, 1926; Carbondale: Southern Illinois University Press, 1974.

————. *Darlinghissima: Letters to a Friend*. Edited by Natalia Danesi Murray. New York: Random House, 1985.

————. *Janet Flanner's World: Uncollected Writings, 1932–1975*. Edited by Irving Drutman. New York: Harcourt Brace Jovanovich, 1979.

————. "Paris Letter." *New Yorker* 1, no. 34 (October 10, 1925): 26–27.

———. "Paris Letter." *New Yorker* 1, no. 46 (January 2, 1926): 35.

———. "Paris Letter." *New Yorker* 11, no. 5 (March 16, 1935): 78–80.

———. "Paris Letter." *New Yorker* 11, no. 21 (July 6, 1935): 50–51.

———. "Paris Letter." *New Yorker* 11, no. 37 (October 26, 1935): 45–48.

———. "Paris Letter." *New Yorker* 12, no. 40 (November 21, 1936): 74–76.

———. "Paris Letter." *New Yorker* 13, no. 6 (March 27, 1937): 56–58.

———. "Paris Letter." *New Yorker* 13, no. 9 (April 17, 1937): 56–58.

———. "Paris Letter." *New Yorker* 13, no. 50 (January 29, 1938): 45–46.

———. "Paris Letter." *New Yorker* 14, no. 22 (July 16, 1938): 57–58.

———. "Paris Letter." *New Yorker* 14, no. 46 (December 31, 1938): 49–50.

———. *Paris Was Yesterday: 1925–1939*. Edited by Irving Drutman. New York: Viking Press, 1972; San Diego: Harcourt Brace Jovanovich, 1998.

Ford, Hugh, ed. *The Left Bank Revisited: Selections from the Paris Tribune, 1917–1934*. University Park: Pennsylvania State University Press, 1972.

Gilbert, Sandra M., and Susan Gubar. *No Man's Land: The Place of the Woman Writer in the Twentieth Century*. 3 vols. New Haven: Yale University Press, 1988.

Gilmore, Leigh. "A Signature of Lesbian Autobiography: 'Gertrice/Altrude.'" *Prose Studies* 14, no. 2 (September 1991): 56–75.

Glassco, John. *Memoirs of Montparnasse*. New York: Oxford University Press, 1995.

Gopnik, Adam, ed. *Americans in Paris: A Literary Anthology*. New York: Library of America, 2004.

Grant, Jane. *Ross, The New Yorker and Me*. New York: Reynal and Company, 1968.

Gross, David. *Lost Time: On Remembering and Forgetting in Late Modern Culture*. Amherst: University of Massachusetts Press, 2000.

Grossman, Anita Susan. "Art Versus Truth in Autobiography." *Clio: A Journal of Literature, History, and the Philosophy of History* 14, no. 3 (Spring 1985): 289–308.

Guggenheim, Peggy. *Out of This Century: The Informal Memoirs of Peggy Guggenheim*. New York: Dial Press, 1946.

Hansen, Arlen J. *Expatriate Paris: A Cultural and Literary Guide to Paris of the 1920s*. New York: Arcade Publishing, 1990.

———. *Gentlemen Volunteers: The Story of the American Ambulance Drivers of the Great War, August 1914–September 1918*. New York: Arcade Publishing, 1996.

Harvey, David. *The Condition of Postmodernity*. Malden, Mass.: Blackwell Publishers, 1990.

Hazlett, John Downton. "Conversion, Revisionism, and Revision in Malcolm Cowley's *Exile's Return*." *South Atlantic Quarterly* 82, no. 2 (Spring 1983): 179–88.

———. *My Generation: Collective Autobiography and Identity Politics*. Madison: University of Wisconsin Press, 1998.

Hemingway, Ernest. *A Moveable Feast.* New York: Charles Scribner's Sons, 1964; New York: Touchstone Books, 1996.

—————. *Selected Letters, 1917–1961.* Edited by Carlos Baker. New York: Charles Scribner's Sons, 1981.

—————. *The Sun Also Rises.* New York: Charles Scribner's Sons, 1926; New York: Simon and Schuster, 1995.

Hemingway, Mary Welsh. *How It Was.* New York: Knopf, 1976.

—————. "The Making of the Book: A Chronicle and a Memoir." *New York Times Book Review* (May 10, 1964): 26–27.

Hollenberg, Donna. "Abortion, Identity Formation, and the Expatriate Woman Writer: H. D. and Kay Boyle in the Twenties." *Twentieth Century Literature* 34, no. 3 (Fall 1988): 499–517.

Horton, Philip. *Hart Crane: The Life of an American Poet.* New York: Viking Press, 1937.

Imbs, Bravig. *Confessions of Another Young Man.* New York: Henkle-Yewdale House, 1936.

Jameson, Fredric. *The Ideologies of Theory: Essays, 1971–1986.* 2 vols. Minneapolis: University of Minnesota Press, 1988.

Jay, Paul, ed. *The Selected Correspondence of Kenneth Burke and Malcolm Cowley: 1915–1981.* Berkeley: University of California Press, 1990.

Jolas, Eugene. *Man from Babel.* Edited by Andreas Kramer and Rainer Rumold. New Haven: Yale University Press, 1998.

Jolas, Maria. *Woman of Action: A Memoir and Other Writings.* Edited by Mary Ann Caws. Columbia: University of South Carolina Press, 2004.

Josephson, Matthew. *Life among the Surrealists.* New York: Holt, Rinehart and Winston, 1962.

Kennedy, J. Gerald. *Imagining Paris: Exile, Writing, and American Identity.* New Haven: Yale University Press, 1994.

Kenner, Hugh. "The Making of the Modernist Canon." *Chicago Review* 34, no. 2 (Spring 1984): 49–61.

Kiely, Robert, ed. *Modernism Reconsidered.* Cambridge: Harvard University Press, 1983.

Kreymborg, Alfred. *The Little World: 1914 and After.* New York: Coward-McGann, 1932.

—————. *Our Singing Strength: An Outline of American Poetry, 1620–1930.* New York: Coward-McGann, 1929.

—————. *Troubadour: An Autobiography.* New York: Boni and Liveright, 1925.

Lang, Candace. "Autobiography in the Aftermath of Romanticism." *Diacritics* 12, no. 4 (Winter 1982): 2–16.

Latham, Sean. *Am I a Snob? Modernism and the Novel.* Ithaca: Cornell University Press, 2003.

Lejeune, Philippe. *On Autobiography.* Minneapolis: University of Minnesota Press, 1989.

Lensink, Judy Nolte. "Expanding the Boundaries of Criticism: The Diary as Female Autobiography." *Women's Studies* 14, no. 1 (1987): 39–53.

Lévy, Sophie, ed. *A Transatlantic Avant-Garde: American Artists in Paris, 1918–1939*. Berkeley: University of California Press, 2003.

Loeb, Harold. "Hemingway's Bitterness." *Connecticut Review* 1 (1967): 7–24.

———. *The Way It Was*. New York: Criterion Books, 1959.

Lutwack, Leonard. *Role of Place in Literature*. Syracuse: Syracuse University Press, 1984.

Lytle, Andrew. "*A Moveable Feast*: The Going To and Fro." *Sewanee Review* 73 (1965): 339–43.

McAlmon, Robert. *Being Geniuses Together: An Autobiography*. London: Secker and Warburg, 1938.

———. *The Nightinghouls of Paris*. Edited by Sanford J. Smoller. Urbana: University of Illinois Press, 2007.

McAlmon, Robert, and Kay Boyle. *Being Geniuses Together, 1920–1930*. Garden City, N.J.: Doubleday, 1968; Baltimore: Johns Hopkins University Press, 1997.

McFarlane, Gerald W. *Inside Greenwich Village: A New York City Neighbourhood, 1898–1918*. Amherst: University of Massachusetts Press, 2001.

Mellon, Joan. *Kay Boyle: Author of Herself*. New York: Farrar, Straus, and Giroux, 1994.

Mellow, James R. *Charmed Circle: Gertrude Stein and Company*. New York: Praeger Publishers, 1974; New York: Owl Books, 2003.

Muldoon, James, ed. *Varieties of Religious Conversion in the Middle Ages*. Gainesville: University Press of Florida, 1997.

Munson, Gorham. *The Awakening Twenties: A Memoir-History of a Literary Period*. Baton Rouge: Louisiana State University Press, 1985.

Neuman, Shirley. *Gertrude Stein: Autobiography and the Problem of Narration*. Victoria, B.C.: English Literary Studies, 1979.

———. "The Observer Observed: Distancing the Self in Autobiography." *Prose Studies* 4, no. 3 (December 1981): 317–36.

Neuman, Shirley, and Ira B. Nadel, eds. *Gertrude Stein and the Making of Literature*. Houndsmill, Hampshire: Macmillan Press, 1988.

Nicholls, Peter. *Modernisms: A Literary Guide*. New York: Macmillan, 1995.

Olney, James, ed. *Studies in Autobiography*. New York: Oxford University Press, 1988.

Overton, Grant, ed. *Mirrors of the Year: A National Review of the Outstanding Figures, Trends and Events of 1926–7*. New York: Frederick A. Stokes Company, 1927.

Parini, Jay, ed. *The Norton Book of American Autobiography*. New York: W. W. Norton and Company, 1999.

Parke, Catherine N. "'Simple through Complication': Gertrude Stein Thinking." *American Literature: A Journal of Literary History, Criticism, and Bibliography* 60, no. 4 (December 1988): 554–74.

Pascal, Roy. *Design and Truth in Autobiography*. London: Routledge and Paul, 1960.

Perreault, Donna. "What Makes Autobiography Interrogative?" *Biography: An Interdisciplinary Quarterly* 13, no. 2 (Spring 1990): 130–42.

Pierce, Constance. "Gertrude Stein and Her Thoroughly Modern Protégé." *Modern Fiction Studies* 42, no. 3 (Fall 1996): 607–25.

Pilling, John. *Autobiography and Imagination: Studies in Self-Scrutiny.* Boston: Routledge and Kegan Paul, 1981.

Pizer, Donald. *American Expatriate Writing and the Paris Moment: Modernism and Place.* Baton Rouge: Louisiana State University Press, 1996.

Pound, Ezra. *Ezra Pound's Poetry and Prose: Contributions to Periodicals in Ten Volumes.* Edited by Lea Baechler, A. Walton Litz, and James Logenbach. New York: Garland Press, 1991.

———. *Literary Essays of Ezra Pound.* Edited by T. S. Eliot. New York: New Directions, 1968.

———. *The Selected Letters of Ezra Pound, 1907–1941.* Edited by D. D. Paige. New York: New Directions, 1950.

Putnam, Samuel. *Paris Was Our Mistress: Memoirs of a Lost and Found Generation.* New York: Viking Press, 1947.

Raab, Lawrence. "Remarks as Literature." *Michigan Quarterly Review* 17 (1978): 480–93.

Rainey, Lawrence. *Institutions of Modernism: Literary Elites and the Public Culture.* New Haven: Yale University Press, 1998.

Reaves, Gerri. *Mapping the Private Geography: Autobiography, Identity, and America.* Jefferson, N.C.: McFarland and Company, 2001.

Riding, Laura, and Robert Graves. *A Survey of Modernist Poetry.* London: Heinemann, 1927.

Rodriguez, Suzanne. *Wild Heart: Natalie Clifford Barney and the Decadence of Literary Paris.* New York: HarperCollins Publishers, 2002; New York: Ecco Press, 2003.

Rogers, W. G. *When This You See Remember Me: Gertrude Stein in Person.* New York: Rinehart, 1948.

Root, Waverley. *The Paris Edition.* Edited by Samuel Abt. San Francisco: North Point Press, 1987.

Sayre, Robert F. *The Examined Self: Benjamin Franklin, Henry Adams, Henry James.* Princeton: Princeton University Press, 1964.

Schultz, Susan M. "Gertrude Stein's Self-Advertisement." *Raritan* 12, no. 2 (Fall 1992): 71–87.

Seigel, Jerrold. *Bohemian Paris: Culture, Politics, and the Boundaries of Bourgeois Life, 1830–1930.* Baltimore: Johns Hopkins University Press, 1986.

Severijnen, Olav. "The Renaissance of a Genre: Autobiography and Modernism." *New Comparison: A Journal of Comparative and General Literary Studies* 9 (Spring 1990): 41–49.

Shirer, William L. *20th Century Journey: The Start, 1904–1930.* New York: Simon and Schuster, 1976.

Smith, Sidonie. *A Poetics of Women's Autobiography: Marginality and the Fictions of Self-Representation.* Bloomington: Indiana University Press, 1987.

Smith, Sidonie, and Julia Watson. *Reading Autobiography: A Guide for Interpreting Life Narratives*. Minneapolis: University of Minnesota Press, 2001.

———, eds. *Women, Autobiography, Theory: A Reader.* Madison: University of Wisconsin Press, 1998.

Smoller, Sanford J. *Adrift among Geniuses: Robert McAlmon, Writer and Publisher of the Twenties*. University Park: Pennsylvania State University Press, 1975.

Stearns, Harold. "America and the Young Intellectual." *Bookman* 53, no. 1 (March 1921): 42–48.

———. *America and the Young Intellectual*. New York: George H. Doran, 1921.

———, ed. *America Now: An Inquiry into Civilization in the United States by Thirty-Six Americans*. New York: Charles Scribner's Sons, 1938.

———, ed. *Civilization in the United States: An Inquiry by Thirty Americans*. New York: Harcourt, Brace, and Company, 1922.

———. *Confessions of a Harvard Man: The Street I Know Revisited*. Edited by Hugh Ford. Santa Barbara, Calif.: Paget Press, 1984.

———. "A Prodigal American Returns." *Scribner's Magazine* 91, no. 5 (May 1932): 293–95.

———. *The Street I Know*. New York: Lee Furman, 1935.

Stein, Gertrude. *The Autobiography of Alice B. Toklas*. New York: Harcourt, Brace, and Company, 1933; New York: Vintage Books, 1990.

———. *Everybody's Autobiography*. New York: Random House, 1937; Cambridge, Mass.: Exact Change, 1993.

———. *The Geographical History of America*. New York: Random House, 1936.

———. *How Writing is Written: Volume II of the Previously Uncollected Writings of Gertrude Stein*. Edited by Robert Bartlett Haas. Los Angeles: Black Sparrow Press, 1974.

———. Review of *Troubadour: An Autobiography*, by Alfred Kreymborg. *Ex Libris* 2, no. 9 (June 1925): 278.

Stone, Albert E. *Autobiographical Occasions and Original Acts*. Philadelphia: University of Pennsylvania Press, 1982.

Tate, Allen. *Sixty American Poets, 1896–1944*. Washington, D.C.: Library of Congress, 1945.

Tavernier-Courbin, Jacqueline. *Ernest Hemingway's "A Moveable Feast": The Making of Myth*. Boston: Northeastern University Press, 1991.

Testimony against Gertrude Stein. The Hague: Servire Press, 1935.

Thomas, John. *Dry Martini: A Gentleman Turns to Love*. New York: George H. Doran, 1926; Carbondale: Southern Illinois University Press, 1974.

Thomson, Virgil. *Virgil Thomson*. New York: A. A. Knopf, 1966.

Toklas, Alice B. *What Is Remembered*. New York: Holt, Rinehart, Winston, 1960.

Turner, Catherine. *Marketing Modernism between the Two World Wars*. Amherst: University of Massachusetts Press, 2003.

Van Gessel, Nina. "Re-Casting the Midwives of Modernism: Autobiographies of American Expatriate Women Publishers and Editors." Ph.D. diss. McMaster University, 1996.

Weber, Ronald. *News of Paris: American Journalists in the City of Light between the Wars*. Chicago: Ivan R. Dee, 2006.

Weiss, Andrea. *Paris Was a Woman: Portraits from the Left Bank*. San Francisco: Harper Collins, 1995.

Wetzsteon, Ross. *Republic of Dreams, Greenwich Village: The American Bohemia, 1910–1960*. New York: Simon and Schuster, 2002.

Wheeler, Kenneth W., and Virginia Lee Lussier, eds. *Women, the Arts, and the 1920s in Paris and New York*. New Brunswick, N.J.: Transaction Books, 1982.

"Why Do Americans Live in Europe?" *transition* 14 (Fall 1928): 97–119.

Wickes, George. *Americans in Paris, 1903–1939*. New York: Doubleday, 1969.

Williams, William Carlos. *The Autobiography of William Carlos Williams*. New York: Random House, 1951; New York: New Directions, 1967.

Wilson, Edmund. *Axel's Castle: A Study in the Imaginative Literature of 1870–1930*. New York: Charles Scribner's Sons, 1931.

Wineapple, Brenda. *Genêt: A Biography of Janet Flanner*. Lincoln: University of Nebraska Press, 1989.

Wolff, Geoffrey. *Black Sun: The Brief Transit and Violent Eclipse of Harry Crosby*. New York: Random House, 1976.

Wood, Tom. "Origin of the Term Lost Generation." *Lost Generation Journal* 1, no. 1 (May 1973): 3–5.

Wordsworth, William. *The Prose Works of William Wordsworth*. Edited by W. J. B. Owen and Jane Worthington Smyser. 3 vols. Oxford: Clarendon Press, 1974.

INDEX

Guggenheim, Peggy, 117–18

Halpert, Samuel, 29
Harcourt, Alfred, 51
Hartpence, Lance, 25, 34
Hemingway, Ernest, 1, 57, 71, 78,
  96, 106, 123, 127–28, 137, 142–
  43, 145, 147, 151, 156, 163, 166;
  and Gertrude Stein, 46–47, 52,
  60, 61, 139, 167; and influence of
  his fiction, 6, 100, 126, 144; origin of "Lost Generation" phrase
  and, 1, 6, 58–59; and views of
  contemporaries, 141–42; as writer of autobiography, 139–41
Hemingway, John Hadley
  (Bumby), 128
Hemingway, Mary Welsh, 17, 140,
  146, 163
Hoffman, Leigh, 38
homosexuality, 52–53, 60, 68, 118
  125–26, 156–58

Imbs, Bravig, 97–98, 119, 178, 179;
  and affection for Paris, 103; on
  escaping America, 101–2; in
  French countryside, 113–14;
  and Gertrude Stein, 58, 60, 61,
  110–12; and views of contemporaries, 108–9

Jolas, Eugene, 47, 48, 106, 152, 164;
  expatriation of, 171–72; and
  little magazines, 173–74, 181–82;
  newspaper work of, 180–81
Jolas, Maria, 47, 164, 170–71,
  172–73
Josephson, Matthew, 84, 144–45
Joyce, James, 108, 111, 118, 126,
  127, 130, 136–37, 151, 152, 167,
  173–74

Kreymborg, Alfred, 42, 44, 70;
  expatriation of, 21, 27–31; and
  modernism, 20–21, 24, 26, 31,

36, 37–38, 39; and rejection of
  industrial age, 24–25, 36–37; as
  writer of autobiography, 21–24,
  38–39, 44

Lardner, Ring, 81
Lewis, Sinclair, 26, 105, 151
Lewis, Wyndham, 141
Lindbergh, Charles, 127
Lipschitz, Jacques, 47
Little Review, 123, 136
Loeb, Harold, 7, 28, 143–44, 145,
  167, 168
Lost Generation, 5, 30, 31, 44, 65,
  68, 82–83, 92, 94, 96, 100, 101,
  102, 118–19, 144, 149, 159–60,
  166, 169, 180, 182; enduring in-
  terest in, 2–3, 161–62; origin of
  the phrase, 1, 6, 9, 58–59, 179; as
  pejorative, 4; as subject of revi-
  sion, 10, 96, 138, 139, 145, 147,
  155–56, 162–63, 167, 178
Love in Chartres (Asch), 7–8
Lowell, Amy, 151
Loy, Mina, 125

The Making of Americans (Stein), 14,
  46, 51, 128–29
Mansfield, Katherine, 141, 155
Martin, Flossie, 106
Matisse, Henri, 3, 41, 43, 46, 49–50
McAlmon, Robert, 51, 61, 85,
  125, 144–45, 147–48; and sexual
  identity, 156–58; and views of
  contemporaries, 150–51, 152
McBride, Henry, 54, 61
Mencken, H. L., 81
Miller, Henry, 100, 106, 129, 165,
  179
modernism, 4–5, 11, 92, 162;
  American culture and, 3–4;
  cultural complicity of, 159–60;
  diversity in, 153–54; elitism of,
  12–14, 36–37, 51; interdisciplin-
  arity and, 31–32; populism and,

62–63; critical and commercial neglect of, 41–42, 50–51, 53–54; and Ernest Hemingway, 60, 139, 142; as mentor, 60–62; origin of "Lost Generation" phrase and, 1, 58–59, 65, 179; as salonist, 56–58, 109–12; and sexual identity, 52–53, 60, 109, 128; success of, 14, 51, 54–55; and views of contemporaries, 39, 46–48; as writer of autobiography, 42–43, 44–46, 49, 119

Stein, Leo, 41, 55

Stein, Michael, 41

Stella, Joseph, 105

Stillman, Ary, 105

The Sun Also Rises (Hemingway), 6, 82–83, 100, 105, 126, 129, 144, 151, 166, 169

Surrealism, 99, 105

A Survey of Modernist Poetry (Riding and Graves), 5

Tate, Allen, 32, 101

Taylor, Graeme, 157–58

Tender Is the Night (Fitzgerald), 8, 58

Testimony against Gertrude Stein, 47–48

This Quarter, 141, 149

Thomas, John, 5–6

Thomson, Virgil, 57–58, 111

Three Lives (Stein), 41, 43, 49, 50–51, 62, 126

Toklas, Alice B., 48, 52–53, 57, 60, 61, 111–12, 119, 126, 128–29, 135; as autobiographical voice, 44, 45, 46, 48, 49–50, 55–56

transition, 38, 42, 47–48, 84, 106, 127, 152, 167, 173–74, 181–82

Tropic of Cancer (Miller), 100, 129

Tunney, Gene, 127

Ulysses (Joyce), 118, 126, 136–37

Untermeyer, Louis, 5

Vail, Lawrence, 117, 153

Van Vechten, Carl, 48

Walsh, Ernest, 141, 149, 152, 155, 156

The Waste Land (Eliot), 28–29

Wheelwright, John, 167

Whitehead, Alfred, 48–49, 55

Williams, William Carlos, 14, 28–29, 35, 151, 157

Wilson, Edmund, 5, 33

Yeats, W. B., 151